HARDPRESS

ISBN: 9781313779807

Published by:
HardPress Publishing
8345 NW 66TH ST #2561
MIAMI FL 33166-2626

Email: info@hardpress.net
Web: http://www.hardpress.net

Date Due

THE PHILOSOPHY OF THE BIBLE

DAVID NEUMARK

THE PHILOSOPHY

OF THE

BIBLE

BY

David Neumark

Professor of Jewish Philosophy
HEBREW UNION COLLEGE
CINCINNATI

CINCINNATI

ARK PUBLISHING COMPANY

1918

PREFACE.

THIS book attempts the first scientific and popular presentation of the history of thought in biblical Judaism. The views laid down in this book are based on a minute study of the literatures concerned, biblical, Graeco-Jewish, and talmudic. For the arguments on which these views are based, the student is referred to my previous publications on the subject.* Nevertheless the presentation is so arranged that, from the references given, the reader will always be able to verify my statements from the text of the Bible. Notably I have made it a point to give all the references necessary to an independent verification of my statements in cases where I had to treat of subjects as yet not fully discussed in my previous publications.

This Preface is written on the *tenth anniversary* of my *first sessions* at the Hebrew Union College. The plan of this book is based on the experience acquired in actual teaching, "The Philosophy of the Bible," representing a part of the ground covered in the lecture-

*(1) Geschicht der juedischen Philosophie des Mittelalters vol. I, George Reimer, Berlin 1907, II, 1, 1910.
(2) Jehuda Hallevi's philosophy, Hebrew Union College Catalog, 1908.
(3) Crescas and Spinoza, Year Book of Central Conference of American Rabbis, 1909.
(4) Tholdoth ha-'Ikkarim be-Yisroel, vol. I, Moriyah, Odessa 1912; for the second volume cf. the
(5) Outline in the article " 'Ikkarim" in the Sample-Volume of the Hebrew Encyclopedia "Otsar ha-Yahduth," Warsaw 1906.
(6) Essays and articles in periodicals and occasional publications.

course on Jewish Philosophy in the Collegiate Department. My German book, "History of Jewish Philosophy" is arranged according to *Problems*. This book presents the subject *chronologically*. Smaller literary units, however, are treated jointly, as set forth in the course of the presentation on apt occasions.

I hope the book will be of help to readers, students and teachers of the Bible.

A Table of the Sources of the Torah, an elaborate *Table of Contents*, an exhaustive *Index*, and complete *Bible References* in the Massoretic order, greatly facilitate the use of the book to students, teachers and preachers.

DAVID NEUMARK.

Cincinnati, Ohio, December 4, 1917.

CONTENTS

Historical truth and literary motif. Babylonian
influence (1-2).—Monotheism and the sexual motive
in Divinity (2-4).—Sexual motif in biblical literature (4-6).—Differentiation of the ethical God-conception from the cosmological (6-7).—Motif of
Attributes. Divine attributes and names, names
of angels (7-9).—Speculative element in Babylonian
and early biblical God-conceptions. The social
aspect of divine Justice, Fatum (9-11).—Prophecy
and free will, personality and responsibility in
general Semitic theology (11-12).—Divine Mercy
in Semitic theology. The rivalry between the God-
conceptions of rigid justice and mercy in Israel: El
Kanna, Elohim, EHJH, JHVH (12-14).—The
national Name of God (14-15).—The practical postulates of the new God-conception. The Covenant
at Sinai (15-16).

and develops theory of Mercabah. More interest in early history. Return to ethical God-idea of holiness. Cosmogonic interest. Motif of attributes (115-118).—Ways of JHVH central problem, Adonay, El Shadday, Adonay JHVH, Cabhod, Cloud, Cherubs: Presence of JHVH, Mercabah in restored Temple. Ethical God-conception with a cosmological touch (118-121).—Reaction in means of revelation, and progress in conception of prophet's calling. Ruah (Spirit) in contrast to flesh. Difficulties in question of free will (121-124).—Discussion and solution of the problem of justice. Emphasis laid on individual responsibility and repentance. Eschatological elements: Ruah, Sheol, Bor (124-129).—Artistic postulates in worship, music (129-131).—Influence upon the development of literature 131-132).—Influence on legislation: Sabbath, circumcision, capital punishment, sin-offering (132-134).—Weakening of universalistic-messianic hopes. Conception of History. Reunion of Israel and Juda (134-137).

This prophet belongs to the Jeremian School. His fight against Persian Dualism (140). Cosmological Proof, Israel's Selection, Metaphysical conceptions, Thirteen Attributes (141-142).

General plan of the book of Job. Use of divine names (142-144).—The general argument in Defense of Justice. The special arguments of Eliphaz, Bildad, Zophar, and Elihu (144-148).—Job meant to represent the oscillating currents of his age, affecting *all* principles of Judaism (148-151).—Job's wavering attitude in eschatological questions (151-154).—Cosmogonical elements in the discussion of creation. The Cosmological Proof in the Revelation in Storm (154-157).—Free will, Fatum, Determinism. Reaction in conception of medium of prohpetic revelation, progress in conception of function of prophecy, speculative prophecy (157-160).—Cultural life, music, plastics. Date and literary development of the book of Job (160-162).—Development of literary composition in Hebrew Literature. Job a problem-drama. Other problem-dramas: Jonah, Ruth, Song of

INTRODUCTION.

1. SCOPE OF THE BOOK

THIS book has for its object the presentation of the spiritual development of Judaism in biblical times in its theoretical principles as well as in the expressions these principles found in the cultural manifestations of life. All currents and tendencies, lawful and unlawful, have been accorded equal attention. This procedure finds its justification even in the fact that it is the *history* of the spiritual development of Judaism which is the object of this book. And history teaches us that almost every one of the currents treated here, has enjoyed at some time or other a certain measure of authoritative standing. However, our aim is not only to register the facts in Judaism's spiritual development, but also, and primarily, to understand and to present in the light of historical evolutions that form of biblical Judaism which, in spite of all internal and external changes, has been preserved through the ages up to our own day. This aspect of our presentation made it imperative for us to pay especial attention to that path in the development which marks the gradual evolution and consolidation of what may be considered *authoritative Judaism* in the making. Corresponding to this aim special attention has been paid to the development of the Pentateuch, the *Torah*.

The presentation is so arranged that each one of the *four periods* into which the biblical time has been divided, concludes with a decisive phase in the

history of the Torah: The *first* period (first chapter)
concludes with the proclamation of the *First Book of
the Covenant* as "Torah"; the *second* (second chapter)
with the proclamation of *Deuteronomy* as "Torah";
the *third* (third chapter) with the proclamation of the
enlarged *Priestly Code*, together with Deuteronomy,
as "Torah"; and the *fourth* (fourth chapter) with the
proclamation of *our* Pentateuch as the *Torah.*

This history of the Torah is based generally on
the results of modern biblical criticism.   In many
points, however, we differ with the views in vogue.
The differences in detail will be brought out in the
course of the presentation.   Here it will be sufficient
to mention *two cardinal points* of difference as the
result of the very numerous revisions in particular
questions: *First,* the conception in vogue among the
critics that prophetic Judaism as an *unofficial* doctrine
was *opposed* to the *official* doctrine of authoritative
Judaism, is to be abandoned.   Not only is there
nothing in the sources to back up this assumption,
but, on the contrary, an impartial examination of the
sources reveals the unquestionable fact that the so
called official Judaism represented by the "Torah"
of a given time has always been the result of the
development of prophetic Judaism in the preceding
period.   This leads up to the *other point* of difference:
The "unoverbridgeable gap" between biblical and
Rabbinical Judaism, spoken of so often and so
tenaciously, *does not exist at all.*   Our presentation
will show the continuity of development in the
spiritual contents of Judaism from Bible to Talmud
with a clear outlook into later periods.

The foregoing will be sufficient to orient the student who knows the scientific situation in the questions referred to, as to the method and the practical educational aims pursued in this book. For the orientation of the average reader I republish here my popular article "Biblical Criticism" (American Jewish Chronicle, Nov. 10 and 24, 1916,) which I read in the Convention of the Ohio Jewish Religious Education Association, December 30, 1916, and published in my Hebrew collection of essays "Mik-Keren Zowith" No. 2, Asaph Publishing Company, New York, 1918.

2. BIBLICAL CRITICISM.

Of late, discussion has been going on as to the compatibility of biblical criticism with popular Judaism. Many have written and spoken on this question in the course of the last century, yet the question is to-day almost as unsettled as it was at the beginning of that period. The scope of this article is to review the situation which in itself may constitute something like a solution to the puzzling problem.

Now everybody, or almost everybody, knows what biblical criticism is, still, this intending to be a popular article, it may not be amiss to state first what biblical criticism is. It is essentially this:

According to the view in vogue with the Jewish masses the Torah was dictated by God while Moses was busy writing it down. As to the other books of the Bible, the general belief may be said to ascribe the books bearing the names of certain prophets, like Isaiah, Jeremiah, Hosea, Amos, and so on, to these prophets, the Psalms to David, Proverbs, Song of Songs and Koheleth to Solomon, and Echah to Jeremiah. As to historical books like Judges, Kings, Chronicles, Ruth, and Esther, it may be said that the Jewish masses do not hold any definite view as to who wrote them or by whom they were compiled. The same may be said as to particular questions which force themselves upon every, even the most orthodox and the least learned, reader of the Bible, such as who wrote those parts of the books ascribed to certain prophets in which their death and the events after their death are reported. The Jewish masses do not hold any definite view about these questions, leaving them to the learned who certainly know all about it. Of course there are questions the views about which cannot be stated in any average formulation, varying as they do with the various degrees of education, Jewish and secular. So, for instance, the question as to who wrote those parts in the Torah that speak of Moses, or those parts of other books that speak of their alleged authors, in the third person, is not greatly perplexing even to the unlearned masses, the great majority of them being ready to tell you upon inquiry that it is not unusual for ancient writers to speak about themselves in the third person. The same may be said about the question as to who wrote the last eight verses of the Torah relating of the death of Moses. Even those who know nothing about the pertinent controversy in the Talmud, know in a general way of the idea that the Torah is a pre-mundane being (knowing nothing, of course, about the controversy whether created or eternal), having been written "in black fire upon white fire," and as such is to be taken as a whole without any further questions. Likewise they believe that in cases where events of the future are not *related*, but *prophesied*, there is no difficulty, for instance, in believing that Isaiah could forsee the events prophesied in his book from chapter forty on.

As against this most radical orthodox view of the unlearned masses (and you may find any number of them in the pews of the most reformed temples), there exists quite a large class of learned orthodox Jews who hold a view which may be designated as the traditional, critical attitude based upon certain critical remarks in the Talmud. There we find views which differ from the general orthodox view characterized above. Thus, for instance, that Moses wrote only the fifth book of the Torah (Deuteronomy) and some part in the fourth book, leaving open the question of who wrote the rest of the Torah (the passage in question, Babli Baba Bathra 14-15, which commentators harmonize in different ways with the traditional view, being most likely fragmentary); that the last eight verses of the Torah, relating the death of Moses, were written by Joshua; that the Psalms are not all the work of David alone, but rather of ten different Psalmists, some of whom lived before David (Adam, Malkisedek, Moses) and some of whom were his contemporaries, David being the final compiler of the book of Psalms, as we have it. Similar views and speculations as to authorship we find in the Talmud about other books of the Bible also. Then, too, we find some speculation as to when the different laws contained in the Torah were given, distributing them upon the pre-Sinaitic station of Marah, Sinai, Arboth Moab, and the land east of the Jordan, covering the period of the forty years intervening between the Exodus from Egypt and the entrance into Palestine. Then there are observations in the Talmud about contradictions in the Bible in the historical reports as well as in the laws, contradictions and discrepancies between Moses and the prophets (especially between some laws in Ezekiel and their counterparts in the Torah), and also between the different parts of the Torah itself. All of these contradictions and discrepancies have, of course, found their harmonization in the work of the Talmudists, and also the talmudical remarks about authorship have been harmonized by later commentators with the traditional view. But in spite of this there have always been, as there still are, large numbers of learned Jews who maintain a certain critical attitude in these questions, without, however, attempting to bring their views into anything like a definite systematic shape. As the best representative of this class may be mentioned the great commentator Abraham Ibn Ezra (12 century), who in many a passage of his commentaries reveals in rather enigmatic language that he had doubts and suspicions as to the authorship and the time of certain passages in the Torah and other parts of the Bible. These two views, as they have been existing through the ages, still exist to-day in those sections of Jewry which have no knowledge of modern biblical criticism, which means the bulk of the Jews in all lands.

The first to rebel openly against all harmonizations and to insist upon a critical orientation as to authorship and time of the different parts of the Bible was the philosopher Baruch Spinoza. He utilized the remarks of Ibn Ezra and his own general knowledge of Jewish sources and, feeling himself free of all Jewish traditions, undertook to establish the general idea that the writers of the biblical books all agreed on one point only, viz., that man must live a life of righteousness and equity, while as to all other questions, such as the metaphysical principles of Judaism and historical conceptions (in which latter, however, Spinoza was not greatly interested) the biblical writers differ among, and claim no authority for, themselves. In order to understand the different views laid down in the different parts of the Bible, one must study the Bible and the history of the Jews critically, so as to find out who were the real authors of the books or portions of books under question, in what environments and circumstances those writers lived, and so on. Spinoza himself never took up this task, but his suggestion was taken up by many Christian scholars of the nineteenth century, so that in the course of time this branch of Jewish science has become the almost exclusive domain of Christian, notably Protestant, scholars in Germany and England. There were, of course, a few Jewish scholars who did some work in the field of biblical criticism, such as Geiger and Zunz. But Geiger never went into the main questions, while Zunz, although he succeeded in finding some of the most essential features of the so-called Graf-Wellhausen hypothesis, is never given credit for them (perhaps because he later neglected, almost shunned, this line of work).

This hypothesis concerns itself with the composition of the Torah, the most important and the most far-reaching question of biblical criticism—a question in the face of which the question whether Isaiah the son of Amoz or a so-called Isaiah the second, is the author of the prophecies of the book Isaiah beginning with chapter forty, or other questions of that kind, fade into utter insignificance. The gist of this hypothesis which has since found many different formulations, is about this:

The Torah is the product of a long literary and religious development. Somewhere in the ninth and eighth centuries before the present era there existed two historical books covering the period from Abraham to the death of Moses (or of Joshua, according to some). The author of the one they call Elohist (or E) because he uses the name of God Elohim, that of the other Jahvist (or J) because he uses the name of God Jahveh. Each one of these two books contained an account of the history of the patriarchs and the Israelites, and also some laws, E. containing the laws embodied in Ex. chaps. XX-XXIII, and J (perhaps) those of Ex. XXXIV. Each one of these books enjoyed some authority in a different center of Palestine. Later these two books were fused into one by some writer whom they call the compiler of JE (JE). The new compiler (who may have lived and worked sometime in the seventh century) harmonized the discrepancies as best he could by cutting here and adding there. This book, the new "Torah"

so to say, enjoyed authority to a larger extent than
either of the two when alone, representing as it did
the unification of the two great forces of spiritual
endeavor. Later, in the time of King Josiah, in
the year 621, a new book was published by the spiritual
leaders of the time, including the king, the book
which is known under the name D́euteronomy (D)
as the fifth book of Moses (minus chaps. I-IV,
XXVII and XXIX-XXXIV which are considered as
later additions). This book contains an historical
introduction, largely a brief review of history (Deut.
V-XI), as given in JE, a collection of laws (Deut.
XII-XXVI), essentially an enlargement of the laws
contained in JE (Ex. XX-XXIII, called the first
Book of the Covenant, and Ex. XXXIV, called the
little Book of the Covenant), and a concluding
admonition setting forth the consequences of disobedience (Deut. XXVIII). This book (D) is
supposed to have ousted the book JE and its laws
from the place of authority it occupied, and to have
placed itself in authority in it́s stead.   Later, in the
time of Ezra, we find two more books, one called the
Priestly Code (P) and the other the Book of Holiness
(H).   Each of these two books contained a short
historic review, P beginning with the creation of the
world and H with the exodus (the present writer,
however, holding that also H contained a report of
creation and early history), and a collection of laws
(P: Ex. XII, XIII, XXV-XXXI, XXXV-XL;
Lev. I-XV, XVI (?), XXVII; and almost all laws
found in Num.; H: Lev. XVII-XXV with some exceptions belonging to P; Num. XV, 37 f. and a few

others scattered), H containing also a concluding admonition (Lev. XXVI), like Deuteronomy (XXVIII). Later these two books were fused into one (PH) in the same manner as J and E into JE.

At the time of Ezra, then, there existed three distinct books, JE, D, and PH, each one of which had an historic introduction and a collection of laws. The question when these three books were fused into one, the Torah in its present form, is a matter of controversy, the general belief being that it took place in the time of Ezra (the present writer preferring the later date, about a century after Ezra). But all critics agree that the present Torah is the product of a long development and consists of the constituent parts mentioned above. This explains why we find some historical events as well as some laws repeated as often as five times, corresponding to the five distinct sources (E, J, D, P, H), and also accounts for contradictions and discrepancies both in historical reports and in formulations of laws, contradictions and discrepancies which the final redactors thought they had harmonized sufficiently, but which were discovered by the Talmudists and the old Jewish commentators as well as by the modern critics, with the difference, however, that the former (with very few exceptions) reharmonized them, while the latter took them as indications that our Torah represents a fusion of different "sources" (this being the technical designation for the constituent books) into one book. These indications coincided, in the minds of the critics, with recent discoveries, such as the cuneiform tablets and the like.

In the wake of this hypothesis and the newly discovered oriental sources there came a new orientation in the meaning of the message of the prophets and in the spiritual position of Israel among the nations of the ancient world. The prophets, according to the critical view in vogue, denounced the specific Jewish, notably the sacrificial, ritual as in fact all organized religion and ritualism altogether, and preached a pure ethical (social) message. In a word, our Torah or the constituent parts thereof each in its time, was denounced and repudiated by the prophets who insisted that *only* the ethical laws are worthy of being embodied in the national religious charter or Book of the Covenant; some hyper-critics going so far as to hold that some of the prophets were opposed to all and any written law or Torah. Israel, according to this view deserves credit only as a mediator in bringing the message emphasized by his prophets to the world, since in all essentials Israel inherited all those teachings from other, older nations. Even the belief in one God, monotheism, is by no means a creation of Israel, as older nations had already outspoken leanings towards monotheism. This, of course, is the view of the most radical non-Jewish scholars, the conservative among them harmonizing to an extent the results of criticism and the newly discovered oriental sources with the old traditional view of the prophets being essentially in harmony with the Torah, and of Israel as deserving a certain amount of credit for achievements of his own. As to the sources on which ancient Israel drew the doctrines, teachings and laws embodied in

the Torah and the rest of the Bible, there are differences of opinion among the scholars. It depends
largely on the special field of endeavor to which a
scholar has devoted himself. The Arabists have
traced all back to ancient Arabic culture, notably
the Kenites, to whom they give credit for the Jahveh
God-conception; the Assyriologists are inclined to
give all credit to Assyrians and Babylonians, the
Sumerists to the Sumerians, as surely as the Egypt-
ologists to the Egyptians.

How did the Jews react to this conception of things?

The orthodox among the learned Jews first denounced all biblical criticism as heresy, without
attempting a scientific refutation. Later they made
concessions to the criticism of the other parts of the
Bible, insisting, however, on the unity and authenticity of the Torah. The late Dr. Jacob Barth, professor at the Theological Seminary and the University
of Berlin, for instance, admitted hesitatingly that
the last chapters of the book of Isaiah (chaps. XL f.)
are not the words of Isaiah ben Amoz. At the same
time some have tried to refute with scientific arguments the above hypothesis concerning the composition of the Torah. Dr. David Hoffmann, professor at the Berlin Seminary, wrote several books and
essays in refutation of that hypothesis, with a view
toward establishing the authenticity of the Torah.
In doing so, however, he had (as the present writer
has shown elsewhere) to make many concessions
which to the truly orthodox Jew are almost as inacceptable as the theory of the radical critics. Notably, he had to admit that in the course of the forty

years intervening between the exodus and the entrance into Palestine many a law had to be changed and adapted to some illegal practices produced by changed conditions.   Then, too, Hoffmann confined himself to the legal portions of the Torah, neglecting altogether to account for the contradictions and discrepancies in the historic portions.   This task was taken up recently by a younger conservative scholar, Dr. Siegmund Jampel (Rabbi in Schwedt, Germany, I think), who in a number of articles and essays tried to justify the historic accounts of the Torah (and some other parts of the Bible), to harmonize them with or to defend them against other oriental sources.   But aside from the fact that he, too, had to make some concessions inacceptable to the orthodox Jew, he has so far confined himself to special questions, without succeeding in presenting an acceptable comprehensive view of all the chief problems involved.

Among the Jewish scholars of the liberal wing there were such as made concessions from the very start as far as the principle goes, but contradicted in details, which attitude enabled them to present the history of the spiritual development of Israel and his contribution to the advancement of mankind in a favorable light, avoiding the unpleasant features connected with this point in the view of radical critics (Geiger, Samuel Hirsch, Graetz).   A scholar of our own generation, Dr. Jacob, rabbi in Dortmund, Germany, attacked the critical theory about the Torah on scientific grounds, accepting, however, the general principle, and without attempting a comprehensive

THE PHILOSOPHY OF THE BIBLE

systematic presentation of the religious and literary
development leading up to the Torah in its present
form. So far, the present writer is the only one to
have attempted a systematic presentation comprising
all essential questions of the composition of the Torah
and of the whole religious and literary development
leading up to the Torah in its present composition.
In the first volume of my Hebrew work, "History
of Dogmas in Judaism," and in my German work,
"History of Jewish Philosophy," I have accepted
the above hypothesis in its essential points, but have
shown that the critics have overlooked the most
vital facts in the religious development of Judaism.
They overlooked the central controversy in ancient
Judaism about the angels, as to their role as mediators
between God and man, and even as to their existence.
In consequence of this oversight they were in the
dark as to the attitude of the different prophets and
biblical writers in the question of creation. Missing
these two vital points they necessarily failed to see
the influence of these questions upon all other questions of creed and law, as in general they missed the
relation of the prophets to the authoritative Books
of the Covenant of their respective generations.
They overlooked, in a word, the most decisive features
of the development of the God-conception in ancient
Israel with which all other questions of import are
bound up so closely that in missing this they could
not but miss all the rest. The reason why these
scholars with their excellent equipment and their
great achievements failed to grasp the Jewish spirit
in the course of its development, I cannot now state

any better than I have in the foreword to the second
volume of the History of Jewish Philosophy:

"And not only is it impossible to comprehend and
to present the Jewish Middle Ages without orientation in Jewish antiquity, but also the other way:
The Old Testament scholars and the Hellenists who
decline to orient themselves in Rabbinic, especially
in the *philosophic*, literature of the Jewish Middle
Ages, have, all of their valuable achievements notwithstanding, *remained outside*. They have *not*
penetrated into the spirit of the Jewish way of thinking in the biblical and Greek periods. . . Judaism
is a whole entity and must be approached and comprehended as such."

Non-Jewish critics often say the Jews are not fit
to read the Bible with the right unbiased critical
spirit.   And it may be that they are right to a certain
extent.   Although it was a Jew, Spinoza, who started
modern biblical criticism, it may be so indeed that
the reverence of the Jew for the Bible was a handicap
to his progress in this field, and that he was indeed
in need of help from outside.   But now, while paying
our gratitude for the assistance received, we are entitled and bound to pass the word back.   Only a Jew
who has imbibed the Jewish spirit in a genuine
Jewish education and has devoted his life to the study
of Judaism in all of its phases, may hope to be able
to follow the Jewish spirit in its triumphal course
through the ages.

Seen in this light, the idea that the prophets
were opposed to the "Torah" of their time, because
they were opposed to the sacrificial cult or to ritualism

and organized religion on principle, vanishes like fog before the sun. And also the view that not Israel, but other, ancient peoples are to be credited for what is good and valuable in the religion of Israel, proves to be the product of ignorance as to what Jewish religion really is. Of course, it is not always ignorance alone that misleads some of the radical non-Jewish critics. At times there is what the late Dr. Schechter expressed in his famous epigram: "Higher criticism—higher anti-Semitism." If I now add that there have always been Jews who in their articles or books on the subject would slavishly copy the radical views mentioned, with all they imply, to the detriment of Judaism, I have said all I care to say in this connection about the attitude of Jewish scholars toward biblical criticism.

As to the masses, I have already indicated at the outset that both the orthodox as well as the reformed are almost wholly in ignorance about these questions. The question we have to face now is: Is it right to keep them in ignorance?

In the light of the foregoing it will be readily seen that the leaders of orthodox Judaism from their standpoint are doing the right thing in not giving their people a chance to become informed about the critical view. Not being able to give an adequate scientific presentation of the questions involved in harmony with their belief in the authenticity of the Torah, they do best to let faith alone in its sublime inapproachability. The orthodox leaders, in the vast majority, are entitled to our respect for their faith, as also to our confidence in their sincerity that they really believe what they say they believe. And if they, knowing of the arguments of the critics, still hold tenaciously to their faith in spite of the fact that they are not able to refute the essential arguments against their belief and still less to give a comprehensive systematic view of the main questions —they are fully justified in excluding this subject from their pulpits, schools, Bible classes, publications and lecture platforms, if they do so, or to brush the critical views aside by a summary declaration that they are rank heresy and scientifically untenable at that, if they really believe that they have refuted them. Of course, the orthodox, also, advance popular arguments in favor of the traditional view of prophecy in general and of the authenticity of the Torah in particular, but these arguments must be carried on without any technical literary amplifications. The orthodox rabbis naturally do study the literature of biblical criticism either in their seminaries or privately, at any rate they ought to do so, and large numbers of them certainly do. But while it may be well possible to give some instruction in this subject in popular classes for adults and the more mature youths, it is hardly worth while to do so, since the ultimate aim of the instruction is the upholding of the traditional view which the pupils in question have already acquired in their early religious education. The harm that may come to the orthodox Jews from outside information about biblical criticism appearing casually in newspapers and magazines, is quite sufficiently met by occasional summary refutations in the orthodox pulpit and press.

Far different from this is the situation we face in the reform camp. Reform Judasim not only may accept the principles of criticism, but is actually in need of some such principles. If there happened to be no biblical criticism at all, reform Judaism would have to formulate of its own accord some critical view comprising all the questions involved, or—to disappear from the face of the earth. With reform Judaism it is a question of life and death—"to be or not to be." Reform Judaism rejected the old traditional view of the Torah and its authenticity, right at the start. The first move to abolish or to relax in the practice of any biblical law of a ritual or dietary nature meant the repudiation of the old idea of prophecy and of the absolutely binding authority and the authenticity of the Torah. The remainder of authority that the Torah has retained in our camp must have some basis to rest on. Now we, the rabbis and teachers of the reform wing, base this authority on the principle formulated by Spinoza, although we differ from him in essential aspects of the question (cf. my Crescas and Spinnoza). We believe in the divine inspiration of the prophets and the biblical writers in those essentials in which they agree or which they gradually developed, taking their lasting differences in minor points of creed and ritual to be the changeable human element in the divinely inspired religion of Judaism. This principle is the magna charta of reform Judaism, a basis solid and reliable. But what about the masses, the unlearned? What is to them the basis of their Judaism? It is no exaggeration to state that to the bulk of the reform

Jews the basis of their reform Judaism is the old orthodox belief in the authenticity of the Torah, with the addition that somehow or other the rabbis of every generation (and, in fact, of every congregation) have authority to change matters in accordance with the demands of the times. Of course, the rabbis, most of them, weave into their sermons and lectures now and then some remarks indicating their critical views. But these remarks as a rule belong to those parts of the sermon or lecture which fall to the ground without leaving any trace in the minds of the people (You know there are such stretches in every sermon and lecture). To say that the orthodox view of the matter does not harm the people, is to admit that reform Judaism cannot stand on its own feet and is, therefore, willing to accept whatever assistance it may get from the fund of orthodox principles which it protests to have abandoned.

And then, too, even the little information reform Jews do get on these most essential questions very often does them more harm than good. The sources on which the less learned rabbis and teachers of Bible classes and lecturers draw are very often polluted with the anti-Jewish bias which is to be found in most of the books on biblical criticism. You can hear from reform pulpits that the prophets were opposed not only to the sacrificial cult, but also to ritualism in general, although the rabbi concerned keeps up a certain ritualism in his own synagogue. You can find in books and essays written by reform rabbis and teachers the old stale anti-Jewish talk about the prophets having been opposed to organized religion, while those essayists and writers themselves are engaged in the service of organized religion. Even the best among our rabbis and teachers, who, by their learning and sagacity are able to pick out the grain from the chaff, show alarmingly the lack of a comprehensive systematic *Jewish* view of the questions so vital to reform Judaism. What then about the less learned, who, the less they know, the more they insist on talking learnedly on these questions before their audiences. They kill the Jewish spirit in the hearts of their listeners without realizing what is taking place. They do not give their audience any systematic instruction in biblical criticism, but they present to them enough of the anti-Jewish talk of non-Jewish authors and their Jewish imitators, to shake them in their religious sentiments. The result may be said to amount to this: Large numbers of reform Jews hold the same views on these questions as our orthodox brethren, but for the minus sign attached to it: The Torah was written by Moses, and so on, but they do not believe it. And to appreciate how great the harm is, we must consider that also our religious schools are caught in this net of ignorance and indolence. On the whole our children get the same ideas about the questions under discussion here as the children in the orthodox schools. But in the higher classes they are simply told that reform Judaism differs in many points from the old orthodox Judaism, without being made to see whence reform Judaism derives its authority.

The result very often is that the brighter children, when they get as far as the confirmation class, are shaken in their religious foundations on the laying of which parents and teachers had been working all these years.

It may well be said that the failure of reform Judaism to make more headway than it has, and to have a firmer hold on many, notably on the most intelligent and most educated in the ranks of the reform congregations, is due to the chaotic conditions which I have just described. We need systematic instruction in these questions in the higher classes of the religious schools and in smaller Bible classes where work of that kind can be accomplished. We need popular publications on these questions, accessible to the average intelligent reader. And we need a reassertion of ourselves. We must not suffer the anti-Jewish spirit in Jewish schools and Jewish institutions. Everybody is free to think and to write what is good in his eyes, but our Jewish institutions must be free to teach *Jewish* Judaism. We must remove "the abomination that maketh desolate" from the temple of the Lord. Reform Judaism built on the ground prepared for the most part by scholars of an anti-Jewish spirit and an anti-Jewish bias, is built on sandy soil. But reform Judaism built on a solid Jewish basis, on a critical view permeated with the Jewish spirit that has dominated the ages of our development in his creative evolution, will wield much more power within and without than is the case at present.

3.   THE SOURCES OF THE TORAH

By giving here a *Table of Sources* of the Torah I do not mean to suggest that the only right way of reading the Torah is to read each constituent source separately.   On the contrary, I believe that the Torah, as well as the rest of the Bible, should be read for religious edification in the traditional way without paying attention to any kind of biblical criticism whatsoever.   The Bible has fulfilled its great mission for religious and moral progress of humanity by the un-analysed ensemble of the psychological impression it leaves in the heart of the reader.   But the fact of the matter is, *we need both.*   We must read the Bible without any further critical orientation for its potent psychological efficiency in the upbuilding of religious sentiment and moral character, but we also must read the Bible, and most especially the *Torah*, critically, if we are to have an adequate scientific view of the history of thought in Judaism in biblical times.   The influence of the Bible, as read in the traditional way, upon the mind of the modern Jew or Jewess will be much the stronger for the adequate knowledge of things acquired through scientific study.   And it is for this reason that I give here the table of sources of the Torah.   The intelligent reader will get the gist of the book without orienting himself in the details of analysis and synthesis of sources.   But his knowledge will be more firm and adequate, if he will read the sources of the Torah each by itself, and imbibe the distinct impression from the reading of each source as isolated from the other constituents of the composition.

The following Table of Sources is the one generally in vogue among critics, as compiled by *Driver*. In instances where I differ with this table, it will be expressly stated.

I.   GENESIS.

To the *Priestly Code* (P) which constitutes the *frame* of the entire Torah in its present shape, belong the following parts: (a, b, c stand for first, second, third, part of a verse):

I, 1-II, 4a; V, 1-28, 30-32; VI, 9-22; VII, 6,11,13-16a.18-21.24; VIII, 1-2a,3b-5, 13a, 14-19; X, 1-7, 20, 22,23,31-32;XI, 10-26,27,31,32; XII, 4b, 5; XIII, 6, 11b-13a; XVI, 1a, 3,15,16; XVII; XIX, 29; XXI, 1b, 2c-5;XXIII; XXV, 7-11a, 12-17,19,20,26c; XXVI, 34,35; XXVII,46-XXVIII,9; XXIX, 24,29; XXXI, 18b-c; XXXIII, 18a; XXXIV, 1,2a,4,6,8-10,13-18, 20-24,25 (in part), 27-29; XXXV, 9-13,15,22b-29; XXXVI (in the main, some elements evidently drawn from another, unidentified, source); XXXVII, 1,2a (to "Jacob"); XLI, 46; XLVI, 6-27; XLVII, 5,6a,7-11,27c,28; XLVIII, 3,6,7 (?); XLIX, 1a,28c-33; L, 12,13.

And also in other parts of the book there are some elements of P, but they are so organically fused with elements from other sources as to make an analysis impossible.

To the *Younger Jahvist* (J$_2$) belong the following parts:

II, 4c-III, 24; IV, 1-26; V, 20; VI, 1-4,5-8; VII, 1-5,7-10 (in the main; there are here elements from P), 12,16c-17,22,23; VIII, 2c,3a,6-12,13c,20-22; IX, 8-19, 21,24-30; XI, 1-9,28,30.

What remains of the book of Genesis after the deduction of the parts belonging to P and J₂, belongs to the Elohist (E) or to the Jahvist (J), in some cases, however, the fusion is much too organic and is left without analysis (JE):

J: XII, 1-4a,6-20; XIII, 1-5,7-11a,12b-18;

E: XV: JE

J: XVI, 1c,2,4-14;

XIV, the battle of the Kings, belongs to a special source, evidently a later reproduction of an old account.

J: XVIII, 1-XIX, 28,30-38;

E: XX, 1-17 (18);

J: XXI, 1a,2a,7 (?),   33;

E: XXI, 6-32a (32c),

The verses in brackets seem to belong to the redactor of JE.

J: XXII, 15-18;   20-24;

E: (XXI, 34); XXII, 1-14;   19,

J: XXV, 1-6, 11c,18,21-26a,27-34;

J: XXVII, 1-45; XXVIII, 10,   13-16,

E: 11,12,   17,18,

J: XXVIII, 19,   2-14,

E: 20-22; XXIX, 1,   15-23,25-28,30;

J: XXIX, 31-35; 3-5, 7, 9-16,

E: XXX, 1-3b 6, 8, 17-20b

J: XXX, 20, 24-43; XXXI, 1,3,

E: 20c-23,

J: 46, 48-50;

E: XXXI, 2,4-18a,19-45, 47, 51-54

In chapter XXXI there evidently are some elements from P, notably in 22a.

J: 4-14a, 23, 25-33;

E: XXXII, 1-3 14b-22, 24,

J: XXXIII, 1-17, XXXIV, 2c,3,5,7,11,12,19.

E: 18c-20;

J: XXXIV, 25 (part),26,30,31; 14 (?)

E: XXXV, 1-8,

J: 21,22a;

E: XXXV, 16-20

J: 12-21 25-27 28b

E: XXXVII,2c-11 22-24 28a 28c-30

In XXXVII, 2c-21 the analysis is uncertain; in 22-24 there are additions of the redactor.

J: XXXVII, 31-35 XXXVIII; XXXIX;

E: 36;

J: 38-XLIV, 34;

E: XL,XLI, 1-45,47-57; XLII, 1-37

In chapter XL there are traces of J, as also in XLI, 1-45; XLIII, 14 and 23c: E.

J: 28-XLVII, 4,6b

E: XLV,1-XLVI,5

J: 13-26,27a,29-31;

E: XLVII, 12,   XLVIII, 1-3

J: XLIX, 1c-28a; L, 1-11,14

E:XLVIII, 8-22 (13,14,17-19 J?);   15-26

2.   Exodus

P: I, 1-5,   7,   13,14   23b-25;

J: 6,   8-12,   15-23a

E: 15-22; II,1-14

J: 7,8   16-20,   IV, 1-16,

E:III,1-6   9-15,   21,22;   17,18

P: 2-VII, 13;

J: IV, 19,20a   22-VI,1

E: 20b,21

P: 19,20(a)   21c,22

J: 14-18

E: VII, 12 (part)   20b,21a

P: VIII, 1-3

J: VII, 23,   25-29,

E·   24,   4-11a

P: VIII, 11-15   8-12

J: 16-IX,7   13-21,

E: 22,23a

J: IX 23b-34,   X, 1-7,   13b   19

E;   35,   8-13a   14a

P: 9.10;

J: 28-29; 4-8,

E: X, 20-27 XI, 1-3

P: XII, 1-20 28 37a 40 - 51;

J: 29, 30

E: 31-36 37b-39 42a

P: XIII, 1, 2

J: 21, 22;

E: 17-19

JE: XII, 21-27; XIII, 3-16

P: XIV, 1-4 8, 9 15-18 21a

J: 5-7 10a 11-14 19c, 20

E: 10b 19a

P: 21c-23 26-27a 28, 29

J; XIV, 21b 24, 25 27b 30, 31;

E:

P: (19)

J: - 22-27;

E: XV, 1-18 20, 21

As against this analysis I have shown in Tholdoth that some of the passages about the hardening of the heart of Pharao cannot be ascribed to the Priestly Code.

P: XVI, 1-3 6-24 31-36; XVII, 1a.

J: 4, 5 25-30 1b, 2

E: 3-6

P:		XIX, 1, 2a	
J: XVII, 7			
E:	8-16; XVIII;	2b.	
J:		20-25;	
E: XIX, 3-19 (in the main)		XX, 1-XXIII, 33;	
P:		15-18a	
J: XXIV, 1, 2,	9-11		
E:	3-8	12, 14	18b
P: XXV, 1-XXXI, 18a			
J:			9-14
E:		18b; XXXII, 1-8	15-29
E: XXII, 30-XXXIII, 6 (in the main), 7-11			
P:	-	29-35; XXXV-XL;	
J: XXXIII, 12-XXXIV, 28.			

In our presentation we differ in many essential points from the views at the basis of this analysis, notably as to passages on the *golden calf* and the *thirteen attributes* in chapters XXXII-XXXIV, those on the *Cherubs, Urim ve-Thumim, Hoshen* and *Ephod,* and others on erection and equipment of the Tabernacle and the holy service.

3. LEVITICUS.

P: I-XVI;	XXVII;
H:	XVII-XXVI;

Our presentation differs with this analysis as to the *scape-goats* in XVI which we ascribe to the Book

of Holiness, as also in the analysis of chapters XVIII
and XX as to the distribution of the laws on capital
punishment and Khareth.

4. NUMBERS.

| P: | I, 1-X, 26; | XIII, 1-17a | 21 |

| JE: | XI; XII; | 17b-20 | 22-24 |

| P: XIII, 25, 26a (exc. of Kadeshah) | 32a |

| JE: | 26b-31 | 32b,33; |

| P: XIV, 1, 2 (in the main) | 5, 7 | 10 | 26-30 |

| JE: | 3, 4 | 8, 9 | 11-25 |

| P: | 34-38 | XV; XVI, 1a |

| JE: XIV, 31-33 | 39-45. | 1c, 2a |

| P: XVI, 2b-7a (7b-11) | (16, 17) 18-24 | 27a |

| JE: | 12-15 | 25, 26 |

| P: | 32b | 35; XVII, (1-5) 6-28; XVIII; XIX; |

| JE: XVI, 27c - 34 |

| P: XX, 1a | 2 | 3c, 4 6-13 | 22-29; |

| JE: | 1b 3a | 5 | 14-21 |

| P: | 4a | 10, 11; | XXII, 1 |

| JE: XXI, 1-3 | 4c-9 | 12-34; | 2-XXIV, 25; |

| P: | 6-19; XXVI-XXXI; |

| JE: XXV, 1-5 |

| P: | 18, 19 |

| JE: XXXII, 1-17 (in the main) | 20-27 (most) |

| P: XXXII, 28-32 (33) | 33-36 |

| JE: | 34 | 42 |

xlii THE PHILOSOPHY OF THE BIBLE

I believe that in the passages about the distribution of the land the elements of *Urim ve-Thumim* and *Lot* do *not* belong to P, as generally assumed; cf. Tholdoth and Crescas and Spinoza.

5.   DEUTERONOMY.

Deuteronomy is distributed upon the following constituent sources: 1. D—Deuteronomy proper; 2. D₂—later redactor of Deuteronomy; 3. P; 4. JE, and some special sources:

1 and 2:

D:	I, 1, 2, 4-III, 13	18-IV, 28	32-40
D₂:	14-17	29-31	· 41-49
D:	V, 1-XXVI, 19;	9, 10	
D₂:	XXVII, 1-4,7c,8	11-13(14-26);	
D:	XXVIII; XXIX, 1-8		11-20;
D₂:	9-28; XXX, 1-10		
D:	XXXI, 1-13, 24, 27	XXXII, 45-47;	
D₂:	28-30;		
D₂:	XXXIV, 11, 12.		

3: P: I, 3; XXXII, 48-52; XXXIV, 1(some words from JE). 5b, 7-9.

4: JE: XXVII, 5-7a; XXXI, 14, 15, 23; XXXIV, 1a (parts), 1b-5a, 6, 10.

5: *Special sources:* XXXI, 16-22; XXXII, 1-44; XXXIII;

FIRST CHAPTER

PRE-SINAITIC PERIOD.

WHOEVER approaches the historical documents of the Bible with the determination to examine and judge them without prejudice to the right or to the left, cannot help recognizing the *historical kernel* even in those sections, where contradictions and evidently legendary traits in the various reports, as also, and especially, certain political, religious-cultural and literary-artistic *motifs*, indicate beyond a doubt that this or that biblical writer deviates, at any rate *objectively*, from the historical truth in certain details. From this point of view it is justified, if not to follow the radical Babylonians (like *Jensen* and others) in their exaggerations, so at least to assume, in accordance with the report of the Torah, that the spiritual development of the *Abrahamites*, the ancestors of a prominent part of ancient Israel, was a continuation of the development in ancient Babylonia. This, indeed, is confirmed by a comparison of Babylonian-Assyrian literature with Biblical (-Talmudical) literature. Such a comparison makes it clear at once that the spiritual development of ancient Israel moves along the same lines as the ancient Babylonian development within which the former presents itself as a religious and cultural reform-movement. All reports, pointing as they do into opposite directions, indicate that the Abrahamites, the Hebrews, have gone on their wanderings through a spiritual, and probably also through a racial, cross-breeding with other nations, in Egypt and around the Sinai-Peninsula, melting afterwards into a loose national unit with the *Israelites* in Canaan. (Some believe that the Abrahamites originated in Canaan whence they emigrated to Babylonia, only to *return* later into the land of their origin. According to this view the Abrahamites reunited themselves later in Canaan with their *own tribes*.)   But in spite of all these various elements which entered into the development, the Babylonian element remained the chief movent of the reform movement; the more so as almost all of these foreign elements were *Semitic* in their origin, depending on Babylonia-Assyria in all things religious and cultural.

But what was the *driving power* in the Abrahamitic reform-movement? A comparison of Babylonian-Assyrian religious literature with Biblical literature results in the following orientation:

In the center of the religious and cultural life of Babylonia was the *sexual motif*. This motif prevented the Babylonians from progressing on the road to monotheism upon which they, indeed, had started in the course of their development. So long as the sexual motif dominates in the sphere of the Divine, there can be no idea of an *intellectual, incorporeal* divine Being. This feature is more decisive than that of *arithmetical unity*. Gods that are born are no absolute cosmological potencies; gods that are subject to any passion whatsoever are no absolute ethical ideals. It was of no avail to the Babylonians, even though, at times at least, they really did recognize one of the gods as "God of gods" and did unite upon him many, though never *all*, of the attributes. This "King of the gods" (whether it was Ea, Anu, Marduck or Ashur) could not do without the female half, and this alone was sufficient to destroy the arithmetical, and, even to a still greater extent, the cosmologico-ethical unity of the divine being.

This, then, was the first step in the progress of the Abrahamites beyond the Babylonians on the road to religious and cultural progress. They realized that the divine Being must be exalted above this most aggressive of all human passions, the sexual motive, altogether, in order to be able to be really just and impartial. The efforts that were made to overcome this motive, led to the conception of an *incorporeal*, intellectual Being. A being exalted above the sexual cannot be presented in a perfect *image*, a fact which led gradually to the conceiving of the idea of a Being of pure spirit and to the prohibition of making an image (מסכה) of God.

This insight into the nature of the Divine gradually revolutionized all forms of life, religious and cultural. It is safe to presume that this exalted conception of God was first conceived by *one* great personality, (which, of course, was the product of the accumulated efforts of the past), and that even in the next following generation those were only few who were able to fathom this great idea and utilize it in their lives. Moreover, it would seem that even in the leading intellectual circles the progress was going on at a very slow pace. The narration of the "Sons of God," or the *Angels*, who took unto themselves

wives from the "Daughters of Adam" according to
their own choice (Gen. VI) shows clearly that, even
within the *literary period*, when they could not
ascribe the sexual motive to God any more, they
would not hesitate to ascribe it to the *angels*.   Nevertheless, the oldest literary material in its totality
warrants the assumption that the leading circles
were well aware of the fact that a real reform of life
in religion and culture can never be achieved, unless
the sexual motive will be eliminated entirely from the
sphere of the Divine.   An orientation in the historical
narrations of the Bible indicates clearly that almost
all sections in which the sexual motive plays any part,
belong to the oldest documents of the Bible.

By saying this we admit, of course, that the biblical
writers alluded to were not able to free themselves
entirely from the sexual motif in their literary production.   However, a comparison with Babylonian-
Assyrian, and general Semitic, parallels to those
narrations shows beyond a doubt that these writers
whose productions were the primary sources of our
Biblical narrations, were progressing greatly in decisive points on the road to ethical monotheism.

It was by no means an easy task to do away with
the sexual motive.   To do so meant to rob the people
of their *religion*, their *literature* (written or oral),
their *art*.   Perhaps it was just the restraint the
writers imposed upon themselves in this regard, that
helped them to bring the people to a realization of
one divine Being exalted above others, as *God*.   *God*
is exalted above the sexual motive, the *gods*, however,
the *angels*, remain to these writers (whose type we

have before us in Gen. VI, lf.) so as the people knew and loved them. The angels have intercourse with men, and some nations trace their pedigree up to them as their divine ancestors. The angels continue to appear in human form, while God himself is thought to be exalted above this form of manifestation. This was the degree of intellectuality of the divine Being attainable for that early period, which later has become the origin of the prohibition to make an *image of God* (Ex. XX, 23) and which was codified in the *Sinaitic Book of the Covenant* (Exodus XX-XXIII, with some omissions). But by and by the postulates of these prophetic writers went further than this, in that they excluded also the angels from the sexual motive, even though not yet from appearing in human forms on earth. The early history of the nation, in which the ancestors were presented as of divine origin, was rewritten by these writers (or bards, or story tellers). In this new version God and the angels retained but a *providential relation* to the family affairs of men. And these relations are of such a nature that through them the *purity of the family* of the Abrahamites stands out prominently as against the corruption of other nations, some of whom owe their existence to an act of incest, like Moab and Ammon (Gen. XIX, 30-38, as compared with the story of Sarah-Pharao, Sarah-Abimelech and Rebecca-Abimelech). These efforts were leading up to an even more rigid intellectual conception of God. Exaltedness above sexuality and corporeality was being expressed by the word "holy." This word, קדש, assumed an eminently ethical meaning, already in pre-Sinaitic times, even though it was not as pregnant with meaning as in later times.

Thus we have arrived at another point in which the God-conception of the pre-Sinaitic writers differentiated from the Babylonian conception. Of course you can find any number of ethical attributes with the Babylonians as well as with other Semites, but none in the sense of *ethical holiness*, as they are to be found in the Bible (and later in Plato). Now to this *Plus* with the Abrahamites on the one hand there is a corresponding *Minus* on the other. The divine attribute of *Creator*, as also all other cosmological attributes so often met with in Babylonian literature, disappears entirely from the literary products of the Abrahamites (not to be taken up again until *Jeremiah*). A monotheistic conception of creation was out of reach to these writers, especially on account of their belief in the existence of eternal angels. The cosmogonic myths familiar to them were entirely too much permeated with the sexual motive, as also with the motives of strife, envy and rebellion amongst the gods, as to invite these writers to reshape them in the monotheistic spirit. Evidently for this reason they neglected all cosmogony, devoting themselves to the *national history* without paying any attention to the origin of mankind. The oldest known sources of the Torah, the *Elohist* and the older *Jahvist*, start their narrations with Abraham (the Elohist sets in Gen. XV, the older Jahvist Gen. XI-end). This elimination of the cosmological element from the God-conception dates back to pre-Sinaitic times, as it would appear from the fact that we do not find any inkling of a cosomological attribute in the *first Book of the Covenant*, a book in which we well may look for a comprehensive expression of all efforts and achievements in pre-Sinaitic times.

This differentiation of the point of view in the God-conception brought about a radical alteration in the *literary motifs* of the writers. There are in Babylonian-Semitic literature all kinds of motifs dominating in the conception of history and legend, such as astrologico-magical, national-political, eschatological and others, while the motif of attributes, that is to say the motif which presses all narration and all song into service to emphasize the ethical monotheistic God-conception, was barely in its incipient stages. Also the Abrahamitic writers utilize all these motifs, including the sexual, but the motif of attributes comes with ever increasing definiteness into the center of interest. All literature and all speculation aim in the first line at the elucidation of the ethical God-conception. Some instances of the motif of attributes as an artistic motif of literary composition we will see in products of later periods, but the extensive use of this motif goes back to those pre-Sinaitic times in which the prophets and the writers of Israel's ancestors were shaping the monotheistic God-conception by gradually combining the *attributes* and *names* of all the gods and uniting them upon one divine being, thus depriving all the other gods, the *angels*, of all of their names and attributes. In the Bible (except for the late book of *Daniel*) an angel has no proper name nor any attribute of his own. Asked for his name, he gives an evasive answer, although he does have a temporary name according to the function that happens to be incumbent upon him.[1] Of course, the passages alluded to here are found but in post-Sinaitic literature, since there is no literary product identifiable as a whole as pre-Sinaitic. But the fact that the exclusive claim of the one God upon all names and attributes has condensed, already in the Sinaitic Book of the Covenant, into the prohibition of calling other gods by their names (Ex. XXIII, 13), warrants the assumption that this phase of development had already been reached in pre-Sinaitic times.

As divine *names* they considered in those days (even as, to a certain extent, also in later times, talmudical and medieval) all *attributes*, such as "merciful," "gracious," and the like. Nevertheless, certain designations of the divine Being differentiated early as *names*, or, still better, *proper names*, of the one God, in contradistinction of other appellations which were understood as expressive of certain divine qualities. Of these names two stand out most prominently: *Elohim* (אלהים) and *JHVH* (יהוה). The name *Elohim* which goes back to the common Semitic *El* (אל), and which was in use among the Abrahamites in previous periods, was gradually replaced by the name of *JHVH* which goes back to the older *Jah* (יה). *Gradually*, for there evidently has been a time in which the national proper name of God with the Abrahamites was *EHJH* (likewise a

---

[1] Compare Gen. XXXII, 30, 31; Jud. VI, 22; XIII, 17-8 with Ex. XXIII, 20-21; Josh. XXIV, 19; wherefrom it would seem that the angel in Ex. XXIII, 21 had the name of קנאל

compound with *Jah*). Traces of the rivalry between these two names are still to be found in the Bible (the most distinct trace in Ex. III, 13-15), and in this rivalry there are involved certain facts the discussion of which shall permit us a deeper insight into the higher phases of the development of the God-conception in pre-Sinaitic times:

While the elimination of the cosmological interest meant originally a lessening of the *speculative* element undoubtedly present in Babylonian literature, it was, on the other hand, just the deeper ethical conception of a divine Being exalted above all human passions that has been leading up to the conception of a divine Being exalted above all human forms of appearance. Thus the desire of the spiritual leaders of the people to formulate a more practical God-conception, a conception of the divine Being that involves the postulate of a better life, has repelled that speculative element which was in no immediate relation to life, only to lay more stress upon that speculative element by which life can be influenced in a direct and decisive way. As a first step in this direction we have recognized the one from the ethical concept of holiness to the eminently metaphysical speculative concept of the intellectual essence of God. This feature concerned the life of the *individual*. God as the ideal of holiness was undoubtedly a very apt, at any rate the best conceivable, instrument with which to try a reform of life within the province of the individual. But if this instrument was to be made effective, it had to be perfected in two directions. In the first line the old *doctrine of retribution* had to be adapted to the new God-conception, and, in turn, the God-conception had to be completed in such a manner as to comprise also the *social aspect* of life, the relations between man and man. Quite indifferent to the deeper cosmological questions, the oldest representatives of religious literature in Israel manifest a much more open mind to all questions affecting the ethical life. In their way of treating the two questions alluded to, they, indeed, show a deep understanding of the fact that in the ultimate analysis there is *one* question only, that of the *divine Justice.* Only the belief in a *just* God makes it imperative upon man to be just toward his fellowman. Again, only of a just God can man expect the reward due to him for the sacrifices he has to bear in shaping his own life and his relationship to his fellowman according to the postulates of ethics. As a matter of fact the oldest literary elements still traceable show beyond a doubt that it was the concept of divine Justice which engaged all the speculation of the thinking men in Israel's hoary past. Of course, also the other Semitic nations knew the attribute of divine justice and the doctrine of retribution. But there were all kinds of gods with conflicting tendencies whose purposes were crossing and double-crossing each other. *Injustice, too, had its divine representatives.* And this had to be so, it could not be otherwise, as long as the gods themselves were subject to human passions, differing from man only in that their passions were *super-human*, or rather, *inhuman.* And there is one more important feature. The Semitic gods *could not* be looked upon as the source of justice. Were they not themselves under the sway of *Fatum*, just as men were? There also were *fights* among the gods, and there is only *one* just party to a fight. Quite different under the dominion of the conception of a unique Being that is exalted above all passions and possessed of omnipotence from the sway of which there is no escape, for either angel or man. Then the idea of justice had to be taken up in all seriousness. The only God is not under the rule of a Fatum, and nothing prevented Him from ruling the world in Justice.

In consequence of this also the concept of *Prophecy*, common to all Semitic peoples, underwent a deep-going modification. The prophets are no more those witchcrafters and soothsayers who can perform miracles by which they are able to subdue even the gods, and who know the means by which to shift the figures within the fatalistic order of things. The prophets in Israel are becoming ever more and more the messengers of God whose function it is to teach men to try to be as good as God is; and only for the purpose of enabling them to perform this duty God equips them with the power to do wonders.

The further development along these lines led up to a stricter conception of *man's personality*, of *ethical* and *religious responsibility*. Among other Semitic peoples the notion of responsibility was very limited. Responsibility in its ultimate meaning was nothing but the helplessness of man within the fatalistic order of things. True, the gods also were subject to Fatum, but by virtue of their better knowledge of the magical means and their greater power to bring them into play, they were not as helplessly lost as man was. In the following we will see that the conception of *prophecy* and *free will* were going through a certain development even in later times. But as compared with the Babylonian and common Semitic notions of these beliefs we may well say that these concepts, as cherished by Israel's ancestors, display a certain amount of ethical maturity and logical consistency.

In its first stages this speculation has led to the concept of a God of the most rigid justice, to the *"El Kanna"* (אל קנא), the "God of Vengeance," the "Consuming Fire." "The holy *Elohim*, the zealous God" (Joshua XXIV, 19), corresponds to this phase of development in the pre-Sinaitic God-conception. But the *reaction* was bound to come before long. The concept of *Grace*, in vogue among the Semitic gods, the *arbitrary grace*, could not be harmonized with the new God-conception. On the other hand, a God that knows no mercy, had no prospect of endearing himself to the hearts of the people. And then, too: A God with no grace and no mercy would educate man also to be hard and cruel. The Semitic peoples believed in certain gods that defend the cause of the weak and the poor. A certain part of the crops of field and flock was *tabooed*, reserved by some god for the priest and the poor. But under the dominion of *one* Being in the exclusive possession of all names and attributes, the weak and the poor could have no protection whatsoever unless that only Being is equipped with the pertaining attributes. And also the people in its entirety which was believing in its being a chosen nation destined to a great future, must have felt that rigid justice with no mercy imperiled the realization of this future.

It is to this period that we have to look for the first efforts of the thinkers and writers to designate God by the attributes of "merciful," "gracious," and the like. Further reflection on this question, notably the endeavour to remove the evidently conflicting conceptions of the "gracious and compassionate God" and the "zealous God," was gradually leading up to attempts of uniting these attributes in one *formula* by way of compromise. These were the first efforts toward a *definition of the ethical God-conception.* In its *most complete form* we have the ethical definition of God in the Bible in the formula of the *Thirteen Attributes* (Ex. XXXIV, 6-7), but this formula, being the product of a later period, was the result of preceding formulas of the same kind, less expressive and less known. This was bound to lead up to an endeavour to coin a new Name for God. The zealous God of rigid justice had been known by the name of *Elohim*, but how were they to designate their God-conception by *one* word, by a *name* which would stand as a *sign* for the attributes united in the *compromise formula?* And then, too, there was a *national* aspect to the question. *Elohim* was common-Semitic, but the God-conception of future Israel had already been so much of a new coinage that it was also urging for a new name of national coinage. For a time this function was filled by the name of *E HJ H* (אהיה). But it seems that this phase of the development coincides with that period in which the reaction against the God of rigid justice was still so strong that the element of *arbitrary mercy at the expense of justice* was prevailing in the attempted definitions of God. For this probably is the meaning of *E HJ H*. As long as the God-conception of rigid justice was dominating, the belief was spread that the presence of Elohim spelled great danger, a belief that made the *intermediation of angels* necessary. The latter, too, were rigid enough, yet their intermediation meant mitigation of rigid justice. Then, with the rising of the conception of the God of mercy, the opposite conception developed: The presence of God mean† great, unlimited, or, at least, but little limited, mercy. Accordingly, they formed the name of EHJH— "I will be (with thee)." But while the names *Elohim* and *E HJ H*, the God-conception of rigid justice and that of absolute mercy, or at least of far-reaching mercy, were rivaling each other, certain efforts came to the fore which tried to define God as a Being which rules with rigid justice, at the same time, however, bringing, also, mercy into play, according to *certain principles.* And the promoters of this new compromise God-idea, they, too, covered their new God-conception with a new name: JHVH. The traces which the name EHJH left in the Bible, clearly indicate that the name JHVH had to go through a contest with its older rival, one not at all too easy, but from which JHVH came out victorious.

Insignificant as the question of names may appear to us today, the conception of a Being that

regards rigid justice, which, however, at the same
time dispenses mercy according to definite rules,
would never have developed that great power which
it has been called upon to exercise, were it not for
the new name that became the bearer of that new
conception. And this is especially true as regards
the *national* consolidation of the people. The new
name won the hearts of many prominent individuals
and their groups for the new God-conception, and led
up to the forming of a certain unity of national consciousness on the basis of a *Covenant* between this
national unity and the God of Justice and Mercy.

This was a task not easy of accomplishing, as it
is also evident that it took a development of centuries to accomplish it. The postulates of the new
God-conception, in each and every phase of its
development, called for a *thorough reform of the entire
system of life*, in all of its private and public manifestations, in religion, culture, art and custom.
The attempt to oust the sexual stories about the gods,
so dear to the people, as, for that matter, the entire
ancient Semitic conception of the essence of the
gods, by the new conception of the holy, just, or just
and merciful, God, was a task almost hopeless on its
own account, but much the more so on account of the
practical postulates involved: The making and
worshipping of images to be forbidden; the worship
to be deprived of all that lends to it the character of
mysterious exaltation; to be mindful of rigid purity
of the family; to forego the exercise of might for the
sake of right; moreover, to mind the weal of the
weak and the needy far beyond all postulates of

right — these were postulates so new and so radical
that it required hundreds of years before even a small
fraction of the people was ripe for them.   However,
the power of the new ideas was great; the prophets
of JHVH were indefatigable; the small band was
becoming ever larger, it kept on growing in numbers
and in spiritual power.   And at the time when that
phase of development had been reached in which the
name JHVH made its appearance as the emblem
of the national flag—at that time that small band
of enthusiasts, in the midst of a people which in its
great masses was as yet unripe for the covenant
with JHVH, felt strong enough to venture the great
step of proclaiming the *Covenant at Sinai.*

FROM THE COVENANT AT SINAI TO THE DEUTERONOMIC COVENANT (621 a.)

CERTAIN indications in Bible and Talmud, as also in the documents brought to light by the excavations of the last decades, irresistibly corroborate the suggestion hinted at above that the Abrahamites, in the course of the struggles concomitant to the invasion of Palestine, entered relations of political alliance and spiritual as well as bodily assimilation with certain autochthonic tribes.

The passive resistance of the people against the doctrines and ordinances of the Sinaitic Covenant and their realization in life was now strengthened by the new active influences of the new Semitic environment, and most especially by the influences of those autochthonic elements with which the Abrahamites came into close contact, and, by and by, were assimilated into a loose political and religious community. And the more they gave up their previous *nomadic freedom* in their efforts toward gaining permanent settlements, the stronger grew the influence exerted by the now permanent environments and intimate contacts. And difficult as it may be to have it ever made out with any degree of certainty, there seems to be much justification for the conclusion that the original Abrahamitic element was predominating in the South, while the Israelitic element was predominating in the North. And whatever the truth may be about the traditional

story of the original unity of North and South and
their later separation, for our purpose, that of clearing
up the outlines of the spiritual development, it is
sufficient to refer to the fact contradicted by none,
that between North and South there were contentions
not only of a political, but also of a religious nature.
Indeed, it is but natural that the Israelitic element
of the North had historic-mythological traditions
and religious-cultural ideals of so definite a character
that they were well liable to retard even more the
reform movement started with the Sinaitic Covenant.
Reading the historical books of the Bible, especially
the book of Judges, with due attention, one can
hardly resist the definite impression that certain
narrations were originally independent conceptions
of early national history, developed in different
centers of the Northern tribes, and but later cor-
sespondingly modified and fitted into the frame of
pragmatic history. The fact that there was a backsliding after the Sinaitic Covenant is expressed by
tradition in the narrative of the *molten image* (מסכה)
the Israelites are said to have made after the Sinaitic
Covenant. Likewise our suggestion that backsliding and retardation in the monotheistic development
are to be charged, in part at least, to the Northern
tribes, appears strengthened by the *later Judean
interpretation* that the molten image in that tradition
was a *golden calf*, thus the *political* and *religious
national emblem* of the Northern Kingdom. The
literary documents of biblical times came down to
us in a very composite shape, the various conflicting
elements and influences being molten together in a

fashion often so organic that a complete analysis into
their original constituent elements is a task almost
impossible of accomplishing.   Moreover, in the course
of the development there have taken place certain
crossings of conflicting traditions and ideas which
variously caused an alteration, and oft-times nearly
a reversion of the standpoints of the conflicting
groups, at least in particulars. Nevertheless, in
spite of all this uncertainty in particulars, there is
one fact that is established beyond all doubt. The
Deuteronomic Covenant was carried out in *Judea*,
and, notably, *after* the destruction of the Northern
Kingdom, at a time when the latter was dependent
on Judea in all matters religious, and after all preceding attempts at reform while the Northern Kingdom was still in existence, had proved futile. Thus
it shall be well possible to refer now and then to the
bearing of the conflicts between North and South
upon the course of the spiritual development in the
period enclosed by the first two Covenants:

There is one pivotal point from which all phases
of the development under discussion can be explored
and gotten full sight of. I refer to the *question of
angels*.

Let us compare the *Admonition* (תוכחה) contained
in those concluding verses of the first Book of the
Covenant which stamp it as the Deed of the Covenant,
with the parallel section in the Deuteronomic Book
of the Covenant, chapter XXVIII: At once we
become aware of the fact that the *Angel*, the very
bearer of the Covenant in the first Book of the
Covenant, is entirely missing in the concluding

Admonition of the Deuteronomic Book of the Covenant.   Continuing to orient ourselves in this direction, we soon find that in the *entire* Book of Deuteronomy (inclusive of the later additions) the existence
of angels is not only never asserted but rather expressly denied.   This is especially evident from one
passage in Deuteronomy, VII, 1-5, when compared
with its parallel in the first Book of the Covenant,
Ex. XXIII, 20-32.   All that is being said in the
latter passage of the *Angel* as *Mediator*, the former
says of *God Himself*.   At once it becomes evident
that we face here a deepgoing, portenteous dogmatical
controversy.

A thorough study of the history of that period,
as its literary echo resounds in the Bible, conveys to
us the suggestion that this controversy formed the
center of all that movement which found its temporary
conclusion by the Deuteronomic Reform, and also
that the entire spiritual development of that period
was going on under the influence of this controversy
which started asserting itself very early and was
keeping on increasing with the advance of time.
The phenomena referred to here are variously over-
lapping into each other's sphere in a very complicated
manner; it is, nevertheless, well possible to analyse
the problem of the development in its totality into
four component problems, the separate discussion of
which will make the presentation more transparent.
These four component problems are:
1. The Conception of Early History.
2. God-conception and Divine Names.
3. The General Dogmatical Development.
4. The Religious-Cultural Life.

1. THE CONCEPTION OF EARLY HISTORY

Considering the fact that the narrations in the sources E and J are so intimately bound up with theophanies and angels, it becomes evident that the effort to overcome the sexual motive in the sphere of the divine was greatly furthered by the opposition to the doctrine of angels. And since the opposition to the angels developed chiefly in Judea, as we will soon see, it would be easy to show that as far as the process of purification is concerned, the Israelitish conceptions of early history remained far behind those of Judea. If we compare some of the narratives in the *Book of Judges* with those of *Genesis*, we soon shall find that narratives which came down to us in a shape nearer the original Israelitish conception, have achieved but a lesser degree of purification than those which had gone through a decisive Judean influence, as for instance those in the book of Genesis. And among the latter, too, various degrees of purification are perceptible in their various parts. And in these also the less purified motives could be traced to an Israelitish origin, though not always with sufficient certainty. In general it may well be said that the Judean source (which is the younger one), the *Jahvist* (J), presents the higher degree of the development. At times, however, it happens that a report in the *Elohistic* source (E, which is the older one), would appear more purified than its parallel in the Jahvistic source (cf. to this whole question Gesch. d. jued. Philos, II. 1, at the beginning of the second chapter, and my essay: The monotheistic redaction of the national mythology, in the Hebrew monthly "Hatoren," New York,

1913-1914). But these details shall not be discussed here. For our purpose here it will be sufficient to present the *results* of the *whole development* at the time of its completion at the end of this period, results that testify best to the driving force of the preceding development:

When after many backslidings and religious aberrations the prophets had come to the conclusion that the position of the angels in the religion of Israel was decidedly obstructing the much-desired purification of the God-conception and its penetrating into the rank and file of the people, they could not escape the further conclusion that it was necessary to remove everything reminding of the authoritative sanction of that doctrine. And so when it came to the redaction of the Deuteronomic Book of the Covenant, they ventured a thorough *revision* of the *early history*. For, apart from the fact that angels occupy a prominent place even in the purified narratives of the early history, the rigid monotheistic reform party must have taken offence at the ill-concealed remainders of the old legends. And of such ill-concealed remainders there were a good many not only in the older, but also in the later versions of the tribal history, such as E and J, and some of them are still perceptible in the *combination* of both, JE. In addition to this, apprehension was growing on account of the sexual motives in vogue in the religious practices of the people in closely pre-Deuteronomic times. So it had become imperative to remove not only the first Book of the Covenant from its authoritative position, but also the book of JE, which was enjoying a certain degree of

authority with the people.   This end they hoped to
achieve by attaching to the new Book of the Covenant,
even the Deuteronomy, *a new version of the national
history* as an introduction.   In conceiving this official
version of the national history they proceeded in a
manner which was as radical as it was simple.   Instead
of going into the troublesome task of refashioning the
early national history, they simply *cut it off*:   They
started the history with the exodus from Egypt, thus
deliberately giving up all of the interesting early
history.   Taking into account the original book of
Deuteronomy (V-XXVI and XXVIII) only, the
three names of the patriarchs, Abraham, Isaac, and
Jacob, are the *only trace* of the early history by means
of which they tried to cover the infinite pre-historic
vacuum.   And even these three names are preferably
replaced by the general designation "Your Ancestors"
(אבתיכם).   For, possibly, even these names were
better avoided, reminiscent as they were of the time
when they still were *names of gods* (cf. Is. LXIII, 16).
To alter the name of the people "Israel" was not
feasible, from the traditional point of view, inasmuch
as according to this tradition Israel was originally
one people; but the name "Israel" as that of the patriarch Jacob is completely avoided.   They did not like
to be reminded of the change of name brought about
by an *angel*.   Moreover, even the last vestige of the
number *twelve* as that of the tribes of Jacob, and thus
a very important *astral motif*, was to disappear entirely
from the national history.   But most decisive is the
fact that all *woman figures*, with all the stories attached
to their names, have disappeared entirely from the

official version of the national history as outlined in Deuteronomy(including the later additions). The only woman whose name occurs in Deuteronomy, Miriam (XXIV, 9), is mentioned only in the part she played "on the road after thou hadst left Egypt," to emphasize the supreme position of Moses as a prophet. Besides, this passage is most likely a later interpolation, as may be concluded from the fact that the entire incident of marriage and children in the life of Moses appears to be advisedly suppressed in the book of Deuteronomy. According to this book (as also according to the Priestly Code) we have to understand that Moses remained single all his life. The Talmudists, feeling this situation, harmonized this with the contradictory reports in other portions of the Torah by the interpretation that as a preparatory step to the Covenant at Sinai Moses separated himself from his wife for ever (cf. Deut. IX, 14; Ex. XXXII, 10).

This radical step taken by the redactors of Deuteronomy can be explained by the conditions of that time:

The political dependence of Judea on Assyria-Babylonia and, in consequence thereof, the imitation of the conquerers in cult and ritual started already under the reign of Ahaz (II Kings XVI, 8), even though for the first the relation was a half-way friendly one. The Reform of Hezekiah had been delayed and, eventually, marred. Then came the rather covered dependence of Hezekiah on the Babylonian empire, (ibid. XX, 12f.). No doubt the Reformer Hezekiah was watchfully counteracting the Babylonian influences in cult and ritual. Nonetheless, the relation to Babylonia started by him, not of his seeking, in spite of his wishes, is, to a certain extent, to be considered as preparatory to the backsliding under the reign of Menasseh whose dependence on the Neobabylonian empire certainly contributed greatly to those motives which made him reform the cult and ritual back to Babylonian standards or to their imitations among Western Semitic peoples (ibid. XXI; 2 Chr. XXXIII). Thus the time preceding the Reform of Josiah was one of deep religious deterioration. Politically and religiously the people was laboring under the destructive influence of Babylonia. If, therefore, the speakers of the people in their defense of the cult of the "Queen of the Heavens" against Jeremiah refer to previous times when this cult, according to Jeremiah's own completing and confirming report, was practised by the kings, the nobles and the people, they certainly mean at least also the time closely preceding the Deuteronomic Covenant (Jer. XLIV, 16f.; cf. VII, 18). These conditions hardly improved in the first eighteen years of the reign of Josiah, the time in the first half of which the spiritual leaders of the people were working towards the aim of persuading and inspiring the young king to carry out their plans of a great Reformation. It is those times into which we have to project the flourishing Ishtar cult "in the cities of Judah and in the streets of Jerusalem."

Confronting this situation, the leaders of the Reform Movement evidently deemed it best to oust all that literature in which certain, even though attenuated, sexual motifs were dominating, liable to further the very Ishtar-cult which they tried to suppress. And this situation accounts also for the little success of this radical step. This Reform may have, indeed, has, succeeded in ousting some offensive elements entirely and in attenuating others, but it *never* succeeded in the attempt to oust entirely the stories of the early history. It was easier to thwart the first Book of the Covenant from its authoritative position than to dispute the narrating literature its semi-authoritative pedestal. And, indeed, the conception of the early history continues to develop in the next period.

2. GOD-CONCEPTION AND DIVINE NAMES.

In the Torah in its present form the most complete definition of God in pre-Deuteronomic times (the Formula of Thirteen) occurs in the Elohistic source (E). True, it is very likely, nay almost sure, that this formula had been developed and consummated in Judea, as it is also sure, that it was contained in the original Jahvistic source (J, before it was combined with E). But since of the two sources E is evidently the older one, it recommends itself to start the presentation of the development of the God-conception by considering the source E first. The more so since E is evidently nothing else but the Israelitish version of the pre-Sinaitic (Judean) development, thus reflecting the development in its totality to a certain extent more faithfully than does J in which the Israelitish influence touches upon rather subordinate points (cf. to all questions treated in the following my Geschichte d. jued. Philosophie II. chap. 2):

The *motif* of *attributes* in E is, in its artistic-literary aspects as well as in its substance, of such a high finish, that it becomes clear at once that we have before us a product of a long development. Under the guidance of this motif, emulated and developed to a still higher degree of perfection by later writers, the biblical historians would conceive their presentations of early History in such a way as to make the very development of the God-conception mirror itself in the course of events, a feature especially emphasized by the use of different divine names for different periods of History. And also writers of later periods of history use the artistic motif of different divine names in order to emphasize the importance of certain events, and to characterize various times and personalities. *Prophets*, too, use this motif in their visions, sermons, admonitions and promises. Everything is in connection with the God-conception, everything is carried by it. This holds true not only of the conception of history, dogmatic doctrines, admonitions and promises, but also of *practical legislation*. It, too, is in intrinsic contact with the God-conception. All this will be confirmed by our presentation, which we now start with an outline of E's God-conception as mirrored in the early national history.

The Elohistic source sets in with Genesis chapter XV. In the report of creation there is no element reminding of this source, nor is there to be found anything in this source that would suggest any interest of the writer in cosmological questions. The development of early history as presented by this writer is one of the *pure ethical God-conception*. To him History begins with *Abraham*. God reveals Himself to the patriarchs through the intermediation of *angels* (and we evidently are to understand that *all* revelations took place through angels even where it is not stated so expressly—this probably having been the case in older versions).   The patriarchs knew the *God of rigid justice* only, by the name of *Elohim*. Accordingly, not only all persons mentioned in the narrative, but even the author himself, in presenting that early period, uses the name of *Elohim* to the exclusion of all other names.   This, the writer confining himself to the use of that divine name in the presentation of a given period which according to his conception of history was the dominating attribute of that period, is an artistic literary device which variously found imitation by later writers.   In E's conception of history God was ruling the world originally according to the demands of rigid justice, an attribute covered by the name of Elohim.   The sin of the brothers against Joseph appears retaliated by the oppression of Israel in Egypt.   It was but after God had decreed to redeem Israel, that the change started by God revealing Himself to Moses under the name of EHJH, and giving him a *sign* of *Mercy*.   And it was only after the Israelites had made the *Massecha* (cf. above and in the following), that Moses prayed to God for a revelation of His "ways", or attributes, and that, in answer to that prayer, God revealed to him the name of JHVH and the Formula of Thirteen as the ideogram of which that name stands.   And this occurs on the Mount of *Sinai*, out from the Cloud (Ex. XXXIV, 5-7):

"And JHVH passed by him, and exclaimed: JHVH! JHVH is God, merciful and compassionate, long-suffering, rich in Grace and Loving-Kindness. Remembering merit unto the thousandth generation, forgiving Sin, Misdeed and Erring, but never blotting out (sin) entirely, (rather) visiting the sins of the fathers upon their children and children's children unto the third and fourth generations!"

There upon Moses prays that JHVH Himself, not the angel, may walk before the Israelites. But, in the conception of E, this prayer is not granted. After the introduction of the name JHVH, E uses this name exclusively (with but two exceptions easily accounted for).

The Jahvistic source (J), too, sets out with the patriarch *Abraham*. After a few short notes on Abraham's family, (Gen. ch. XI, conclusion), this writer utilizes, right in the first divine revelation to Abraham, certain elements which we shall recognize later on as the primitive elements of a *formula of attributes* parallel to the Formula of Thirteen (comp. Gen. XII, 2, with Num. VI, 24-27). Accordingly, it is already this first representative of monotheism, Abraham, who is made acquainted with the name JHVH used so far only by the writer himself (who, then, did not care for the artistic device of using the divine name corresponding to the period under consideration). Of course, in accordance with the scheme outlined above, this revelation does not occur without *preparatory steps*. Abraham builds one altar at Sichem, then one at Bethel, and right here he is distinguished by the revelation of the *great name* (Gen. XV, 2-8). Then the Covenant is entered into on the ground of the Formula of Attri-

butes (XV, 13-f.). After the backsliding at Sinai
there is an appeal to these Attributes of Mercy, the
result being the *elimination of the angel as inter-
mediator* (thus differing from E in this point).

As in other questions, such as the distinction
attached to certain places in the lives of the patriarchs and the like, we notice also regarding the question of who was distinguished by the first revelation
of the name JHVH a certain rivalry between the
respective conceptions in Israel and Juda.   Of course,
in the conception of E, too, the patriarchs are founders
of the Jewish nation, and Israel one of the patriarchs,
the grandson of Abraham.   But we can understand
his aversion to the idea of the God-conception having
reached its highest stage of development by the
patriarch Abraham. His desire was rather to
indicate through his conception of this development
that also the elements that entered but later into the
body of the nation, contributed some valuable
features to the Jewish God-conception.   Consciously
or unconsciously, the general tendency in Israel was
to emphasize the gradual development of the Jewish
God-conception.   In the Judean conception Abraham
signifies at once the beginning and the end of the
development of the God-conception.   The great
name, JHVH, and, consequently, also the Formula
of Thirteen, has already been revealed to Abraham.
The *Elohist*, on the other hand, replaces Abraham by
Moses, a feature that conveys the suggestion that
the beginnings of the relationship between Israel and
Juda go back to the time of the Sinaitic Covenant.
Another feature that seems to have entered the motif

of development in E, is the desire to give some expression to those general Semitic tendencies which were present in Israel to a greater extent than in Juda. Also E wishes to represent the final God-conception, JHVH, as the ultimately only one, but on account of stricter adherence in Israel to the idea of angels as intermediators, this, rather official, writer, notwithstanding his being inspired by prophetic ideas, may have intended to protect the name *Elohim* which, by its plural form, is reminding of the angels, from being ousted entirely. In Juda, on the other hand, there seems to have been a prevailing tendency, concomitant to the growing opposition to the doctrine of angels, to oust the name Elohim entirely from the authoritative national document. And, finally, it is well possible that the difference in the use of divine names is further indicating that in the Formula of Mercy in J there was a wider range for the play of mercy than in E's formula of Thirteen. The *far-going postulates of mercy* in J's *story of Sodom* (Gen. XVIII-XIX; omitted by E) may point in this direction, as also the above mentioned exceptional use of the name Elohim in the case of non-Israelites and of sinners by E. The attribute of rigid justice, as indicated by the name Elohim, has not been abrogated altogether.

And there is another fact which points to the existence of the tendency in Juda to bar the name Elohim entirely from being used as the *proper name* of God: Elohim is not used as the proper name of God in any Judean source provably younger than the J-source. Those in the books of Joshua, Judges, and

Samuel in which Elohim is used as a proper name, belong to the older Israelitish sources, or the name is used in the *evolutionary motif*, only to introduce the name JHVH at a given turn; or, else, in order to identify both names, Elohim and JHVH, as designating the identical divine Being (cf. 1 Sam. IX, 1-10; X, 1; 2 Sam. VII, 18-29).   And if we orient ourselves well in the Bible, we soon realize that this tendency, originating in Judea, was decidedly successful all along the line: We do not find Elohim as the *proper name* of God in *any* literary product, Judean or Israelitish, that is provably younger than the Jahvistic source (except for a few *Psalms* where this usage has its special reason, as we shall see later on.)

This leads up to an orientation in the development of the God-conception and the divine names among the *prophets*.   We are inclined to believe that the sources E and J are older than *Amos* and *Hosea*.   For even if the common elements be more than just common elements going back to an older common source; and even if we were justified in considering certain phrases and ideas in those sources as drawn upon these prophets, it would prove only, what has never been controverted, that the sources E and J have come down to us only after they had been variously refashioned, and with numerous later interpolations. The prophecies of Amos and Hosea are younger than these two sources of which J is the younger one (and perhaps also for *this* reason of a more progressed monotheism).   Be this as it may, we shall soon see that the development of the God-conception and the divine names among the prophets was going on under the influence of those tendencies of which we have noticed more in the Jahvistic than in the Elohistic source.

Amos whose prophecies generally are considered the oldest that have come down to us, never uses Elohim as a divine name in the absolute status (the same is true of Joel, chaps. I and II, which I consider the oldest of the prophecies that have come down to us). This Israelitish prophet who, nevertheless, most probably hailed from Juda and was standing under Judean influence (Am. I, 1; VII, 12), may have evaded the name Elohim out of opposition to the mediation of angels to which he never refers in his prophecies. Also the emphasis laid by him upon the *holy name* which is being shamelessly desecrated by the Ishtar-cult in the practising of which father and son meet each other at the *hierodoule* (II, 7; IV, 2), point clearly in this direction. The elimination of the sexual motive from the sphere of the divine led to the incorporeal God-conception, to the name of "Holy Elohim," but the prophet declines Elohim as a divine name and attaches the attribute "Holy" to JHVH. Yet Amos could not ignore the name Elohim altogether: all prophecies of Amos are borne by the *motif* of attributes. All the prophetic meditation hinges around the question whether or not, and to what extent, the attributes of mercy, as contained in the Formula of Thirteen, will prevail. Especially is this the case in the *Five Visions* at the end of the book VII, 1-IX, 4). Only in the first *two* visions the prophet succeeds in cherishing hopes for the prevailing of the attribute of mercy, while the three last

ones fill him with despair.   No mercy is in sight.
In such a moment of despair, the thought comes upon
the mind of the prophet to discontinue, temporarily
at least, the use of the name of mercy, JHVH, and
to introduce in its stead JHVH Elohei Zebuoth
(יהוה אלהי צבאות) as a *temporary* name of God
(VI, 8-14).   This composite name is to remind the
people that in the time of visitation mercy would
prevail only to a very limited extent.

    Hosea is the *prophet of Mercy* par excellence.
So much are his prophecies permeated by the motif
of attributes, and so full is his language of paronom-
astic allusions to the Formula of Thirteen that some
scholars have been led to believe that Hosea was the
final redactor of that Formula.   Now this alone would
sufficiently account for the fact that this *Israelitish*
prophet uses JHVH exclusively as the proper name
of God, so much so that he raises an emphatic protest
against the temporary name JHVH Elohei Zebuoth
introduced by his older contemporary Amos, insisting
that the exclusive name of God is JHVH, nothing
else.   But the context in which this occurs, indicates
that Hosea's exception to the name Elohim is due
also to the fact that Elohim was generally in use for
the designation of *angels* to whose *mediation* Hosea
was professing strong opposition (XII, 3-7; cf. chap.
VIII against the Calves of Samaria, the symbols of
the angels.)   Hosea who, in his prophecies, shows so
much interest for Juda, was, as also shown by his
preference for the name JHVH, under the influence
of Jerusalem.   It is in harmony with this attitude
that Hosea takes exception to the *women stories* of

Jacob-Israel, contrasting him with the *prophet* (Moses; XII, 13-14; perhaps an allusion to Ex. XVIII, 2, according to which passage Moses separated himself from his wife in order to devote himself fully to the service of the people). This is, furthermore, in accord with the strong emphasis laid by Hosea upon the contrast between Juda and Israel-Jacob in favor of the former. In general, so intense is the interest of Hosea in the fight against the sexual motive in the sphere of the Divine that he tries to fight it, as it often happened in the history of spiritual development, by descending upon the enemy's own ground (chaps. I-IV, especially IV, 11-14 against the cult of Ishtar and hierodoules): In the relationship of Israel to the Ba'alim the sexual motive is the guiding element, while in his relationship to JHVH it is that of faithfulness and exclusiveness (chap II). It is in this spirit that Hosea gives us the *first* definition of God as expressly contrasted with the human: "For I am *God* and not *man*, (I am) a Holy One in thy midst" (XI, 9). But while in former times (cf. Joshua XXIV) the attribute Holy would be identified with "zealous God," Hosea insists that the attribute Holy brings it about that mercy will be prevailing even amid the predicted judgment (XI, 8-11). JHVH, the name of mercy, is the exclusive name of the God of Juda-Israel, moreover, the exclusive name of the *only* divine Being. *All* other names for the designation of gods, of Ba'alim, must be blotted out, should not come upon the lips of man (II, 19). Hosea's definition of God in contradistinction to man signifies a perceptible progress in the direction of the metaphysical deepening of the God-conception. And also one other feature of progress in that direction is perceptibly started by this prophet. The definition of God in the Formula of Thirteen regards only the relation of the attributes of Mercy to those of Justice. Alongside of that Formula we also find the attributes of *Might* and *Eternity* in the Bible, specially indicated in passages where the *great historic doings* of God are spoken of. It is different, however, with the attribute of *Wisdom*. It is hardly indicated, and then incidentally only, never in a Formula including the Thirteen and all other attributes. It is with Hosea that the first elements of the attribute of wisdom loom largely to the fore, but at first only in the *theocratic* phase of it, in that the people are called to realize their blindness in depending on their own counsels instead of following the counsels coming to them from the Wisdom of God. A decided progress in this direction is noticeable with Isaiah, the great Judean prophet.

Isaiah begins his prophetic career at a time pregnant with great events. All the minor states of Western Asia were menaced by the Assyrian giant, Aram and Israel were menacing Juda for her refusal to ally herself with them against the common foe. Isaiah preaches against this alliance, he predicts with great enthusiasm the downfall of Israel as being immediately imminent, but at the same time he cherishes the hope that afterwards the *Remnant* of Israel will unite with Juda into one real Kingdom of God. This may be the reason why the contrast between Israel and Juda does not make itself felt in Isaiah as strongly

as it might otherwise be expected. The prophet was
looking forward to the very near future in which
united Israel will have his religious center in Jerusalem.
And also personal propensities of the prophet play
a great part in this matter. Our prophet, being, on
the one hand, the great opponent of the Northern
Kingdom, was, on the other, at any rate in the beginning of his career, an adherent of the doctrine of
Mercabah and angels upon which rested the right of
the separate religious being of the Northern Kingdom
(cf. in the following). But for all that, Isaiah signifies
the highest degree of religious development in pre-
Deuteronomic, or even, considering the God-conception only, *pre-Jeremian* Judaism. For, summing
up the entire period preceding the formulation of the
monotheistic theory of *creation* and the *cosmologico-
metaphysical* God-conception by *Jeremiah*, as the
period of the pure *ethical* God-conception, we may
say that Isaiah signifies the most adequate expression of
this period. In the deduction of the God-conception
from the concept of *holiness* Isaiah goes further than
all of his predecessors. Alongside of the proper name
JHVH he uses the phrase "the Holy One of Israel,"
an attributive designation of God coined by Isaiah
himself. In the *prophecy of consecration* (ch. VI),
the verse "Holy, Holy, Holy, is JHVH Zebaoth, full
is all the earth of his Khacod," which has come to be
known almost as the *creed* of Judaism, is the introduction of a *new name of God*. In this formula the
attribute "Holy" in itself is, of course, not a new one,
yet not only the emphatic accentuation, but more so
the combination with JHVH Zebuoth imparts to this

formula the value of a *new orientation* in the God-conception. Isaiah believes in angels, but he declines them as *mediators* between God and His people, leaving them the mere function of appearing to the prophet in his first vision of consecration (VI, 6-9). The strong emphasis laid upon the attribute "Holy", specifically in connection with this vision, intends evidently to neutralize the otherwise anthropo-morphically styled appearance of God in this vision (VI, 1). As to the designation "JHVH Zebaoth," evidently also of Isaian coinage (this in spite of the occurence of the composition in the books of Samuel and Kings, passages bearing marks of later inter-polations), it reminds of "JHVH Elohei Zebaoth" in Amos, and is a feature of development along the same line. Isaiah never uses Elohim as the proper name of God, and in this regard he goes much further than Amos, in that he declines the use of "Elohei" even in combination with Zebaoth. Nor does he share the standpoint of Hosea inasmuch as he accepts the surname Zebaoth declined by Hosea, using it very frequently. Isaiah considers the application of the attributes of mercy as expressed in the Formula of Thirteen to be out of the question under the circum-stances. In contrast to the formula of the divine *attributes of mercy* he coins a formula of the *attributes of evil* of the people which bar the efficacy of the attributes of mercy (I, 4). The allusions to the Formula of Thirteen in Isaiah are very slight and few in number, and even these few are retouched with the more comprehensive *motif* of justice (IX, 16; XVI, 5; XXIX, 18-19; XXXIII, 2-5). The attribute

of *Long-suffering* especially seems to have been
given up by Isaiah. For not only is this attribute
never appealed to by the prophet, but it appears to
have been expressly abolished (VIII, 1-4). All data
converge in the indication that Isaiah, like Amos,
favored a temporary name of God which was indicative of a reduced measure of mercy, but at the same
time, in spite of his being an adherent of the belief
in angels, declined to use the name Elohim, even in
combination with JHVH Zebaoth. It is in this that
the Judean attitude asserts itself in Isaiah. JHVH
Zebaoth with Isaiah means the mighty Lord of
Hosts of angels, who has the power to rule the world
in accordance with the postulates of rigid justice.
Having given up the Formula of Thirteen in some of
its essential parts, Isaiah felt the need for a new
definition of God. And in this he shows an outspoken preference for *epigrammatic formulas*. New
coinages of allusive *names* and *formulas* present in
the prophecies of Isaiah the relationship between
justice and mercy, as also a more comprehensive
and metaphysically endeepened definition of the
divine Being. Such are: the formula of attributes
for rulers in the sense of the theocratic idea (III, 2-3);
the names given to children, such as "God with us"
(VII, 13: עמנואל; cf. אהיה), "Hurry for booty,"
"Speed up pillage" (VIII, 1-3) and "Wonder (of a)
counselor of the *mighty* God, the Father of *Eternity*,
the Prince of Peace" (IX, 5; שלום stands for *Mercy*;
cf. next chapter.) These names in their totality,
express the attributes of mercy and justice, of wisdom,
might and eternity in the God-conception of Isaiah.

A more finished definition of God by Isaiah appears in the comprehensive formula of the *metaphysical attributes:* And there shall rest upon him the *Spirit of God*, the Spirit of *Wisdom* and Understanding, the Spirit of *Counsel* and *Fortitude* (Might), the Spirit of *Knowledge* and of the *Fear of the Lord* (XI, 2). This formula signifies an earnest endeavor to define, in a metaphysical way, the divine essence, the source of justice and of mercy, as expounded in the prophet's own explanation added to this formula (cf. *Plato:* Sophia, Andreia, and Sophrosyne (Fear of God) are the *cardinal attributes* of all active reality). And, in general, it was Isaiah who first defined God as *Spirit*, "Ruah," in contradistinction to *Man* (Body) and *Flesh* (Is. XXXI, 3). And also another *new word-coinage* we owe Isaiah: "Elilim" (אלילים) "Nothings," as a designation for idols, is a linguistic creation of the theology of Isaiah. In former periods we find, even with good monotheistic writers, certain notions of the "other gods" which are far from denying them all entity and all power (cf. Jud. XI, 24; 2 Kings, III, 27). To be sure, they considered the other gods as beings inferior to the God of Israel, but they did not deny them all existence. It was, then, Isaiah who attained the insight into the nothingness of the other gods, and who gave it expression in a new linguistic coinage. In Isaiah Judaism achieves its highest stage of development in pre-Deuteronomic times. Indeed, the literary product of the following century is so meager that we may well proceed immediately from Isaiah to *Deuteronomy*.

The book of Deuteronomy, the Book of the Covenant of Josia, is the most comprehensive expression of the party of extreme monotheists which discarded the doctrine of angels entirely, to the extent of denying the existence of angels altogether. Deuteronomy avoids Elohim as the proper name of God, but very often uses the combination of JHVH and Elohim with possessive suffixes, like: "JHVH your God," "JHVH thy God." Deuteronomy obliterates designedly all the vestiges of development in the God-Conception. According to its presentation the name of God has always been JHVH, a point in which it follows the Judean source (J). And yet, the authors of Deuteronomy belong to those (of the Jeremian School; cf. next chapter) who continued and developed the opposition to the attribute of *Long-suffering* started by Isaiah. Not only is there no mention of this attribute, while other elements of the Thirteen are quoted, but it is expressly declined (VIII, 10). It seems, then, that Deuteronomy uses the word Elohim with possessive suffixes in order to lay stress upon the idea of rigid justice inherent in this word to a greater extent than in the name JHVH which covers the Formula of Thirteen. Isaiah's usage of JHVH Zebaoth to express the same idea was not acceptable to the promoters of the Deuteronomic Covenant, its meaning being at that time "God of hosts (of angels)". It was quite different with the name Elohim. This word gradually, especially after the established victory of the name JHVH, came to mean "angels." Now the reader of Deuteronomy often experiences the marked feeling as though "JHVH thy (or your) God" means to say: "JHVH Thy Elohim," JHVH who alone carries out all that is usually ascribed to the Elohim (the angels) which in reality do not exist at all.   In fact, the formula of unity in Deuteronomy seems to express nothing else but this: "Hear, O Israel, JHVH is our Elohim, JHVH is One!"—there are absolutely no Elohim beside Him.   And it is this more than any other feature which marks the progress in the Deuteronomic God-conception.   In the metaphysical formulation of the pure ethical God-conception Isaiah signifies the consummation of the biblical development, Deuteronomy merely codifying the achievement of Isaiah, in that it brings the law in harmony with the pure spiritual nature of the Supreme Being, by the absolute prohibition of images.   But over and above this achievement Deuteronomy teaches the real *arithmetical* and *dynamic unity* of the Divine Being, a point which in pre-Deuteronomic times always was obscured through the belief in the existence of (eternal) angels.   Isaiah and Deuteronomy combined signify the achieved goal of the development of the pure ethical God-conception in Juadism: the *one unique spiritual God.*

3.   The Other Essential Principles.

Ethical monotheism is inseparably bound up with several principles without which the moral order of the world is inconceivable.   These are:

1. *Prophecy*, 2. *Man's Freedom of Will*, 3. *Retribution*, and 4. *Essentiality* and *Substantiality* of the *Soul of Man.*

Now to a certain extent these principles are taken for granted to be the basis of every religion.   Thus we may say that these four principles were with the

Abrahamites a part of their old tradition. However, no matter how true this is, these principles, too, underwent a long and eventful development. This regards their *conscious and distinct* formulation as well as the *emphasis* laid upon them. And then again, in connection with their distinct formulation, there was a certain development in the *purification* of these principles in that they were freed from the contradictory features inherent in them.

As compared with Semitic paganism the progress in these principles, even in the fashion they present themselves in the oldest parts of the Bible, is most obvious:

Prophecy gradually ceased to be a sort of *witchcraft* by which man could learn in what way he could gratify the various passions of the gods so as to secure their favor. Even in the oldest narratives of the Bible the prophet is looked upon as a man who stands for justice and is engaged in the service of loving kindness and charity. The prophet is the *image* of his God. The intercourse of God with the prophet is also gradually being conceived from a subtler standpoint. The idea of man's *freedom* is gaining ground, wrestling it inch by inch from the dominion of the general Fatum encompassing the divine and the human alike. *Retribution* ceases to be an act of *retaliation* and *vengeance*, as looked upon in pagan religion, and develops in the sense of that justice which reclaims, heals and redeems even while it punishes. The *Soul* of man comes more and more to be considered an independent god-like entity. But for all that, if we compare the oldest parts of the

Bible with Deuteronomy, we soon become aware of the fact that, like the God-conception, the principles connected with the same also went through a purifying development.

In the older parts of the Bible *prophecy* still labors under a certain element of witchcraft and sorcery, and the angels mostly play a great part in the prophetic visions.[1] But alongside of these older elements there are long stretches in the Bible in which God's intercourse with the prophets takes place without any magic adornment, and also without the mediation of angels. Moreover, at places there is an obvious effort to slight the older notions of prophecy and to replace them by a higher, more spiritual conception of divine revelation.[2] Particularly it would appear that there was some growing understanding between the different schools of writers to eliminate the mediation of "the angel" (or the angels) altogether from the scene of the *Revelation*

---

[1] Cf. Gen. XVI, 7-15; XVIII; XIX; XXI, 17-18; XXII, 11-18; XXVIII, 11-16; XXXII, 2-7, 25-31; XLVIII, 15, 16; Ex. III, 1-6; IV, 1-9, 24-26; VII ff.; miracles and plagues in Egypt; XIV, 19; XV, 25; XXIII, 20 f.: XXXII, 34; XXXIII, 2-12, 19-23; Num. XI, 24-29; XII, 1-8; XXI, 8,9; XXII, 20-35; Jos. VII, 10-18; Jud. II, I-5; VI, 11-24; XIII, 2-23; 1 Sam. V, 1; VII, 2; IX, 1; X, 16, 20, 22; XIX, 20-24; XXII, 15; XXIII, 2-12; XXVIII, 6-25; XXX, 7-8; 2 Sam. II, 1; V, 19-24; VI, 3-12; XXIV, 1, 16, 17; cf. the parallel 1 Chr. XXI; 1 Kings VIII, 6-12; XIII (esp. v. 18); XIX, 7; XXII, 19-22; 2 Kings I, 15; II, 1-18, and in general the narrations about the miracles of Elijah and Elisha.

[2] Jud. VI, 7-10 obviously against Jud. II, I-5: the "prophetic man" (איש נביא) *replaces* "the angel of JHVH" (מלאך יהוה); I Sam. III, 1-4: revelation reduced to a *voice* coming from the unkown; 1 Kings XIX, 11-12: divine revelation neither in storm, nor in earthquake, nor in fire, but in a still whisper, as against verse 7.

at Sinai: we find them in *no* source.[1]   Thus the suggestion is near that there was a certain movement
against the part of angels in prophecy, and so strong
had this movement become that even those prophets
and writers who otherwise were in the habit of employing angels in their accounts of revelations, agreed
to eliminate them from the revelation at Sinai.   The
same is to be said of *dreams* as a means of revelation.
Divine revelation, we are told, comes to prophets in
dreams, but Moses is exempt from this, his, then,
is a higher, more direct form of revelation (Num.
XII, 6-8).   Here it is clearly stated that dreams as a
means of prophecy signify a lower phase of revelation.
Fortunately, the sources permit us to fix with a
certain degree of exactitude some chronological data
of this important development.   *Isaiah* is the last
pre-Deuteronomic prophet in whose prophecy angels
play any part (ch. VI).   And seeing that this is the
case in the *vision of consecration*, and again that in
this very vision the angels as mediators between God
and Israel are expressly eliminated, it would appear
quite likely that it was but Isaiah himself who, in
spite of his belief in the existence of angels, gradually
came to the conviction that the Mercabah-visions
usually connected with a divine revelation, are mere
illusions which in the higher forms of inspiration are

---

[1]   Deut. XXXIII, 2 is to be read ממריבת קדש; comp.
the parallel in the *Song of Deborah* Jud. V, 4, 5,
although it would seem that this latter source preserved
(in another passage) a vestige of the older conception in
which the angel entered into the scene of revelation at
Sinai; comp. the מלאך יהוה in Jud. V, 23 with Jud. II,
1-5 and Ex. XXIII, 20; cf. my Gesch. d. jued. Philos.
II, 1, p. 80.

not necessarily a part of the prophetic experience, and thus may be eliminated entirely. This would be quite in accordance with the high phase of development in the God-conception achieved by Isaiah. Indeed, Isaiah seems to describe the higher form of revelation as being a *voice* heard in the *ears* of the prophet (V,; XXII, 14). And, in general, Isaiah fights the lower mantic forms and all crafts of sorcery with great emphasis and in seething terms (VIII, 19-21). Of course, the efforts to oust the lower mantic forms go back to older times, prohibitions to that effect having already been enacted in the first Book of the Covenant (Ex. XXII, 17) and in the time of Saul (1 Sam. XV, 23; XXVII, 3, 9, 21). From the latter case we can infer that even after the suppression of necromancy, if the law mentioned should really have succeeded in suppressing it, the *dream* was still being considered a legitimate means of revelation (v. 6). But the insight that the dream is beneath the dignity of a divine revelation, may also have been achieved before the time of Isaiah: King *Solomon* is the *last* of pre-Deuteronomic biblical personalities of whom divine revelation in a dream is reported. This account seems, indeed, to be the last pre-Deuteronomic document in which the dream is recognized as a legitimate vehicle of revelation. The prophets between Isaiah and Deuteronomy stand on the ground prepared by Isaiah (Mi. II, 11; III, 5-12; V, 11; Zeph. III, 4).

The Book of *Deuteronomy codifies* the result of the development in the conception of prophecy as outlined in the preceding. In describing the scene at

Sinai Deuteronomy does not go so far in its pro-
gressive spirit as to give up the *fire* out of which the
Voice came (V, 4, 5, 19-23), but it at least gives up
the *thundering and lightning*, as also the *sounding of
the trumpet*, features that play so prominent a part
in the older accounts (cf. Ex. XIX, 16-19; XX, 18).
It seems that in describing the great scene at Sinai
even the Deuteronomists thought it necessary to add
at least one ornamental equipment, "the mountain
burning afire."   But the *laws* about prophecy as
enacted in Deuteronomy profess a very high cor-
ception of prophecy (XIII, 2-6; XVIII, 9-22).   The
vehicle of revelation as used at Sinai, "the Voice out
of the fire" is expressly *abrogated* for *all future*, replacing it by a higher form of inspiration, expressed
in the words: "and I will place my words in his
mouth."   This shall from now on be the *only* form
of revelation for all *Jewish* prophets (XVIII, 15-18).
This is an open repudiation of the older conception
of things according to which God reveals himself to
non-Jewish   prophets   also   (Num.   XXII),   using
dreams and enigmatic visions in revealing Himself
to prophets other than Moses, thus distinguishing
Moses not only at Sinai but also in later revelations
(Num. XII).   Deuteronomy prohibits not only all
lower mantic forms and all the inferior forms of
intercourse with God in usage among other nations
(XVIII, 9-14), but declares as false prophets *all*
who speak in the name of *dreams*, even though they
are good Jews (XIII, 2-6).   "Dream" and "Dreamer"
in this section of Deuteronomy is synonymous with
"false prophecy" and "false prophet," respectively.

And this linguistic usage continues for the next two centuries, even beyond the time in which the reaction sets in.[1]   *Miracles* and other magical signs are no longer a proof for the veracity of a prophet, according to the Deuteronomic laws, especially in cases where the prophet tries to induce the people to transgress divine injunctions (Deut. XIII, 2-6).   The prophet has only one task, to instruct the people about and to inspire them for the pure ethical and religious life. The only sign that a prophet is expected to offer is the prediction of future events, provided he does not try to use the sign as a proof for the permission to transgress a divine law (XVIII, 21, 22; modified later by Jeremiah; cf. below.)

Freedom of man's will is the *general premise* in the first Book of the Covenant (especially emphasized at the conclusion, Ex. XXIII, 20 f.) as well as in the other sources.   Nevertheless, the belief in eternal angels seems to have had its retarding effect also upon the development of the idea of man's freedom toward its higher and purer ethical conception.   In the evidently very old elements of the later source J₂

(Younger Jahvist), for instance, we find the view that while man's will is free, God tries to prevent him from using it fully, lest he should become too *mighty*. nay, "like one of us" (Gen. III, 22; VI, 5; XI, 6). Again in E, as also in other Israelitish sources, we meet with utterances tending greatly to reduce the sphere of man's freedom in that they suggest the

[1] Cf. Jer. XXIII, 25-32; XXVII, 9; XXIX, 8; Sech. X, 2; in the *exilic* prophecy Joel III, 1 (cf. Tholdoth ha-'Ikkarim I, p. 30-31) it is already the reaction that influences thought and language; cf. below.

idea of God now preventing man from carrying out his sinful intentions, now again inducing him to sin in order to make him fall into disaster and ruin.[1] These strange tendencies toward a fatalistic restriction of man's freedom are found with *none* of the pre-Deuteronomic prophets beginning with *Amos* (or Joel chap. I and II; cf. above). This goes to show that the conception of man's freedom was growing in purity and firmness with the progress in the development of the God-conception by the prophets, especially with the growing weakening of the belief in angels which we were able to verify with all the prophets, including Isaiah. And in this, too, Deuteronomy signifies the consummation and the systematic expression of the preceding development. Here man's free will is asserted in unequivocal terms and solemnly emphasized (V, 26; VIII, 11-18; XI, 26 f. and, most especially, the Thochaha in ch. XXVIII). The alteration Deuteronomy effects in the account about *Balaam* is particularly noteworthy. According to Deuteronomy Balaam was *not prevented* from carrying out his intention of cursing Israel (as related in Num. XXII-XXIV), but Balaam *did* carry out his intention and *did* curse Israel in accordance with his free will, but God *converted* the curse into a blessing (Deut. XXIII, 6).

Objectively taken, the questions of *freedom*, *Retribution* and *Soul* are closely interdependent with

---

[1] Cf. Gen. XX, 6; XXXI, 29; Ex. III, 19; IV, 21 and *all* passages treating of the hardening of the heart of Pharaoh against God; cf. Tholdoth I, p. 87-88; Num. XX-XXIV: Balaam; 1 Sam. II, 25; XXV, 26; cf. verses 33, 34, 39; 1 Kings XVIII, 37.

each other. But while the first indications of this interdependence in the subjective consciousness of the biblical writers as to the question of freedom is noticeable in post-Deuteronomic developments only, the connection between the question of retribution and soul clearly manifests itself long enough within the period of the Deuteronomic development. If we compare pre-Deuteronomic biblical literature with the corresponding Babylonian, or Egyptian literature, we soon notice the rather strange fact that the biblical writers, unlike the Babylonian or Egyptian, speak exclusively of retribution in *this* world, having nothing to say about retribution in the *Hereafter*. For even in those few passages where the *Sheol* is spoken of (*fifteen* times, perhaps also Is. VII, 11), there is no definite suggestion that retribution in the hereafter is aimed at.

But a thorough inquiry into the data involved leads to the following orientation as to the facts in the case (cf. Tholdoth I, 2, chaps 3 and 4):

In the Egyptian "Book of the Dead" we find a rather well developed system of retribution in the hereafter. And since there can hardly be any doubt that the biblical writers knew of this Egyptian, and, for that matter, the entire general Semitic eschatological mythology, their silence about this important feature of religion certainly has its definite reasons.

To begin with, one could not say that there is absolute silence on this subject even in pre-Deuteronomic biblical literature. In two places at least the question of *eternal life* is being dealt with even though with negative results (Gen. III, 22; VI, 3;

these passages are most likely of the later source
J₂, but evidently elements of old mythology). Likewise the "taking away" of *Enoch* and *Elijah* certainly
go to show that the idea of *eternal life for man* was
not unknown to the pre-Deuteronomic biblical
writers (the passages in question being considered as
pre-Deuteronomic by the best authorities). Now
these instances are of great importance inasmuch as
they contain direct *eschatological elements*, clearly
connecting, as they do, the idea of eternal life with
man's *merit and guilt*. Still, there is another passage
which is perhaps even more important and of a more
decisive nature: Elijah prays: "Grant that the soul
of this child return upon his body." And God
answered his prayer, "and the soul of the child returned upon his body, and he revived again." (1
Kings XVII, 21, 22). Here it is stated clearly, and
with all desirable definiteness, that the soul of man
is an *independent substance*, an *individual entity*,
which, when man dies, leaves the body, and which
may again return upon the body, when God so
ordains. And in the light coming from this passage
the eschatological interpretation of another passage
becomes quite suggestive (1 Sam. XXV, 29). The
distinction between *flesh* (בשר) and *spirit* (רוח),
as between two *different substances* is also found with
Isaiah, and this, too, in close connection with the
God-conception (Is. XXXI, 3; cf. II, 22 and XI, 2).
And here we are at the very point of view from which
the discussion of the attitude displayed by the
biblical writers on these questions, is to be undertaken and carried through. The different conception

of God gradually produces a different conception of man's soul also.   The soul as conceived in Egyptian and Semitic eschatology is but the body reduced, be it in some shady existence in the Sheol or driven through all those strange phases known in the doctrine of *migration of the soul*.   With these beliefs there were connected all kinds of abominable practices of *worship of the dead, necromancy,* with all its idolatrous feasts and rituals which only too often served to cover up the worst and most shameless orgies of passion.   The new God-conception refused all connection with these beliefs and rites.   The masess, of course, knew all of these beliefs and rituals, and certainly only too often did they slide back into these attractive practices of superstition and lust, if the prophets ever succeeded in suppressing them at all, to a certain extent at least.

And this was one of the reasons why writers and prophets were so loath to give definite expression to their views on these subjects.   The people had rather *too much* eschatology.   The narrating sources do use the *word* "Sheol," but only in the meaning of "grave," which the word had come to denote, and never in its eschatological meaning.   The prophets, *Amos* (IX, 2.), *Hosea* (XIII, 14) and *Isaiah* (V, 14; XXVIII, 14-18) do, indeed, speak of the Sheol, but in all of these passages it is the *popular beliefs and notions* that the prophets utilize.   Moreover, it is mostly evident from the context that the prophets, in utilizing these popular conceptions, intend to point at the political and cultural influence of Egypt which they considered so detrimental to Israel and Juda, and which, therefore, they were fighting so eloquently and so emphatically. At times they condescend to the language of the people in order to drive it home to them that even the Sheol, if there be any, is in the hand of God (cf. Proverbs XV, 11; verse 18 reminds of the later conception of Sheol, Hell). As to Isaiah, this aspect of the matter suggests itself more definitely with him than with the other prophets. For it is clear that the abominable necromantical usuages in vogue among the people which Isaiah condemns so strongly and so indignantly (VIII, 19. 20; XXIX, 4), are attributed by him to the Egyptian influence which he condemns, for religious, moral and political reasons (XIX, 1-3; XXII, 12-14: the death feast described here is known to be of Egyptian origin; XXVIII, 14-18). It is the "Egyptian Spirit" (XIX, 3: רוח מצרים ; cf. verse 14) from which all the eschatological notions and abominable practices originated, and which, therefore, was opposed so strongly by Isaiah and the other prophets as incompatible with the new, strictly monotheistic God-conception.

And there was another reason why prophets and writers in pre-Deuteronomic times were more loath to indulge in eschatological utterances than their post-Deuteronomic successors. And this reason, too, is in connection with the higher God-conception. The ancient Babylonian, as also the later Jewish, development, bears witness to the fact that the *cosmological* God-conception postulates a more individual conception of retribution than does the pure ethical God-conception. The doctrine of retribution with the Babylonians, whether referring to this world or the hereafter, is essentially of an individual character.

In the first line it is the individual to whom the threats and promises of the gods are addressed. And even in cases where national fears and hopes are the subject of the threats or promises, it is always some representative individual whose weal and woe are involved. This holds true especially of Egyptian eschatology which, in conception and finish, is built entirely on the credit and debit account of the individual. The cosmological God-conception, even in its higher phase of development, produces a certain contrast between the individual and the *outer world*. In the ancient cosmological theology of Egypt and Babylonia this contrast was very intense, to the degree of antagonism. In Israel a decisive change came about with the elimination of the cosmological element and the development of the pure ethical God-conception. The *egotism* inherent in the individual conception of retribution gradually gave way to the growing sentiment of *social justice*. The individual discovered his fellow-man, his neighbor. The hitherto paramount question of how the individual is to *get his right*, begins to yield to the one of how the individual is to *guarantee the rights of others*. Now the eschatological doctrine of retribution is largely the outflow of the sentiment of justice, inasmuch as its function has always been to appease the sentiment of justice, not satisfied in this life, through better prospects in the life hereafter. But in spite of this its lofty origin this sentiment is largely the *sentiment of the individual*. With but few exceptions each and every individual deems himself right and not sufficiently rewarded in this life, wherefore he expects his final adequate

reward in the life hereafter, just as he expects the
punishment of *those others*, the *unjust*, in the future
life.   Thus eschatological doctrines of retribution are
essentially conceived under the aspect of the *individual
account*.   Each and every individual has his own
balance.   With the development of the pure ethical
God-conception, however, this viewpoint underwent a
gradual obliteration.   The old Semitic and Egyptian
eschatology had to be discarded not only on account
of the above mentioned pagan exercises attached to
it, but also because the doctrine of absolute individual
retribution had been becoming less and less compatible
with the progressing development of ethical monotheism.   The divine attribute "visiting the sins of the
parents upon the children" and its counterpart
"remembering merit unto the thousandth generation,"
as conceived in the pure ethical definition of God in
the Thirteen Attributes, corresponds, indeed, to the
growing enlightenment that the doctrine of absolute
individual retribution is in keeping neither with the
realities of life nor with the higher ethical postulates.
The *national consciousness* in the old narrating
sources (E and J) is so intense that the postulate of a
wholly individual account of sin is not considered at
all.   All promises, as a reward for good conduct, are
of a national character.   Seized by the potent national
spirit which permeates these narratives, the reader,
ever so much leaning toward the individual view of
retribution, will feel satisfied in the end that it is the
very right thing for retribution not to tally completely in the life of the individual, but rather to
balance up in a *national-historical accounting*, as it

were. It is a very high conception of *historical personality* that holds sway in these sources. Each and every one of these grand life-sized figures of the patriarchs tells you at first sight that he represents the future history of the great nation in his own life; that his soul is a definite, independent, entity which, like a mirror, reflects all future events in all the wealth of the varied developments in the history of the nation-to-be. But that intense realization of the spiritual personality does not draw conclusions in the individual eschatological direction. On the contrary, the intense national sentiment can well afford to do without individual eschatology. There is an equalizing justice *on earth*, in the *history of the nation*, if not in the life of the individual. This caused them, as it made it possible for them, to *do without* any eschatological doctrine of retribution *altogether*, at least as long as they had not yet found any higher conception of that doctrine. All promises occurring in these sources, as also in the first Book of the Covenant, are of *this world*, and, with very few exceptions, of a national character. Even good or poor crops and other happenings of this kind which clearly affect the individual first, are promised or predicted to the nation as a whole (cf. the Thochaha in the first Book of the Covenant, Ex. XXIII, 25.26). This holds true of all pre-Deuteronomic prophets. Their doctrine of retribution is of *this world*, and *national in the main*. National *in the main*, but *only* in the main. The national note in the pre-Deuteronomic doctrine of retribution simply corresponds to the fact which is generally recognized in our day also, that the scene of equalizing justice is to be sought in the first line within the bounds of the natural units. However, the discovery of the fellow-man within the national unit was bound to lead up to the same discovery outside of the national community also. And again it is in *contrast* to the oppression of the stranger experienced by the Israelites in *Egypt*, that kindness and humane treatment of the stranger are enjoined and emphasized in the first Book of the Covenant (Ex. XXII, 20; XXIII, 9-12). Egypt had a well developed doctrine of retribution in which the ethical note of justice was not entirely missing. But the ethical note was not only compatible with individual and national selfishness, but, moreover, the postulate of complete individual justice had, in a measure, its root in the very promptings of selfishness. It was natural for the prophets whose messages were not of a legislative, but rather of a political nature, that they very often took a severe stand against the other nations. For the relation between *nation and nation* is generally different, and, indeed, less ethical than that of the nation to helpless individual strangers in its midst (cf. 1 Kings, XX, 31; 2 Kings, VI, 21-23). And yet, here, too, the uniting force of the ethical God-conception comes to the fore in the *universal hopes* of the prophets of which we will speak later on.

And in this, too, we find the *consummation* of the development in *Deuteronomy*. One of the most important measures taken by the Deuteronomic reformation was the removal of the necromantical practises and all other pagan rites connected with them (2

Kings XXIII, 24, referring to Deuteronomic Law:
"Be *sound* with *J H V H* thy Elohim!", cf. Deut.
XXIII, 9-13).   In the *nationalization* of the doctrine
of retribution the Deuteronomic document goes
beyond all older sources, including the prophets.
All historic personalities with all their individual
affairs and interests disappear almost entirely before
the all-dominant national entity. Promises and
threats are addressed to the nation as a whole, to
an even greater extent than it is the case in all the
older sources (cf. especially the Thochaha, chap.
XXVIII). And although Deuteronomy is against
the attribute of "Long-suffering" it retains those
attributes that conceive the whole doctrine of retribution under the national aspect (V, 9; the human
judge, of course, must adhere to strict *individual
responsibility*—XXIV, 16). And here again the
national aspect is not one of selfishness toward the
stranger; on the contrary, in this, too, Deuteronomy signifies a *very decisive step forward.* The
national policy required it, of course, that at times
they had to act on the principle of "war is war,"
but even for times of warfare very humane laws are
enacted.[1]   And again, the prevailing of the strength
of the stranger over the nation is threatened with as

[1] XX, 10-20; the verses 15-18 (19) decidedly make an impression
of a *later interpolation*.   They are in sharp contrast to the
humane enactments around them.   Besides, the harmonization which these verses are to bring about, cannot be effected
at all, if we compare the humane enactments here with the
older practice reported in 2 Kings III, 19-25, where the
nation affected is not one of the "seven nations."   And
then, too, the prohibition of the felling of a "good tree"
extends to *all* nations without any exception.

one of the greatest curses. Nevertheless it is just the treatment of the stranger in the Deuteronomic law that signifies the decidedly humane character of this Book of the Covenant. Not only is the *oppression* of the stranger prohibited, referring emphatically to Egypt (XXIII, 8; XXIV, 14.17; cf. XVII, 16), but, beyond that, the *reference to Egypt* is considered strong enough to carry the injunction to *take care* of the stranger (XIV, 21.29; XVI, 11-14; XXIV, 19-22; XXVI, 5-13.). The humane sentiment toward the stranger, contrasted emphatically with Egyptian selfishness, goes so far as to derive from it the duty of not despising any, not even the *Egyptian* stranger (XXIII, 8.9), and to *love* all other strangers. And in order to emphasize this injunction even more strongly, the attribute of "loving the stranger" is embodied in the *definition of the God of Might and of Justice.* The stranger is placed under the special protection of the Jewish Definition of God! (X, 17-20). The *Edomite*, moreover, is called "brother" (XXIII, 8). For all its national exclusiveness, the Deuteronomic Book of the Covenant reaches out for an all-comprising *universal community of mankind.* The range for, equalizing Justice is so wide that the eschatological hopes have no soil left to draw on.

The great step forward which Deuteronomy signifies in the dogmatical development, can also be seen from the *systematic presentation* which all the principles of Judaism of that time have found in this Book of the Covenant. Attentively read, the arrangement of the subjects in Dueteronomy is as follows:

Corresponding to the two Covenants, the Covenant at Sinai and the *renewal* of the same after the
backsliding in the worship of the golden calf, the
historical introduction of Deuteronomy consists of
two sections (V-VIII and IX-XI), each of which offers
an elucidation of the principles of Judaism: Chapter
V: *unity of God* and *prophecy:* chapters VI-VIII:
retribution and (VIII, 11-18) *freedom of will:* chapter
IX: the *violation* of the principle of *unity:* chapter X:
renewal of the Covenant through the new Tablets of
the Covenant (*prophecy*); chapter XI: *retribution*
and (XI, 26 f.) *freedom of will.* The arrangement of
the Deuteronomic *laws* is also in accordance with
this plan: Chapter XII: laws for the safeguarding of
the monotheistic *God-conception:* chapter XIII: laws
on *prophecy* (XIV, 1-21 links with the preceding
idea of the selection of Israel to ethical holiness);
chapter XIV (from verse 22 on)—XXV: laws based
on the idea of *retribution*, especially those of a forensic
nature, *civil* and *penal:* chapter XXVI: Confession
of faith in divine *providence* (on the basis of retribution), and chapter XXVIII: *admonition* through
threats and promises (freedom of will and retribution;
cf. to this whole matter Tholdoth ha-'Ikkarim, I,
p. 42-43).

4.   THE RELIGIOUS-CULTURAL LIFE.

The spiritual development of Judaism presented
in the preceding covers what may be styled the
authoritative line of the development of the *prophetic
postulates.* And while it is true, in a general way,
that there has always been a certain correspondence

between the prophetic postulates and the level of the religious and cultural life, due orientation in the sources reveals the indubitable fact that often the most appalling backsliding into pagan practices in all forms of religious and cultural life occurs at times when the authoritative theoretical progress records its highest successes. And, again, however extreme in their postulates prophets and lawgivers may have been, it is to be expected beforehand, as it really happened, that the unlawful religious practice and the *pagan form of culture* in the life of the people made their influence greatly felt in nature and tendency of the postulates of prophets and lawgivers. On the one hand the extreme excesses of life were bound to evoke attempts at a reform likewise extreme. On the other hand, however, the obstinacy of realities was bound to compel even the most radical of reformers to consider opportune compromises with the conditions and powers that be. This was necessary in order to convert at least a part of their high ideals into reality, hoping that any, even the slightest, step forward in the realm of real life would greatly enhance the ideal and bring life ever nearer to it. What the spiritual leaders told the people about God and other religious beliefs may have appealed to them very much, but the difficulty was rather in the *conclusions* that the leaders were drawing for practical life. And those conclusions and postulates were the more difficult to live up to, as all forms of culture were almost inseparably bound up with pagan *religious* beliefs and rites. The people could well recognize this or that prophetic doctrine in theory without,

however, being able to part with the forms of life
dear to them and in vogue in their environment.   In
such a state of affairs the people were only too ready
to avail themselves of whatever remnant of paganism
and of whatever inconsistencies there were to be
found in the teachings of their leaders, in order to
defend their conventional forms of life as being well
compatible with the authoritative teachings.   And
then, too, there were the political conditions which
were stronger than the will of both the prophets and
the people.   The political sovereignty of one people
over another in those times meant the almost in-
evitable dominance of the cultural and religious forms
of the conquerer in the life of the conquered.   This
imperiled not only the prophetic God-conception as
such, but even more so those practical postulates
which the prophets derived from the ethico-monotheistic God-conception.   Semitic, and Egyptian,
religion was essentially *ritual*, a system of rites and
exercises by which one could remain on friendly
terms with the gods.   And those rites and exercises
were of such a nature that they often called for
actions, as holy and god-pleasing, which the prophets
of Israel abhorred as the greatest abominations.   In
such situations some of the prophets would take a
very radical attitude toward certain religious practises and would go in their denunciation of such
practises beyond what the authoritative law of the
Jewish Community really warranted.   As a result of
this we find that, aside from the contrast between
theory and life in general, there also was a certain
contrast between the *prophets* and the *law*.

Under the aspects just characterized we get the following outlook upon the development of the religious and cultural life of the Jews in the period beginning with the Sinaitic Covenant and extending to the Deuteronomic Covenant.

We have already intimated above that we interpret the tradition of the backsliding of the people after the Sianitic Covenant as a reflex of the fact that the enthusiasm for the reforms inaugurated by that Covenant which may have reached the masses of the people for a while, relaxed soon afterwards, and that the people therefore soon returned to their idols and their idolatrous life. Be this as it may, the fact is warranted in all biblical sources that the various attempts at reform failed again and again, and that, with a few interruptions, the whole span of time intervening between the two Covenants was replete with backslidings and aberrations, the interruptions in Juda being more frequent and of longer duration than those in Israel. These backslidings had their causes not only in the cultural conditions of life, the influences of the environment, the power of custom, and the mental inertia of the people, which rendered it unable to grasp the ideas of its leaders to reform life accordingly, but also in the *half-heartedness* of the new doctrine itself. In times of more or less victorious wars with the other tribes of Canaan the national-religious enthusiasm may have been powerful enough to bring the people a little nearer to the ideas and postulates of their leaders. In times of peace, however, or in times when they were entertaining friendly alliances with surrounding nations, and most es-

pecially in times when, through the force of circumstances, such as alliance or subjugation, they came
under the influence of the great world-powers, Assyria - Babylonia or Egypt,—in times like these the
people hardly could see why and wherefore they
should deny themselves so completely to the Ba'alim
and other idolatrous deities. Are there no other
divine beings beside JHVH? Are there no *angels?*
And could not Peor, Khemosh, Milkom, Dagon, and
other gods of the nations, enjoy their existence at the
side of JHVH as his angels? Of course, the rituals
of these gods required certain practices that were
objectionable according to the law of the Book of
the Covenant and the teachings of the prophets.
But the people had all reason to believe that in the
service of the gods they well could do things otherwise objectionable. Take the worst of these practices, *Ishtar* and *Moloch-worship: Unchastity* and
Murder. Why, does not the national tradition tell
of intermarriage between heaven and earth (Gen. VI),
and of a human sacrifice ordained by *Elohim* (Gen.
XXII)? True, the first Book of the Covenant prohibits
a *Massechah,* an image of Elohim or images of any
gods (Ex. XX, 23; XXXIV, 17; the prohibition of
images in the decalog, Ex. XX, 3, was taken over from
the decalog in Deuteronomy). But this cannot
possibly mean a general prohibition of images.
For not only was the Micah-image (Jud. XVII) known
in tradition as a meritorious work devoted to JHVH,
and as an institute the priest of which was no less a
man than the *grandson of Moses* (ibid. XVIII, 30),
but even of Moses himself they knew that, at the

command of God, he made the image of a Seraph, and ordained its worship as a mediator between JHVH and his people (Num. XXI, 9). And this Seraph was with them at the Temple in Jerusalem as a sacred symbol of a mediation Seraph in heaven. Why then, not erect also Matsebhoth and Asheroth (2 Kings, XVIII, 4)? And as to the *Cherubs*, they, too, seem to root in an old tradition from the time of Moses. At any rate, there *were cherubs* in the temple at Jerusalem, and *calves* in the temples of Bethel and Dan. Our tradition, coming from Juda (where it underwent certain revisions in the time of its final redaction), as it appears to the critical reader, presents the cherubs as legitimate, as against the calves in Israel, which are marked as an abberration from JHVH. The fact, however, is that 'Agalim were just as legitimate as Cherubim, both being elements of the *mysterious Mercabah-image*, hardly intimated in pre-Deuteronomic literature (Ex. XVII, 16 (?); 2 Kings, XXII, 19; Is. VI), but depicted in full detail in later products (Ez. chap. I). Indeed, we strike here a point of pre-eminent significance. In Israel they could not think of giving up the worship of images, and were it only for the one reason that in the difference between 'Agalim and Cherubim they had the best weapon against the claim of Jerusalem upon the character of a central sanctuary, and thus the most efficient justification of their separate existence, religious and political. The difference between Cherubim and 'Agalim seems to have been in connection with certain astronomical phenomena: The cherubs probably reach back to the period of *the Twins* (gemini), in which sign the sun moved in the most ancient times of traceable history. Thus in ancient Babylonia a pair of cherubs was symbolic of the divine power, a significance attached to them even later, at a time when the sun long ago (2500 a.) had receded from that sign into the sign of the *bullock* (taurus). Hammurabi's reform of the calendar in accordance with the changed astronomical situation had no influence upon the development of the notion of cherubs with the Abrahamites (Juda). Quite different, however, was the situation in Israel. The Israelites went through a more intense Egyptian influence. The Egyptians were *bullock-worshippers* (Osiris-Apis, Serapis). Added to this was the influence of post-Hammurabian Babylonia, an influence to which Israel was more exposed than Juda. The difference between the Judean and the Israelitish calendar to which tradition refers (1 Kings, XII, 32.33), seems, indeed, to be of the same nature as that between the old Babylonian and the Hammurabian calendars, thus growing out organically from the difference between Cherubim and 'Agalim.

The difference between Cherubim and 'Agalim mirrors itself also in the different versions of the tradition concerning the first backsliding of Israel after the Covenant of Sinai (Ex. XXXII). The writers of Israel naturally do not admit that this aberration consisted in the Israelites making a golden *calf*. How could they admit that the worship of a calf as the symbol of the divine was illegitimate, in face of the fact that this symbol formed the very center of the JHVH worship in Bethel and Dan?

The 'Egel-tradition was handed down to us from Juda, expressing therewith marked hostility and contempt for the central symbol of the Israelitish temples of JHVH. In Israel the writers would speak only of a *Massechah*, but never of an *'Egel-Massechah*. In the tradition of Israel it was *Ahron*, the ancestor of the priesthood in Jerusalem, who wrought the Massechah, in the Judean tradition, on the other hand, the tribe of *Levi* was the only one to keep away from the sinful worship of the golden calf, and so qualified itself as the avenger of that great sin. This controversy extended to other questions also. In Israel they denied the genuineness of the Tablets of the Covenant and the Ark of the Covenant in the temple of Jerusalem. They claimed that the temple of Bethel was in possession of the original *Scroll of the Covenant*, written by Moses himself, and guarded under the "Stone of Testimony" (אבן העדה), a *plain* stone with no writing on it (cf. Josh. XXIV, 26). In Juda, of course, they insisted on the genuineness of the Ark and the Tablets of the Covenant, maintaining that "*All* the Words of the Covenant" (not only the Ten Commandments) were written on the Tablets. (All pre-Deuteronomic passages mentioning the Ark are of Judean origin; the idea of *Ten Commandments* as the exclusive contents of the Tablet seems to be a later development within the Deuteronomic School.)

Thus in North and South they were interested in the doctrine of angels, in the worship of images and in religious relics. Moreover, the question of what kind of images should be worshiped was the religious basis of all political differences. No wonder, then, that the people were always disposed to yield to the slightest pressure and to add the unlawful worship of images to the lawful whenever the occasion called for it. And why should they give up the general age-revered custom of worshipping and sacrificing at public and private *High Places* (במות), equipped with a shrine and a pair of cherubs or calves and some other statues in conformity with the local environment? All this considered, we can well understand that stereotype report that even in the time of the "good kings" the Bamoth never disappeared from Juda. As long as angels were worshiped as mediators and their symbols were revered in the central sanctuary, it was impossible to make the people realize that Ba'alim and Bamoth were unlawful.

Slowly but incessantly these conditions brought the leaders of Juda to the realization that the claim of the central position of Jerusalem could not be justified under the dominion of the theory of angels. This led to the awakening of the heretofore rather dormant opposition to the belief in angels as mediators among the prophets in Juda, and, under their influence, also among the prophets in Israel, since they, too, were desirous of bringing about the unity of the nation with Jerusalem as the center. As long as the great adversary in the North existed, any yielding in the claim of possessing the genuine Ark and the genuine Tablets of the Covenant, or of the genuine Seraph of Moses and the genuine Cherubim of Solomon, would have been interpreted by the people as a weakness. The people in Juda, devoted as they were to the worship of images, lawful or unlawful, could easily be brought to waver in their devotion to Jerusalem, and possibly even to consider the temple in Bethel as the real seat of JHVH. That is why all reforms bearing on this matter, including the attempts of the best kings of Juda, never extended beyond the *unlawful* worship of images. It was not until Israel had been hopelessly trodden down by mighty Ashur, and idolatry had been greatly enhanced under the religious and cultural influence of the conqueror (2 Kings XVI, 2-4, 10-18), that *Hezekiah* dared to remove not only the unlawful Matseboths and Asheroth (Ishtar-statues) and the tolerated Bamoth, but also one of the lawful images, the *Nehushthan*, the *Seraph* of *Moses* (2 Kings, XVIII, 3-12). The foe in the North was no more, and so the first step to do away with the symbols of angels and the entire worship of images could be undertaken. Possibly they had already realized at that time that they would have to remove the entire lawful worship of images, as, indeed, they were then already thinking of the necessity of a *renewal of the Covenant* (cf. 2 Chr. Chaps. XXIX-XXXI). But they did not dare lay their hands upon the Cherubim and the Ark. In times of great distress in war the Ark would still be carried in front of the fighting army. The Cherubs were the symbols of angels whose existence and function were warranted by the first Book of the Covenant engraved in the Tablets of the Covenant. There the "angel of JHVH," the "Mal'akh JHVH," was the central figure, the real bearer of the Covenant.

But in the days of Menasseh the aberrations grew to such horrible dimensions that the "Pessel Asherah" was again placed in the Temple of JHVH, and the

Ishtar-worship flourished "in the towns of Judah and the streets of Jerusalem." It was then that the spiritual leaders of the people, among whom (according to a *talmudic tradition* well borne out by the biblical data at hand) *Zephaniah* and (young) *Jeremiah* played as great a part as the prophetess *Huldah* and the high priest *Hilkiyahu*, recognized that theirs was "a time to act for the sake of God," that the time had come to attack the evil at its very roots.   They won King Josiah for their plan of removing all symbols of the inconsistently monotheistic, nay, almost half-polytheistic past, and of making room for a system of worship carried out on the basis of strict, *absolute, monotheism*.   And so it happened that the *Cherubim*, the *Ark*, and the *Book of the Covenant*, as also all other (magical) relics, such as the heavenly fire, the Urim we-Thumim (the Oracle) and Oil of Anointment, disappeared from the temple in Jerusalem forever.   And this extreme measure was announced to the people, in Jerusalem by the Levites and in the towns of the land by Jeremiah, as the will of God, according to which even the *memory of the Ark* should be blotted out.[1]   The effect of this announcement was so deep and so lasting that the reports about the history of the last kings of Juda carefully avoid any mention of the Ark.   In connection with this action, and as a consequence thereof, the king ordained the destruction of all unlawful images, the cells of Ishtar and her

---

[1] Cf. Jer. III, 16; VII, 4; המה may refer to the cherubs (cf. Ez. X, 20-22 and XLI, 20-21) and be the first intimation that the cherubs were removed; XI, 1-13; 2 Chr. XXV, 3; Mish. Shek. VI, 1,2; Joma V, 2; Thos. Shek. II, 18; Yom hak-Kipp. III, 6, 7; Jer. Tha'an. Hal. 1 and parallels; Bab. Joma p. 53-54; Hor. p. 11-12; cf. Tholdoth I, chap. 3.

hierodoules, all places of Moloch, Khemosh and Milcom, as also all public or private Bamoth, heretofore tolerated as a quasi-legal institution, and all lower mantical forms—all of this not only in Juda, but also in Israel, which had become a dependency of Juda in all matters religious. The report about these acts of reform (2 Kings XXII and XXIII) gives us a survey, as it were, of all forms of idolatry and mantical devices ever practiced in Israel and Juda, which then, on the occasion of the new covenant, were removed and destroyed.

The most serious difficulty anent our orientation in the events around the new covenant confronts us in the question of the removal *of the first Book of the Covenant*. How did they manage to make it plausible to the people that God withdraws, as it were, the first Book of the Covenant in order to replace it by a new one? The biblical report is to the effect that, incident to repairs in the temple, the high priest, Hilkiyahu, found a book in which great disasters were predicted as a punishment for the unlawful practices of the people, and that the fear of that punishment led to the *renewal* of the Covenant (2 Kings, XXII; Jer. XI, 1-13). This report has been harmonized with the traditional view about the origin of the Torah (that the five books of Moses were dictated to him literally by God), by the interpretation that the book found was the *personal copy* of Deuteronomy (the fifth book of Moses), which King Menasseh discarded, disregarding the command that the king should always carry such a copy with him and never depart from it. The "find", according to this talmudical interpretation, did not consist in a *new* scroll unknown before to king and nation, but in the fact that they found that book *unrolled* at the great *admonition*, the *Thochaha*, (Deut. chap. XXVIII), which they took as an *omen* that a great national disaster was threatening. But reading the biblical report under critical orientation in all relevant sources and historical events, it becomes clear at once that the report about the finding of the book presumes the possibility that a new book of Moses was found of which none of all those concerned ever knew anything before. The picture presented by this report of the conditions preceding the renewal of the covenant, is well compatible with the presumption that there could be in existence a book of Moses without any of the contemporaries knowing anything about it. This report reached us in a *later redaction*, and we find there no attempt to clear up the relation of the newly found book to the first Book of the Covenant, but this does not preclude that the original report contained such a statement.   It is not only possible but highly probable that the original report contained something like the following explanation of the find:

Before his death Moses enlarged upon and explained the first Book of the Covenant, and this enlarged book, even the Deuteronomy, was, according to the intention of Moses, to replace what was considered the Book of the Covenant since the days of Sinai (what we call the first Book of the Covenant; Ex. XX-XXIII). The scroll containing this book was throughout these centuries in the keeping of the authorities, and the good kings and priests prior to Menasseh had directed all efforts toward guiding the people in accordance with the statutes and ordinances of this book. But the intention of Moses, to have this book introduced as the final book of the covenant, has never been carried out (cf. Deut. XVII, 17-20: The king should take a copy of the Deuteronomy in the keeping of the Priests and the Levites, and carry it constantly on his person). In the long reign of Menasseh, however, this book was neglected, even by king, priest, and Levite, and so it happened that they estranged themselves ever more and more from JHVH. And now the great disaster announced in this book draws threateningly near. Therefore the king and the spiritual leaders of the people, priests and prophets, considered it as the need of the hour to rally and carry out the intention of Moses, and to introduce this book publicly as the final Book of the Covenant. This book contains absolutely no reference to angels, to images in the temple, or to Bamoth. On the contrary, it contains an absolute prohibition of images and demands the *unconditional centralization of the sacrificial cult* in the temple of Jerusalem.[1] In order to live up to the more rigid requirements of this book, they had to remove not only the unlawful images, but also those images that heretofore had been considered lawful, as also the Bamoth, heretofore tolerated as a half-legal institution. Thus even the Cherubim and the Ark with the first Book

---

[1] Deut. V, 8; VII, 5; chap. XII; an exception to the general rule is admitted in regard to the passah-lamb, which originally was a *house-sacrifice,* and conserved this character even after the centralization. But even this house-sacrifice was now confined *within the walls* of *Jerusalem,* so that all desiring to celebrate the Passah in due form had to pilgrim to Jerusalem; Deut. XVI, 1-7; cf. Gesch. d. jued. Philos. II, 1, p. 209 ff.

of the Covenant, as also all other relics, had to be removed, according to the final intention of Moses.

In this narrative which we presume to have been contained in the original complete report in 2 Kings, chaps. XXII and XXIII, we have to change not more than one point in order to make it present what *we* consider to have been the real course of events, no matter whether the explanation of the finding of the book outlined above was really contained in the original report in the second book of Kings, as we presume, or not. The point to be changed concerns the question of Moses' authorship of the book of Deuteronomy. We do believe that the *spirit* of Deuteronomy in its *inception* goes back to the time of the first Covenant which is covered by the name of Moses. But at the same time we believe that this spirit needed all these centuries of experience, in the struggles with the adverse conditions without and in growing self-realization within, in order to be able to attain, by a gradual development, to that height on which we find him in Deuteronomy. We believe that the book of Deuteronomy, in a *literary* sense, is the product of a very long development. Its theoretical parts (V-XI and XXVIII) consist of prophetic sermons addressed to the people on different occasions, as they developed in the prophetic schools throughout the ages. The legal sections (XII-XXVI) were gradually produced through the practice of individual priests and judges who developed the statutes of the first Book of the Covenant by adapting them, through *interpretation*, to conditions of life more developed and more complex than those at the time of the first Book of the Covenant (in the relation of the legal sections of Deuteronomy to the first Book of the Covenant there already appear the first elements of *Oral Law*). Undoubtedly, however, the collection and the redactional shaping of all these primary elements into one organic whole was the work of the spiritual leaders of that time, Zephaniah, Jeremiah, Chilkiyahu, Shaphan and others. These men carried out this great work with the consent of the king, and presented it to the people as the *testament* of *Moses*. They could do so with a good conscience, being convinced that this, no doubt, was the final intention of Moses. He surely hoped and desired that his people would eventually overcome and eliminate all image-worship, Bamoth and all relics savoring of pagan origin, although he, Moses, himself, was not able to carry out his great ideal in his own time. Of course, there were, even among the *prophets* and spiritual leaders, those who had their great apprehensions against this radical step, even though they may have been favorably inclined toward the principles of the reform in a general way. There certainly were also those who sincerely believed in angels, Cherubim, Ark, Tablets, Urim ve-Thumim, heavenly fire, oil of anointmnet and other ritual institutions to which they clung with their hearts, even though they were opposed to all *unlawful* institutions of that kind. But those rigid monotheists who had been preparing the Deuteronomic Covenant, had won the king to their ideas, and so they were enabled to undertake the great attempt to reform the life of the nation according to the postulates of the most rigid monotheism. They hoped that not only the unlawful but also the lawful worship of images, as also the Bamoth, would disappear entirely. Furthermore, they hoped that the new Book of the Covenant would oust from their authoritative, or semi-authoritative, positions all literary documents opposing their ideas, such as the first Book of the Covenant, the composition E and J and others. They knew, of course, that copies of the first Book of the Covenant and the other writings condemned to be "hidden away" were in existence in considerable numbers in certain literary circles in Israel and Juda. But they hoped that, with the aid of the official authorties, they would be able to keep the opposition down and eventually to overcome it entirely.   In this wise, they hoped, they would be able to clear the path leading to the reformation of the religious-cultural life of the nation on the basis of the new Book of the Covenant.

Corresponding to the movement in the religious life sketched above there was a parallel movement in all higher manifestations of culture: *architecture*, *plastics*, *music* and *dance*, *literature*, *legislature*, as also in the general *attitude to the world without.*

The lawful and semi-legal, and, most especially, the widely flourishing unlawful, worship of images, necessitated a certain development of *sculpture* and *artistic cutting, carving* and *weaving.* This may be gathered notably from the report about the building of the temple by Solomon (only for *copper-work* they had to import a Syrian artisan, who, by the way, was a half-breed Jew; 1 Kings, VI, 13 ff., 40 f.).   Plastics as well as architecture were primarily serving religion, lawful or unlawful.   But these artistic efforts could

not fail to influence private life also. The grand
mansions of Solomon may have overshadowed everything known previously in *architecture* and decorative
art in Palestine. They certainly were not the *first*,
and much less the *only*, artistically finished buildings
in Palestine. On the contrary, the buildings of
Solomon indicate that there was a well developed art,
plastical and ornamental. As to a certain cultivation
of decorative art in dwellings, garments and jewelry,
we have the testimonies of the prophets in their sermons against the careless luxuries of the mighty
(Am. VI, 1 f.). and most specifically against the
immodesty and unchaste obstrusiveness of the
daughters of *Zion* (Is. III, 16-26). Of these forms of
art plastics was particularly dependent on image-
worship, and an attack upon the one meant an attack
upon the other also. From the final prohibition in
Deuteronomy (V, 8; cf. VI, 15-18) of any chiseled or
molten image we gather, on the one hand, that the law
aimed to prohibit even the *mere making* of images,
which were generally used as objects of reverence and
worship, but, on the other hnad, that the law by no
means aimed at the complete suppression of the
architectural and ornamental arts. On the contrary,
the taking over of the Canaanitic houses with their
equipments and the continuation of their building
style are announced as a part of the forthcoming
blessing after the entrance into Palestine; at the same
time, however, the warning is sounded to beware of the
peril that with the *secular* also the *religious* art is
bound to creep in and take hold of their minds (Deut.
VI, 9-15; VIII, 7-20; IX, 1). Thus it may be said

that the plastic and decorative arts in pre-Deuteronomic Palestine were demanded and cultivated not
only by the unlawful but also by the lawful religious
practice.   And everything (including recent explora-
tions) goes to show that this form of art attained a
rather high degree of development and was considerably in vogue (of *painting* we hardly hear anything in
pre-Deuteronomic times).

The same may be said of *music, dancing,* and *singing.*
They formed an important element not only of the
illegal ritual (Ex. XXXII, 6. 17-19), but also of the
legal (2 Sam. VI, 13-17; Jer. XXX, 29).   Furthermore
they were the usual forms in which the people would
give vent to their feelings of rejoicing over great
events in the life of the nation, such events largely
being viewed from a *religious* aspect (Ex. XVI, 1-20;
1 Sam. XVIII, 6. 7; XXI, 12; note the prominent
part that women took in such performances).   And
also in private life, in social gatherings of all kinds,
music and songs were forms of entertainment (cf.
Amos VI, 5).   And they seem to have had so deep an
understanding for music that they tried to dispel
mental depression by means of the soothing influence
of proper tunes (1 Sam. XVI, 15-13; XIX, 9).   And
not only the power to exorcise the "evil spirit," but
also that of attuning the mind for the *prophetic
inspiration,* the "Spirit of God," they ascribed to
music (1 Sam. X, 5).   To our modern way of thinking
this suggests a very high conception of the *religiously*
edifying power of music, and to a certain extent we
may suppose this conception to have been realized in
the old prophetic schools.   However, the authorita-

tive circles seem to have had some grave reason to decline all musical efforts in connection with prophecy and holy service. The Book of Deuteronomy knows nothing about music, neither for nor against it. Nowhere in the Bible is there any positive indication of the reason working here, but there cannot be any doubt that there was some efficient reason for this reticent attitude which we also notice in later ages. (Possibly the reason is to be looked for in the prominent part taken by women in such performances; most likely, however, it was the function of music in *mantical* rites that made music and song an undesirable element in the holy service. For even in the later sources of the Torah in which the *sound* of the *trumpet* appears as an item of the service, there is absolutely nothing about *music* and song of the *Levites* of which the Book of Chronicles knows so much and which, as we also know from other sources, formed so prominent an institution in the second Temple. Indeed, the Talmudists are greatly embarrassed when it comes to finding some *backing* in the Torah for this most prominent service of the Levites at the sacrificial functions in the temple (cf. Bab. 'Arach. 11a and Num. Rab. VI, 11, and further below to the Book of Chronicles).

The intimate connection between *religion* and *literature* in ancient Israel was variously touched upon in the preceding: the gradual overcoming of the sexual motif in the conception of the early history, which meant the elimination of the most tenacious obstacle on the road to the genuine monotheistic God-conception, and the actual development of the ethico-monotheistic God-conception under the motif of attributes, signify the *religious root* of all literary efforts in Israel.   This, of course, is not an exclusively Israelitish trait.   None of the ancient nations had any altogether non-religious literature (the Pythagoreans, for instance, considered even *mathematics* a religious discipline—a view, traces of which we still find with *Plato*).   *New* in the Abrahamitic-Israelitish development is the elimination of the sexual motif dominant in general Semitic literature, and the centering of all literary thoughts around the *motif of attributes*, thus substantiating and solidifying the ethico-monotheistic God-conception.   Except for the Song of Songs in which old elements of a secular erotic nature were evidently utilized, all that has come down to us of biblical literature is of a religious character.   Here and there we find some remnants of a general literature of *Fable* and *Wisdom* of a secular character (cf. Jud. IX, 8-15; 1 Ki. IV, 11-13; 2Ki. XIV, 9 and numerous verses in Proverbs and Ecclesiastes).   But the fact that only these few elements of that literature were preserved, clearly shows that the literary activity was growing on a religious basis *in the main*.   Thus as to its *contents* the entire literature consisted of two branches, one religious and the other secular; the secular branch, of which only little has come down to us, being made up of erotic songs, fables and sayings of wisdom.   One passage seems to point to the existence of a book containing a description of the *animal world* (Is. XXXIV, 16).   But the name of it, "Book of JHVH," may be taken as an indication that the whole presentation served the religious outlook of the subject.   As to its *form*, we distinguish in biblical

literature *prose, poetry,* and *poetically attuned prose,* the
latter form employed in *prophecies,* solemn addresses,
and partly also in fables.   The same division applies
to the form of those writings which served our biblical
historical works as *sources,* and of which hardly more
than the titles have come down to us.[1]

A glance over the present biblical literature, as also
over the titles of those biblical writings which have not

---

[1] These are:
1. The Book of the Story of Adam—Gen. V, 1.
2. The Book of the Wars of JHVH—poetical, Num. XXI, 14.
3. The Sepher hay-Yashar—poetical, Josh. X, 13; 2 Sam. I, 18.
4. The Book of the History of Solomon—1 Ki. XI, 41.
5. The Book of the History of the Kings of Israel.
6. The Book of the History of the Kings of Juda.
7. The Book of the History of the Kings of Israel and Juda. Numbers 5, 6 and 7 are quoted very often in the Books of Kings and Chronicles.
8. The Midrash of the Book of the Kings—2 Chr. XXIV, 27.
9. The History of Samuel, the Seer, and the History of Nathan, the Prophet, and the History of Gad, the Seer, 1 Chr. XXIX, 29.
10. The History of Nathan, the Prophet, and the Predictions of Ahiah of Shiloh, and the Vision of Jedo, the Seer, about Jeroboam, the son of Nebat—2 Chr. IX, 29.
11. The History of Shemajah, the Prophet, and of Iddo, the Seer, a Pedigree—2 Chr. XII, 15.
12. The Midrash of the Prophet Iddo—2 Chr. XIII, 22.
13. The History of Jehu, the son of Hanani, intercalated in the Book of the Kings of Israel—2 Chr. XX, 34.
14. The Rest of the History of Usia, written by Isaiah, the Prophet, the son of Amoz—2 Chr. XXVI, 22.
15. The Vision of Isaiah, the Prophet, the son of Amoz, in the Books of the Kings of Juda and Israel—2 Chr. XXXII, 32.
16. The History of Hosai (or of the Seers)—2 Chr. XXXII, 19.
17. Pedigree—Neh. VII, 5; cf. 1 Chr. V, 17; 2 Chr. XII, 15.
18. The later History of David (treating particularly of the *Census* of the People)—1 Chr. XXIII, 27; cf. XXVII, 24.
19. Collection of "Lamentations" (hak-Kinnoth)—2 Chr. XXX, 25; this may be, in part at least, identical with our "Lamentations" (cf., however, Sepher hay-Yashar 2 Sam. I, 17.)

come down to us, will soon convince us that *pre-Deuteronomic* literature, in which we include also those works which, while finished later, go back to pre-Deuteronomic sources, consisted largely of *History* and *historical orientations*.   This is easily explained by the general character of the pre-Deuteronomic God-conception.   "The Book of the History of Adam" (Gen. V, 1) which is supposed to be an ancient source drawn upon by the younger Jahvist (J_2), may still have contained some cosmogonic elements.   In its primary elements that book may have belonged to the first *written products* of Abrahamitic literature.   But in the progess of the development things shaped themselves so that the more *written literature* gained ground, the more was the literary supply of the people becoming dependent on their spiritual leaders.   And these latter, we know, were rather inclined to suppress the cosmogonic interest of the people in order to cultivate in its stead much the more intensely the *historical interest*.   All narratives and elucidations had the only purpose to present and to *prove* to the people, by the course of history, the merciful workings of God for the benefit of His chosen people.   All arguments of the pre-Deuteronomic prophets and writers are taken from *history*.   The cosmological element was neglected by both of these groups, all of the teachings of Judaism being based upon the ethico-historical argument (cf. Geschichte d. jued. Philos. I, p. 16 f.). The abstract formulations of the theoretical doctrines of Judaism about God, free will and retribution were inacessible to the masses of the people; and if prophets and writers had any hope at all of being able to convey to the people at large anything that might help them to grasp those doctrines, it was only by availing themselves of the interest with which meditations on the national history always appealed to the hearts of the people. While the people were listening to the beloved tales of the early days of the nation, there was a favorable opportunity to conceive those tales from a higher aspect and thus to convey to the people the desired ideals and ideas. And also in this the Deuteronomic Book of the Covenant represents the consummation of the entire development. The theoretical teachings of Judaism are explained here in an *historical introduction* and strengthened by *historical arguments*. And both of them together, the theoretical principles and the higher conception of history, are presented as both introduction to and basis of the *law*.

The *law* makes up a part of *literature*, and some particular laws had already to be treated above, in the discussion of the principles and forms of religion and culture. However, this question must be resumed and completed under its own aspect:

We have already mentioned the fact that the Dueteronomic law is arranged according to the four theoretical principles treated in the introduction of the book of Deuteronomy: God, prophecy, free will, and retribution. Furthermore we have already seen what influence the development of the God-conception and of the concept of prophecy had upon the formulation of the laws pertaining to these principles. Also as regards the principle of retribution we have seen that the reformulation of this principle found expression in corresponding laws.   Here we will show in addition that the firm formulation of the principle of free will, too, mirrors itself in the spirit of the Deuteronomic laws; and again, that the principle of retribution is, in general, much clearer in Deuteronomy, owing to its clearer conception of free will.   Of course, there are no specific practical laws which reflect directly the theoretical principle of free will.   Yet, there are manifold ways in which the workings of this principle are noticeably revealed.   For one thing, one of the distinctions of Deuteronomy is its effort to base the binding power of the law upon *knowledge* and *love*; this in spite of the great emphasis laid upon the principle of retribution.   This principle, of course, is being appealed to again and again as to the most efficacious driving motive in the heart of man.   But at the same time the *ideal* of Deuteronomy is to elevate the fear of *individual* punishment and the hope for individual reward to that high degree of understanding in which the workings of divine providence are *admired* and *loved* even in those of its phases, in which the individual is made to forego his own reward, or to suffer for the sins of others in accordance with the principle of national and universal mutual responsibility.   What Deuteronomy calls *love* of God means the liberation of the will from individual fear and individual hope, replacing them by the recognition of the idea of national and universal retribution. and the love for the workings of divine providence in accordance with this idea.   In the command: "Thou shalt love JHVH thy God." the principle of free will appears in the form of a law.   In a more tangible form the command of free will finds its expression in the greater *independence* of the *judges*. There was some speculation about the question why Deuteronomy failed to embody the detailed laws found in the first Book of the Covenant (Ex. XXI and XXII) in the province of civil and penal jurisdiction. The best explanation of this omission seems to be that the Deuteronomic law confines itself to the principles of justice, leaving the working out of the details and the specific application to the free judgment of the judiciary. The principle of *ius talionis*, evidently dominant in the first Book of the Covenant (cf. particularly Ex. XXI, 23-25), retreats before the principle of greater freedom. The purpose of punishing is no more *vengeance* and retribution per se, but rather the *removal* of the evil and the warning of all who might feel prompted to transgress the law (cf. Deut. XIII, 12; XVII, 12. 13; XIX, 20; XXI, 21). The law of retaliation rests primarily on responsibility as mere accountability of the acting individual, no matter whether or not his will is really free. On the other hand, retribution as removal of the evil and warning to those whose will may become affected by the presence of one who committed a wrong with impunity, is based wholly on the genuine idea of free will. The law of retaliation can easily be fixed in its details: "an eye for an eye," "whatever a man does shall be done unto him." Not so the law of removal and warning . The spirit of this law requires that, in penal as well as in civil matters, all conditions relevant to the individual cases be considered in all their manifoldness and complexity. Therefore the details of the law are omitted and left to the free judgment of the contemporary judges (XVI, 18 f. and XVII, 8-13; cf. 2 Chr. XIX, 5-11).   It is, however, the most important of the laws based on the principle of retribution, the law on *capital punishment*, in which the progress in the formulation of this principle makes itself felt most strongly.   The law of Deuteronomy is the *first* in which we find the death penalty on *adultery* in accordance with the rigourous emphasis laid by it on sexual holiness (cf. above as to its conception of early history).   But at the same time it is this code in which we find capital punishment reduced to what may be considered the minimum for that period: There are a number of crimes on which the death penalty is set in the first Book of the Covenant which are omitted in Deuteronomy (these crimes are: beating or cursing parents, adbuction of man, killing a slave (while exercising disciplinary rights), criminal negligence in the care-taking of one's ox which resulted in a man being gored to death, and sexual intercourse with animals).   The Deuteronomic law, on the other hand, knows of the death penalty only in three kinds of capital crimes: *murder, idolatry,* and *sexual crimes* (each one of the *eleven* cases of capital punishment in Deuteronomy is reduceable to one of these three). In addition to this, Deuteronomy opposes the injunction of the first Book of the Covenant according to which the court itself is the executor in all cases of capital punishment, ordaining instead that the *blood revenger* should be entrusted with the execution in all cases in which there is such a person whom the court can consider so directly affected by the crime that he has a claim upon the rights of self-defence, as it were, (applying to murder and to four cases of sexual crime). Thus the tendency to eliminate court execution as far as possible is apparent. This is the first phase of a movement which later developed into the postulate of abolishing capital punishment. On the extension line of the idea that God rules the world without intermediation of angels, there lies the postulate, that no man, be he even the supreme judge on earth, shall dare dispose of the life of his fellowman, unless he is acting in actual defence of his *own* life. Between this latter standpoint and the one represented by the first Book of the Covenant, Deuteronomy forms a middle phase in that it extends the sphere of self-defense and permits even the execution by the courst itself wherever there is none to take the part of the revenger (cf. my Gesch. d. jued. Philos. II, 1, p. 125-138).

And there is another question in which the new formulation of the principle of retribution was of evident influence. We refer to the question of *sacrifices*. We have spoken above of the efforts toward centralization of the sacrificial cult in connection with the monotheistic formulation of the God-conception. Here it is the question of the sacrificial cult *in general* that we are concerned with. We meet very often with rather slighting utterances about sacrifices in the prophets. This led many biblical scholars to form the view that the prophets were opposed to the sacrificial cult altogether. Many went so far as to speak of two different schools and two different *Thoroth*, the *priestly* Torah, which was hardly concerned with the ethical law, and the *prophetic* Torah, which expounded ethical laws only, to the exclusion of all ritual laws in general and to the disdain of the sacrificial cult in particular.   These two schools, it is further stated, entered a compromise in the end, the result of which is *our* Torah.   This view has no backing in scripture and is altogether untenable.   It is true that the prophets often express themselves in a manner disrespectful to sacrifices, but in all instances their intention is clearly to protest that sacrifices *alone*, without moral improvement, are of no religious value and had better be omitted.   Opposition on the part of the prophets to *all* the sacrifices prescribed for certain periods and occasions by the authoritative Book of the Covenant of the time, is entirely out of the question.   The only thing we admit, is that they were making light not only of private, but also of public sacrifices as long as they were not accompanied by religious contrition and moral improvement (cf. my Gesch. d. jued. Philos. 11, 1, p. 124. 221).   Now, while we believe that the opposition of the prophets was thus exaggerated, it must be admitted that the prophets had their misgivings about sacrifices, scenting in them a certain danger to the moral life of the people. The people were only too ready to rate the sacrifices from the viewpoint of retribution.   Through the offering of a sacrifice they felt their consciences alleaviated, considering the sacrifice as a *legitimate compensation* for *official indulgence* to sin and wrongdoing. Indeed, a closer orientation in the sources reveals a certain development in the attitude of the prophets to some of the *private* sacrifices:

Ancient nations in general and Semitic tribes in particular had a certain systematized ritual in which definite sacrifices were prescribed for definite sins of the individual. Now the fact that in the first Book of the Covenant only public sacrifices and "thy burnt offerings and thy peace-offerings, thy sheep and thine oxen" are spoken of (Ex. XX, 24; XXIII, 17-18),while there is not the slighest hint at the institution of the individual *sin-offering*, can be interpreted in more than one way. We could think there was no need for any prescription, as the sin-offering was regulated by a special law in the possession of the priests, as found, for instance, in Lev. I-VII (a collection of laws which, while later embodied into the Priestly Code, evidently belongs to the oldest material which entered that late code; and also other passages about the ritual of the sin-offering may be presumed to have been in possession of the priests). In support of this view we could refer to the fact that the institution of sin-offering actually existed in both Israel and Juda (2 Ki. XII, 17; Hos. IV, 8). Another explanation would be that the sin-offering as a legally defined institution had developed just in the period of the Kings. But the absolute silence of the first Book of the Covenant about this institution, the ordinance that money for sin-offerings should not be brought to the "House of JHVH," but be handed in (privately) to the priests, who then took care of the offering in a private way, as it were (2 Ki. ibid.), and finally the opposition of Hosea specifically against this kind of sacrifice (IV, 8; VIII, 11; X, 2-8; XIV, 1-3; repentance, not sacrifice!)—all of these facts render it highly probable

that there was a strong opposition against the individual sin-offering long before the Deuteronomic
Covenant, and that it was this very opposition that
brought about the peculiar position of the sin-offeiing,
being, as it were, officially ignored, but *tolerated* as a
private affair to be settled between priest and sinner.
This is evidently also the attitude of Deuteronomy:
The prescriptions about public statutory and private
free offerings are more numerous and more specific
in Deuteronomy than in the first Book of the Covenant,
but the obligatory sin-offering is devisedly *ignored*.
They could not possibly enact a law prohibiting the
sin-offering, but, on the other hand, it could not be
granted the character of a legal institution.   For this
would mean to enter a compromise with sin, to
sanction legally the degradation of the principle of
retribution.   The sinner, this is the attitude of
Deuteronomy in this question, should repent, otherwise due visitation shall surely come upon him
(cf. Hosea).

Coming from the outlined picture of religious and
cultural life in Israel to the question of the attitude to
the outside world, we find the answer, as far as the
large masses are concerned, given in the mere facts:
There was a certain Semitic communion of culture,
in which Israel and Juda were also included.   At the
same time, however, the prophets and the spiritual
leaders of the people succeeded in producing within
this general Semitic culture certain cultural and
religious traits of a marked Israelitish or Judean
peculiarity.   As to the theoretical postulates of the
prophets, to wit, the idea of the *Selection* of Israel, it is

this what we have found, upon thourough orientation in the sources:

Often "the nations" appear as an object of abomination to prophets and lawgivers, insamuch as these
latter had to beware lest too close a communion of
culture, especially *intermarriage*, with the surrounding nations, induce the Israelites to idolatory. Yet, the
nations were to the prophets not only the object of
their worry, but also that of a much deeper concern:
What was the divine intention with those "other
nations?" Are they merely to serve as contrast to
give more emphasis to the selection of Israel? Or,
is there any plan of JHVH's in which the other
nations, too, play a worthy part?

The question involved was: *Universalism* or
national-religious exclusiveness?

To be sure, a certain friendly attitude towards
other nations had often, by virtue of prevailing
political relations, to be admitted even by the extreme particularists, as can easily be seen from the
narratives about David, Solomon, Elijah and Elisha.
But the first universalistic thoughts of a really great
conception we meet with in the kingdom of Israel, are
those in the prophecies of *Amos*:

The call to prophesy Amos considers as a mission
to Israel (VII, 15), as, indeed, he gives clear expression
to the idea of Israel's selection (III, 2), an idea which
he bases on the first Book of the Covenant (II, 4)..
But the general character of his prophecy is nevertheless as universal as the "Torah of JHVH", for the
violation of which he blames the people. His word
of rebuke and warning addresses itself not only to Israel.

but also to all other nations in his political horizon. Moreover, he addresses himself *first* to the nations (I, 3; II, 3; cf. IX, 7), directing then the same warning to Israel (II, 4 f.).   And not only for their iniquities against Israel does the prophet blame the other nations, but just as emphatically for the iniquities they committed against each other (I, 6, 9; II, 1). *Justice from nation to nation* was the first great postulate of this universalistic prophet, convinced that justice from individual to individual within the state or the nation would never be firmly established unless it were covered by the greater justice, justice from nation to nation.   In accordance with this, his messianic outlook, too, is of a highly universalistic character, embracing all nations with equal emphasis. In spite of the many moral shortcomings for which the prophet so vigorously rebukes his contemporaries in Israel, he was in unshaken hopes that in the end they would return to God and so become worthy of the great mission assigned to them, the mission of leading the other nations to the recognition of God, so that they, too, learn to live according to the principles of ethical monotheism (V, 14. 15; IX, 11-12).   This far-reaching universalism of Amos is accounted for by *two circumstances*: *First* there was no Ba'al-worship in Israel at the time of Amos.   Among the bitter accusations of the prophet against his contemporaries there is none on the score of Ba'al-worship. Evidently the effect of Jehu's reform in suppressing the Ba'alim (2 Ki. X, 18-28) was still lasting. *Secondly*, Israel at the time of Jeroboam the Second was a politically independent state of considerable power

(2 Ki. XIV, 25-27). The political independence enhanced the prophet in his hope that there would be no return to extreme idolatry. And this hope in turn furthered the great idea that the national-religious exclusiveness concomitant to the idea of the selection is but a means to a great end, this latter being uniting all nations with Israel to one Covenant of Nations on the basis of ethical monotheism.

The extent to which the circumstances mentioned are responsible for the universalism of Amos, will be even more readily seen when we proceed to consider the attitude of *Hosea*, the younger contemporary and fellow-prohpet of Amos. In his time the great peril, the Assyrian world-empire, was menacingly on the advance. The nation was divided in two parties, the *Assyrian*, who considered submission to the great world-power the only salvation from destruction, and the *Egyptian*, who were seeking an alliance with Egypt, with whose help they hoped to make a last stand against Assyria (V, 13; VII, 11; VIII, 9; IX, 3.6; X, 6; XI, 5; XII, 2). Especially there was great political confusion after the death of Jereboam the Second and the half-year reign of Zechariah, the last king of the house of Jehu. Now comes the time of assassinations of kings, Shallum assassinates Zechariah and succeeds him for one month, Meneham assassinates Shallum and usurps the throne, but remains a mock-king, submitting to the sovereignty of the Assyrian king from whom he had to buy the crown of Israel (2 Ki. XV, 19). And the more the political influence of Assyria continues to grow, the more powerful becomes its cultural and religious influence.

Indeed, Hosea's prophecies are full of bitter accusations of the people on the score of the redounding wave
of passion for the Ba'alim and their services (II,
10. 15. 18. 19; III, 1; IV, 12. 17 a.).   These desolate
circumstances caused Hosea to abandon all universalistic hopes so enthusiastically cherished by his older
contemporary.   Hosea is an *extreme particularist.*
There is nothing of messianic-universalistic hopes in
his prophecies.   On the contrary, Hosea zealously
denounces any and all communion of culture between
Ephriam and other nations (VII, 8).   Quite natural,
how could he cherish any hope for an Israel leading the
nations unto JHVH in the face of the sad reality,
Israel being dependent on other nations and following
them in the worship of idols?   Hosea considers the
Covenant of Sinai as broken, the first Book of the
Covenant as desecrated (I, 9; VI, 7; VIII, 1.12), and
longs for a renewal of the Covenant (II, 21-25):
A renewal of the Covenant with God always means a
more intense national concentration and a stronger
emphasis on religious exclusiveness.   The same idea
we find expressed also by another prophet of that
period (Zech. ch. XI and XII, 7-9).   He draws a
picture of the chaotic political conditions of the time
of "three shepherds in one month" (XI, 8), and,
expressly giving up the great universal idea of communion with all nations (XI, 10), he gives voice to
the longing for a renewal of the Covenant, in words
identical with those of Hosea (comp. XIII, 9 with
Hos. 11, 25; cf. Tholdoth I, p. 30).

In *Juda* the universal messainic idea appears to
have been more powerful than in Israel.   *Isaiah* does

complain of idolatry, and also the political conditions leave much to be desired, the kingdom of
Juda being menaced at the time by Sanherib. But
unlike the prophets of Israel who themselves were
gravitating to Jerusalem, the prophets of Juda were
preaching to a people which, sin-laden as it was, has
been camping around its national center. This may
account for the undiminished cultivation of the
universal messianic ideal in spite of the sad conditions
of the immediate present. All nations will, without
having to give up their separate national existence,
pilgrim to the mountain of the house of JHVH to
join Israel in the worship of JHVH and to learn his
ways (Is. II, 2-4 = Mi. IV, 1-3; Is. XI, 10; XVIII, 7;
XIX, 18-25). This hope must have been even more
enhanced after the liberation from the Assyrian peril.
And even the great backsliding in the long reign of
Menasseh was not enough to shake this ideal hope.
Zephaniah, whose activity coincides in time with the
preparation and the enactment of the Deuteronomic
Covenant, hoped that JHVH would call upon all
nations to participate in the Covenant, that all
nations would respond to this call, "and that all
Isles of the Nations, *each one from its own place*, will
worship Him" (II, 10.11; III, 8.9).

This, however, is the *last* universal-messianic
utterance calling upon the nations to join Israel in the
worship of JHVH as individual national entities,
i. e., without submerging and losing their identity
in Israel. In post-Deuteronomic times the messianic
hope receives a new meaning.

Third Chapter.

FROM THE DEUTERONOMIC COVENANT TO THE COVENANT OF ESRA (444 B. C.)

THE essential characteristics of this period is the *cosmological* development of the God-conception. The pre-Deuteronomic teachings of the prophets were based on pure ethical monotheism. The post-Deuteronomic teachings, on the other hand, were conceived on an ethico-cosmological basis, with a prevailing tendency to emphasize the cosmological aspect. For not only is the God-conception growing richer in its contents through the formulation of the monotheistic theory of creation, but even the ethical attributes of God receive a certain cosmological touch. The ethical outlook upon *life*, the "Lebensanschauung", in which the teachings of the prophets *exhausted* themselves in pre-Deuteronomic times, is being enlarged in the following period so as to comprise a full ethico-cosmological outlook upon the *world*, a "Weltanschauung". The ethical system of life is being founded upon a cosmological basis, by which process Judaism develops its metaphysical element to a greater extent than before.

It is under this chief aspect that the development of biblical Judaism in the subsequent period may be most adequately conceived and presented. The problems and phenomena to be treated are the same as in the preceding period, owing to which fact we will be able generally to observe in the discussion of this period the same order which we observed in the preceding. However, the possibilities of development are more numerous in the present period, the opposing elements more intense. The old controversy between adherents and opponents of the belief in angels as intermediators never ceases, but now new complications are added by the advent of the monotheistic theory of creation. This new doctrine caused the old controversy to be taken up with new vigor and tension. On the other hand, however, it was just this endeepening of the problems involved which called for new ways of solving the new difficulties and of adjusting the new situation. The opposing views either resolved into harmony in a higher unity or they were pushed to the background by compromises entered into for practical purposes. One of the consequences of this situation is that the individual personalities actively engaged in the development of things, be they or be they not known by name, stand out more boldly than in the preceding period. The present period is not only richer in personalities and literary units engaged in the controversies, but also *maturer* in the exhaustive treatment of the problems, as also, and particularly, in the relatively *systematic* way in which views and thoughts are developed. This is evidently to be brought in connection with the fact that the controversies and developments alluded to are largely taking place in the *exile*. To be sure, all those ideas and postulates around which the development swings, have for their object the *new state* expected in the near future. Nevertheless, the fact that at persent the firm ground of reality is lacking under the feet of those who try to create the constitution of the future state in accordance with their principles, gives the development a certain tendency toward the abstract, theoretical and radical. It is easier to be radical in your postulates when you do not have to consider the possibility of being taken at your word and entrusted with the practical task of carrying out those postulates. Again, some phenomena in the cultural life of the people in the present period do not press to the fore as intensely as the parallel phenomena in the preceding period. In matters *religious* the Jews in the exile were much better than they were while in their own country. In matters of no direct religious bearing, however, they were naturally absorbed by their environment (we know that many an element in the sphere of the religiously indifferent customs accepted in those days has come to be considered later as a genuine part of Jewish ritual). Of course, there was a *remnant* left in Palestine. But this remnant, though it most likely was larger than the "Golah", and certainly much larger than it is generally believed to have been, really seems to have been made up of inferior elements. We have but little information about them, and that little we owe to writers in the exile, if indeed it does not belong already to the later period when the returning exiles brought new life to their old home. It seems, indeed, to have been the case as tradition has it, that all those who were possessed of anything like position, esteem, property, knowledge and ideals, went, by compulsion or from their own volition, into the exile in order to help prepare the new future from there.

These peculiarities of the present period make it advisable to group the problems around the personalities or literary units as their centers and present them in the order observed in the preceding period. This, of course, can be carried out fully only in respect to those literary units which call for an exhaustive orientation in all, or, at least, in most, of the important questions which are dealt with here. Such units, on the other hand, as furnish material but to some particular questions, will be fitly linked, in their chronological order, with the larger units as contributing elements, thus asuring a freer and clearer outlook from the aspects won in the more comprehensive orientations.

1.   JEREMIAH.

The prophetic career of Jeremiah extends over a period of at least forty years (626-586) which may be divided into two distinct phases. In the first of these Jeremiah stands more or less on the ground prepared by Isaiah, whom we have to consider the most eminent representative of pre-Jeremian Judaism. He differs from him, however, in the question of angels whose existence, or, at any rate, whose function as mediators between God and man, Jeremiah denies. And also in the opposition to the attribute of *Long-Suffering* Jeremiah is much more decided than was Isaiah. The difference of view, favored by the conditions of the time, developed and condensed into a new formulation of the God-conception by Jeremiah. This great turn in the prophetic activity of Jeremiah, as in the development of Judaism in general, takes

place in about the middle of the prophet's career, in
the first years of the reign of *Jojakim* (608). The
second period in Jeremiah's activity may be designated the *ethico-cosmological*, as, in general, we have
to call the new period in Judaism dawning with
Jeremiah, in contradistinction of the pure ethical
monotheism in pre-Jeremiah times. By that time
Juda had been for some time already under the
influence of *Neo-Babylonia*. Through this new contact with the culture of their old native country the
interest of the Jews for cosmogonic questions was reawakened. The eternal passion of the people for
idols had never been overcome by the pure ethical
conception of God. How much less could there be
any hope to get along with the mere ethical God-
conception at a time when the cosmogonic interest
of the people was aroused, when, on account of that
new interest, the Ishtar-worship was carried on more
intensely than ever before (VII, 17-19; XLIV, 15-26).
Under these conditions Jeremiah certainly had sufficient reason to emphasize *holiness* as a divine attribute.
However, contrary to our expectations, this emphasis
is found in Jeremiah chiefly in a *negative* way only,
in that in his numerous historical reminiscences he
hardly alludes to anything beyond the Egyptian
period (XXXI, 15; XXXIII, 26; cf. Deut.), while his
positive utterances on the idea of holiness are very
rare (II, 3; XXIII, 9; cf. XXXI, 23). Evidently the
pure ethical idea of holiness was not sufficient in the
view of Jeremiah, after the experience of so many
generations in which that idea has utterly failed to
impress the people. Clearly the God-idea had to be

conceived more deeply and to be established on a larger basis. This great turn was accomplished by Jeremiah. The doctrine of angels, that great obstacle on the road to the monotheistic theory of creation (the angels were conceived of as *eternal* entities—cf. Gen. III, 22), had been overcome, the cosmological interest of the people reawakened—thus the essential conditions favoring the formulation of the new God-conception had materialized. This led Jeremiah to the conception of the *monotheistic theory of creation*. JHVH is the sole creator of all things, and his right upon the exclusive worship of man is indisputable. In connection with the idea of God as Creator Jeremiah endeepens the concept of JHVH as the sole, unique, true entity, designating the "other gods" as "non-gods" and "non-powers", thus stripping them of all entity and reducing them to empty phantoms. Of the divine attributes Jeremiah presses to the fore the attributes of *Wisdom* and *Might* (cf. IX, 22, 23). The old definition of JHVH, the Thirteen Attributes, satisfies him no more. This formula was lacking the cosmological element, and, then, too, it contained some attributes of mercy which did not appeal to Jeremiah even before he found the new theory of creation, and which now were altogether incompatible with the rigid justice expected from the sole creator of all things. Even the name of JHVH became too narrow to express his God-conception. The name JHVH became too much reminiscent of the God of the Thirteen Attributes, of too much mercy. Jeremiah, therefore, adopts the combination *J HV H Zebaoth* of Isaiah as a *temporary*

name of God, recoining it so as to make it express
his new theory.   JHVH Zebaoth to Jeremiah is the
JHVH of the hosts of creation, the sole creator of
the universe, who insists on rigid justice in the world
which is *His*, and His only (X, 10; Jeremiah uses
the name JHVH Zebaoth more often than any other
prophet, not less than 68 times!).   The Wisdom and
Might of God manifest themselves in the first line in
creation: but also in his *rulership* in the world, in
Nature (v. 13) and *History*, especially in the *selection
of Israel* (v. 16); it is *the same* divine omnipotence,
the same divine wisdom that comes to manifestation:
With the appearance of the monotheistic theory of
creation the divine attributes have at once been
translated from the Ethical into the *Metaphysical*.

The new God-conception in turn greatly influenced the formulation of the other principles.   Of
prophecy we find in Jeremiah the higher Deuteronomic
conception, repudiating all lower mantical forms,
including visions of angels and dreams (XIV, 13-19;
XXIII, 9-40; XXVII, 9; XXIX, 8).   The calling of
the prophet is to lead the people from the evil to the
good way (XXIII, 2), and also to take a hand in
the political affairs of the time (I, 5-10).   The sign of
the prophet is prediction of future events.   However,
in the case a prophet predicts visitation, God in
His mercy may recall the decree, so that even the
prediction of a true prophet may at times not ma-
terialize (XXIX, 8.9).   Jeremiah deepens the concept
of prophecy also from the cosmological viewpoint:
As Israel's prophetic calling was provided for in the
eternal plan of creation, so also the prophet was cre-

ated for prophecy from the womb (I, 5-19; v. 9:
"I will give my word in thy mouth"—Deut. XVIII,
18; cf. above). About man's *free will* we find in
Jeremiah certain utterances which point to some difficulties he faced in the question of the *responsibility
of the individual*. Is not the way of man predeter-
mined by God? Does not God himself lay stumbling
stones in the way of the generations, fathers and
children? And, then too; is man perfectible at all?
(VI, 21; X, 23; XII, 23; XX, 7; cf. Deut. XXIX, 3).
On the other hand, the prophet is by no means ready
to give up the old fundamental prophetic principle
of free will, and he even coins a new word (שרירות)
to express the idea of free will (VI, 16; VII, 24; XIII,
10; XVIII, 12; XXIII, 17; cf. Tholdoth p. 82-83).
Besides, the postulate of man's free will is implied
in the basic thought of the monotheistic theory of
creation: This theory of creation denies the reign
of Fatum over god and man (X, 2). These contradictory tendencies in the question of free will repeat
themselves, naturally enough, in the question of
retribution, a question which is to be treated in further
connection with the soul problem:

From what was said above about Jeremiah's
conception of prophecy we could infer that the underlying concept of the *individual soul* is intensely one
of *substantiality*. And this definite substantial conception of the individual soul which is expressed
clearly as an item of the new theory of creation
(XXXVIII, 16; cf. Is. LVII, 16), shows its direct
influence also upon the question of free will: This
prophet was *called upon* to prophesy, *aganist his will*,

he was *persuaded* by God to devote himself to this
task (XX, 7-18).   Both, the freedom of will as well as
also the occasional restriction laid upon it, are expressed in this statement.   It is evident that in the
view of Jeremiah the individual soul is subject to
some definite disposition restricting man's free will.
This cosmologically endeepened conception of the
individual soul led Jeremiah (and his contemporaries)
back to the emphasis on the principle of individual
retribution which appears ao much restricted in
Deuteronomy.   He no more sees his way clear
before him to accept the attribute of *Long-suffering*
(XV, 15; XVIII, 23; XX, 12), and so he does not
hesitate to consider the view of the people of his
age in their attitude that the principle of national
retribution according to which the account of sin is
carried from generation to generation, is not a just
one (XXXI, 29.30); these two attributes, "long-
suffering" and "visiting the sons of the fathers upon
the children" being in close connection with each
other (God is long-suffering with the individual
sinner, exacting the full punishment on later generations).   This lends color to the historical phenomenon
that Jeremiah, the first to formulate the monotheistic theory of creation, was also the first to formulate
so relentlessly the great problem of the ages: why is
the wicked prosperous, and the righteous suffering?
(XII, 1 f.).   But the new theory of creation not only
urged new problems to the surface, but also gave
Jeremiah the power, if not to solve, so at least, to
mitigate and to silence the new doubts and perplexities.   JHVH has created heaven and earth,

nothing is hidden from His eyes, nothing limits His omnipotence, and so surely everything is all right in His world, He certainly knows how to bring harmony into the workings of the two seemingly contradictory principles, national retribution and individual responsibility. JHVH is great in counsel and rich in activity, it is not the task of man to search God (XXXII, 17-19). Jeremiah, of course, knew also of the idea of equalizing justice in a future world which was to develop in the wake of the new conception of creation (cf. below), but in this he remained on the ground prepared by Deuteronomy: not one word about the eschatological aspect of justice to the individual.

Corresponding to the decisive influence of Jeremiah's new orientation in the theoretical principles of Judaism also his influence upon the development of the higher forms of cultural life was a very deep and potent one. According to Jeremiah's own descriptions of the unlawful image-worship the artistic sense of the people in his time had attained a considerable degree of development. It is, furthermore, Jeremiah who first mentions *wall paintings* as a form of artistic expression (XXII, 14; more clearly Ez. XXIII, 14), an innovation, evidently imported from Babylonia. But if in the following centuries the Jewish people, under the influence of the new teaching, not only gave up the unlawful image-worship but also developed a certain indifference, nay disinclination, toward plastics, it is Jeremiah who is responsible for this change. And this not only in general, inasmuch as he was the expounder of rigid monotheism (as against the belief in angels) and the originator of the monotheistic theory of creation, but also in particular, in that he zealously denounced all reverence for relics and took an emphatic stand against all cultivation of plastics (II, 27.28; III, 9.16.17; IV, 1.30; VII, 12-19; 29.34; X, 1-16; XIV, 22; XVI, 19.20; XVII, 2. XIX, 5.13; XXII, 28; XXVI, 6; XXXII, 34.35; XLIV, 8-25). Jeremiah's intense aversion to the plastical and decorative arts is accounted for in part by the unlawful cultivation of those arts abroad among the people, as also by the psychological depression of the prophet due to the bitter experiences he had with his personal adversaries. Indeed, also of Jeremiah's literary form we have to say that the absence of marked artistic motifs in his prophecies is probably due to the untoward circumstances under which he was obliged to live and to work (having in mind, of course, particularly the destruction of his book and the restoration of the same from memory). Nevertheless, the *indirect influence* of Jeremiah upon the development of Hebrew literature was greater and more powerful than that of any other one individual personality. Pre-Jeremian literature was essentially of *an historical character*, and we have seen above that this was due to the fact that all religious thinking to which all literature has been almost entirely devoted, was purely ethical. All argument for the existence of God and His claim upon the obedience of man were of a providential-historical nature. No argument from *Nature*! This has now been changed, due to the appearance of Jeremiah with his monotheistic theory of creation. To the historical argument has now been added the cosmological, from natural phenomena. God's claim on Providence in History is based on the idea of monotheistic creation, and it is to this idea that Jeremiah refers the kings of Edom, Moab, Ammon, Tyrus and Zidon in explanation of his opposition to the joining of Juda in their alliance against Nebuchadnezzar "my servant" (XXVII, 5 f.). God's ethical attributes under the guidance of which history developed its course, and the selection of Israel, the goal of the past and the new avenue for the future, are considered under the aspect of *natural law* (XXXI, 31-36; XXXIII, 20-26). This meant the *discovery of nature* in Hebrew literature. The argument from nature helped develop interest in and insight into the workings of nature: The numerous grand descriptions of nature in biblical literature are all post-Jeremian. That the deeper penetration into all problems under the new, the cosmological, aspect was also of great literary import is self-evident. Suffice it to point to the fact that it is Jeremiah's new aspect to which Hebrew literature owes the distinction of having produced the *first philosophic dialog in the literature of the world*, the Book of Job (cf. below). Jeremiah is also the first prophet of whose care for the preservation of his literary estate we have definite information (ch. XXXIII).

Jeremiah's influence upon *legislation* is felt partly in Deuteronomy (cf. above), but also in his prophecies there are ample evidences of his desire to have a hand in the shaping of practical laws. So in the

Sabbath-question (ch. XVII; provided the passage is genuine) and in the question of *slavery* (ch. XXXIV). And in general, Jeremiah develops a *formal concept of law*, independent of its content (ch. XXXV—the *prohibition of wine* to the Rechabim, as an example of faithful adherence to a paternal injunction). The later development warrants the assumption that this formal concept of law was conceived by Jeremiah in connection with his monotheistic theory of creation, although there is no definite passage in Jeremiah to this effect (cf. below to the Priestly Code). Whether Jeremiah had any influence upon the development of the institution of circumcision (favored so much by his later followers) cannot be made out with certainty from the only passage bearing upon the subject (IX, 24,25). At any rate, we may say of Jeremiah, that he, the *priest*-prophet with the formalistic conception of law, in spite of the emphasis he lays upon *ethical law* and *social justice* as the one thing which God demands and expects of man, was no opponent of the ritual law on the principle, and especially that he was no opponent of the *sacrificial ritual* as such. This view, wide-spread though it may be, is as little true concerning Jeremiah, as it is concerning other prophets. This can best be shown by an analysis of *chapter seven*, in which Jeremiah develops his ideas about the subject most fully, ideas which are often repeated throughout all of his prophecies. These ideas are as follows:

1. The City of JHVH and the House of JHVH are holy and distinguished by their connection with

the name of God (VII, 10-14; cf. XXIII, 11; XXV, 29; XXXI, 23; XXXII, 34; comp. also XLI, 5 and LI, 11.51).

2.   God declines the acceptance of sacrifices, or does not receive them graciously, for three reasons: *First*, because Judeans defiled the House of JHVH through idolatrous *images* and idolatrous sacrificial rites, especially through the Moloch-cult. *Second*, because they indulge in idolatrous practices in the *land*, often neglecting entirely JHVH and his House. *Third*, because they lead an immoral and unjust life (VII, 3.5-9.17-19.30.31; cf. III, 24; V, 19; VI, 20; XI, 12; XIV, 12; XIX, 5; XXXII, 31 f.; XLIV, 2.3.5.8.15-29).

3.   It is on account of the sins mentioned that God will destroy the City and the House, or that he has destroyed them. But in the case they repent God would not destroy the City and the House, or he would rebuild them. The belief of the Judeans the Temple of JHVH in itself had the power to protect them, is erroneous (VII, 3-15.20.32-34; cf. V, 19; XXII, 4; XXVI, 6; XXXII, 31 f.; XXXIII, 5; XLIV, 2 f., 15-29).

4.   When the Israelites left Egypt the sacrifices were not the *first* thing God spoke of to them, or commanded them about, this being rather the injunction that they should fulfill the Covenant according to which He was to be their God and they were to be His people. i. e. that they should not worship (sacrifice to) strange gods and that they should walk in his ways, leading an ethical and religious life. Sacrifices were ordained only for the

time after the conquest of Palestine (VII, 21 ff.; cf. Amos V, 25; this view of the matter is the *older* tradition; cf. Gesch, d. jued. Philos. II, 1, p. 124. 216 f.).

5. When the Judeans will return to JHVH, or when JHVH shall have compassion with the "*remnant*", then the (prescribed) public, as well as the private free offerings, especially thanks offerings (comp. below as to the later development), shall be received graciously by JHVH (VII, 3.9b; XVII, 26; XXVII, 22; XXX, 19; XXXI, 6.12.14; XXXIII, 18; comp. also XXXIV, 18: the covenant of social justice is sealed with a sacrifice! Some of these passages were declared to be not-genuine, but this was done by a petitio principii; because they believed, without warrant, that Jeremiah was an opponent of sacrifices on principle, some scholars came to the conclusion that passages expressing any appreciation of the sacrificial ritual must necessarily be later interpolations).

6. There is nothing in the prophecies of Jeremiah that would justify the assumption of a conscious contrast between priest and prophet, to say nothing of a contrast between the *priestly Torah* and the *prophetic Torah*. Jeremiah knows of no other distinction than of that between good and bad priests, as also between good (true) and bad (false) prophets. In fact, Jeremiah scolds the people for their ritual sins with as much zeal as for their moral sins (VII, 4.8.9; comp. IV, 9; V, 31; VI, 13; XXIII, 11; XXX, 34; the proverb of XVIII, 18, quoted by Jeremiah's opponents, has nothing to do with our subject.

The only conclusion warranted by this passage is that in practical questions of the Torah the people would look for instruction from the priest, while in public or private affairs outside the sphere of the law they would look for a special revelation of the "word" of God through the prophet, (comp. Ez. VII, 26; XXII, 26 f.; Zeph. III, 4); comp. XVII, 19-27; declared by some not to be genuine).   The only sacrifices which appear to have been opposed by Jeremiah, are the *sin-offerings.* If we compare Jeremiah with his contemporary Ezekiel, the silence of the former about the institution of the sin-offering must appear very strange, and the only interpretation permissible seems to be the same as that applied to Deuteronomy (cf. above to Deut. and below to Ezekiel), namely that Jeremiah was opposed to that institution altogether.

Jeremiah's attitude toward *universalism* is quite in accordance with what we would expect of him on the strength of what has been said about him in the preceding. The emphasis laid by him on ethical conduct as the condition for the worth of the ritual, as, in general, his monotheistic idea of creation, would rather justify the expectation to find him among the universalists. In fact, we find with him utterances of universalistic leanings: JHVH has chosen "His Servant", the King Nebuchadnezzar, to accomplish through him His historic plans (XXVII, 5 f.). Jeremiah gives the Jews the advice to avail themselves, to a certain extent, of *civil communion* with Babylonia (XXIX, 5; XXXII, 15; XLII, 10); he recommends to the Jews to emulate the Rechabites as an

example of faithfulness in the observance of law
(chap. XXXV); indulges with great interest in
prophecies "on the nations" (chaps. XLVI-XLIX),
showing often great sympathy with the fate of those
nations, rising at times even to visions in which he
sees a hopeful future for some of them (XLVII, 6;
XLVIII, 31.36.47; XLIX, 6.39.)

Yet, the hopelessness of the political situation and
the bewilderment reigning supreme in religious
affairs, especially in the latter part of Jeremiah's
prophetic career, made him despair of the possibility
of the Jews being able to take up and to carry out
the great mission of leading the nations as such, i. e.
as distinct national entities, and making them confess
JHVH and His teachings. Jeremiah, indeed, hopes
that all nations will pilgrim *to Jerusalem* to worship
there the name of JHVH (III, 16.17). But the meaning of this messianic idea with Jeremiah has changed
much from what it was before. The nations will
have not only to abandon their idols (XVI, 19), but
also to offer a *positive confession of faith*, in order to
be admitted into the community of the Jewish people
(XII, 15.17; cf. Ruth I, 16). Jeremiah yearns for a
new Covenant (cf. XXXIV, 8.18.19) in which the law
will be written not only upon (a scroll or upon)
tablets of stone, but also upon the hearts of the
people.[1]

---

[1] XXXI, 31-33. The idea of some Christian scholars that
    Jeremiah was opposed to the written law, and thus antici-
    pated Paulinian antinomism, is not deserving of refutation.
    Nevertheless attention may be called to the following
    passages where Jeremiah refers to the written Torah,
    especially to those where he quotes Deuteronomy to which
    he is supposed, by some of the critics, to have taken a

A new Covenant meant more particularistic exclusiveness, all in harmony with Jeremiah's outspoken
aversion to all forms of the general Semitic cultural
communion.

Again, this new Covenant was to reunite Juda
and Israel under the scepter of David (II, 4; III,
11.12; XIII, 11; (XVII, 26); XXIII, 5.6; XXIX,
14.16; XXX, 3.4; XXXI, 1.18-20.27.41; XXXI, 30.
37-39; XXXIII, 20-26; cf. L, 20.33; LI, 5). With
Jeremiah there begins the reawakening of the great
hope for the restoration of the old national unity.

---

hostile attitude: IX, 12 (cf. XXVI, 4 and Deut. IV, 8-44);
XI, 6; XXXII, 23; XXXIV, 8-16 (verse 8 is a quotation
from Deut. XV, 12;) XLIV, 23. This is, furthermore, in
contradiction with the importance Jeremiah attaches to
the written word, as manifested in the great care he has
taken to preserve his prophecies and to save them from
destruction for the benefit of future generations; cf. XVII, 1;
XXII, 24; XXV, 13; XXIX, 1 f.; XXX, 2; XXXII, 9-14;
ch. XXXVI. Some verses in this chapter (4.27.28.33;
cf. XLV, 1) have led to the suggestion that Jeremiah was
an illiterate. But this explanation of the employment of
Baruch the Scribe by Jeremiah is entirely out of the question.
In XXII, 9-14 it is expressly stated that Jeremiah himself
wrote and sealed the deed and *then* gave it to the official
Baruch for embodiment in the public registry; in XXXVI,
5, 6, again, Jeremiah asks Baruch to substitute for him in
reading from the scroll to the people assembled in the
House of JHVH because of his being prevented from coming
into the House of JHVH; evidently, had it not been for
this obstacle Jeremiah would have read himself. (Also
LI, 60 assures us that Jeremiah could write himself. The
author of this prophecy surely was in a position to know
whether Jeremiah was able to write; had he known of
Jeremiah's illiteracy, he certainly would have expressed
himself in a different way). The question why Jeremiah
employed Baruch the Scribe, is irrelevant, but most likely
he did so because the hand of the skilled scribe was more
legible and more fit for public reading, (cf. XXXVI, 5).

2. EZEKIEL.

The new ideas and postulates as laid down in Deuteronomy failed to inspire the people. The Book of Deuteronomy was indeed called upon to influence and to determine the character of Jewish doctrine and life for all times. But it was destined to accomplish this only in combination with the new *cosmological ideas* of Jeremiah. And this combination was the product of a process quite long and complicated. Before the ideas of Jeremiah shaped themselves so definitely as to develop into legislative postulates, this new trend of thought in its totality, comprising the monotheistic emphasis of Deuteronomy with its opposition against the angels, as also the monotheistic theory of creation in the conception advanced by Jeremiah, had yet to face the opponents arisen in the midst of the prophets themselves. And this struggle was the harder and the hotter, as on the side of these opponents, the *conservatives*, there was the *people* in its great multitudes. The spokesman of the old traditions among the prophets was *Ezekiel*.

It took some time before the opponents of the Deuteronomic Covenant succeeded in mustering their forces and organizing them. It was in the *thirtieth* year after this reformation (Ez. I, 1), at the time when Jeremiah was busy working out and spreading his monotheistic theory of creation, that his younger contemporary and fellow-prophet appeared at the head of the *orthodox* to fight the innovations from his post in the exile, innovations which, although not accepted by the people at large, enjoyed a certain authoritative position and furnished the standard by which to measure the religious life of the people as to its lawfulness.

The return to the *belief in angels* stands in the center of the movement started or, rather, organized by Ezekiel. With great emphasis the belief in angels is being systematized and brought into interrelation with all manifestations of religious life: The *Mercabah*, the divine *Throne* and *Court* formed by angels, is the source from which emanate all divine powers in nature, providence, sanctuary, law and history (I; II, 12-14.22-24; chaps. VIII-X; XI, 22-24; XXVIII 14; XL, 18 f.; XLIII, 1 f.).   With the belief in angels also the interest in the early history was reawakened. With Jeremiah, too, we find some allusions to the pre-Egyptian history of Israel. This is generally due to Jeremiah's cosmological conception of the idea of selection of Israel, which made it necessary for him to go back to the beginnings of the history of the human race. Also Ezekiel may be presumed to have been interested in early history on account of his cosmogonical interest. For in spite of his opposition to Jeremiah's doctrine of creation, and partly because of it, Ezekiel had to meet the reawakened cosmogonic interest of the people, which he did by a refashioning of some Babylonian cosmogonic myths in the spirit of monotheism; as indeed the Mercabah (especially in ch. I) has been recognized to be a reflex of cosmogonic legends (cf. Tholdoth I, p. 68 f.).   But, if, in spite of his greater cosmological interest, Jeremiah is surpassed by Ezekiel in the frequency and the emphasis of his retrospections into the early history, this fact shows clearly that the

extent of the interest in the early history is decided
by the different attitude taken by each of these two
prophets toward the question of angels. Jeremiah
had not yet found the way of orienting himself in
the early history without angels (this was found by
one of his later followers), hence his diminished
interest in the early history. Ezekiel, on the other
hand, enhanced in his determination to defend the
angels by the very opposition of Jeremiah and his
followers, alludes frequently not only to the pre-
Egyptian history of Israel, but also to those phases
in the beginnings of history which link with the
beginnings of creation, and in which the angels play
a more conspicuous part than even in the pre-Egyptian history of Israel (XIV, 14: Noah; XVI, 3.45.46
f.: Sodom; XXVIII, 12.16: Gan Eden, Cherub =
XXXI, 8.9.16.18 = XXXVI, 35; XXVIII, 25: to my
servant Jacob; XXXIII, 24: Abraham; these elements
of early history come from the sources of J₂ in Gen.
I-XI). That the development consummated in
Deuteronomy did not fail to influence Ezekiel, we
see best in the fact that, like Jeremiah, also Ezekiel,
permeated with the spirit of purity dominant in
Deuteronomy, denounces all sexual impurity, especially such as dared to adorn its hideous face with
the halo of a *religious ritual* (VIII, 14.17; XIII, 17-21;
XXIII, 48.49). But neither this influence, nor even
the advanced purification of those legends evident
in the conception of Ezekiel, was sufficient to blot
out entirely the traces of objectionable ideas cleaving
to those old narratives. And Ezekiel was not slow
in recognizing the peril to the purity of life lurking

in these interesting stories so much beloved by the
people. And it may be assumed that it was this
peril that Ezekiel sought to meet with the hitherto
unobserved emphasis laid by him on the old idea of
holiness. As against the new prevailing cosmological
conception of Jeremiah, Ezekiel goes back to the
historical origin of the Jewish God-conception, re-
formulating it on the basis of the idea of the holy
name of JHVH (XI, 16; XIII, 19; XX, 9.22.39.44;
XXIV, 21; XXV, 3; XXVIII, 22.25; XXXVI,
20-23; XXXVII, 26.28; XXXVIII, 16.23; XXXIX,
7.13.21.25.27; XLIII, 7.8). Thus Ezekiel reempha-
sizes the ethical God-conception. And, orienting
ourselves in the book of Ezekiel, we soon become aware
of the fact that this book, in spite of its (more latent)
cosmogonic woof, is framed wholly in the scheme of
ethical attributes and borne entirely by the ethical
motif of attributes. Ezekiel utilizes all the well-
known motifs of attributes employed by his predecessors, presenting his conception of history and his
views on the theoretical principles of Judaism in a
setting artistic in its design and systematic in its
execution.

The point of crystallization in the composition of
the book of Ezekiel is the query into the "Ways of
JHVH", the definition of the ethical God-conception.
It was the "Ways of JHVH" as embodied in the
Formula of Thirteen upon which Ezekiel's contemporaries directed their attacks. And to what length
they went in their rejection of the "Ways of JHVH"
is evident from the fact that they rejected also the
name of JHVH, as representing the Formula of

Thirteen, using instead the name of Adonoy (אדני),
denoting *might* and *force* (XVIII, 25.29.30; XXXIII,
17.20). These "Ways" are the same which to
defend Ezekiel chose as the task of his life: The
"Ways of JHVH", this is the prophet's general
answer, are good, only that man, nation or individual,
has no claim upon any judgment other than such as
corresponding to his own ways (III, 18.19; VII,
3.4.8.9.27; IX, 21; XIII, 22.23; XVI, 27.43.47;
XX, 30.43.44; XXII, 31; XXIV, 14; XXXIII,
8.9.11; XXXVI, 17.19.31.32). In detail the prophet
develops his thoughts in the following conception of
history: JHVH appears to him in the Mercabah,
in His creative power, in which character He is designated by the name of *Shadday* (שדי I, 24, cf. X, 5:
אל שדי), but it is rather in His ethical attributes
that JHVH reveals Himself to man. The visual
sign of the "glory of JHVH", the "Cabhod JHVH",
representing the God of the thirteen attributes (cf.
Ex. XXXIII, 18.19.22), appears in the phenomenon
of the "Rainbow in the Cloud", the *fire*, representing
rigid Justice, turned upwards, the *halo*, representing
Mercy, turned downward. This is the real essence
of God, expressed by the name JHVH, whence the
name "Cabhod JHVH" (I, 27.28). But on account of
the people's sins, and especially as a punishment for
the removal of the cherubs, the symbol of the angels,
from the temple, JHVH turned his face away from
them (cf. VII, 21 and XXXIX, 29). He abandons
the City, thus depriving her of her securest shield
against the enemy. In His stead now appears the
"Mal'akh JHVH", eliminated at the time of the erec-

tion of the temple, resuming his function of dis-
pensing rigid justice; a change indicated in the reversion of the previous vision, the Cabhod now being
turned upward, the fire downward.   Only a number
of individuals, marked by a *sign of mercy* on their
foreheads, will escape.   In this time of judgment the
name of God is not only JHVH (employed in the
book of Ezekiel 213 times), but also, following in
part the suggestion of his contemporaries, *Adonoy*
JHVH (likewise 213 times; cf. especially XXXVI,
22.23).   Not before the rebuilding of the temple in
accordance with the divine will, i. e. purified of all
unholy images, but adorned with the holy image not
only of two cherubs, but of the entire *Mercabah*, as
described by the prophet, will JHVH reestablish his
presence in the midst of Israel, and then the city will
receive the name יהוה שמה, "JHVH is There"—
the name JHVH will then become the exclusive name
of God (Chaps. I; VIII; IX; X; especially as compared
with XLIII, 1-8; XLI, 21 with XLIII, 3 (and X, 20)
and XLVIII, 35; as to Mal'akh JHVH cf. Ez. VIII
and IX with 2 Sam. XXIV and 1 Chr. XXI and
Ez. XXI, 13-20, especially v. 16 with 2 Sam. XXIV,
17 in the light of the version 1 Chr. XXI, 16; also
cf. Num. XXII, 22.23 and Josh. X, 13 f.).

As we have just seen, the God-conception of
Ezekiel is by no means the same mere ethical of the
pre-Jeremian period, the former having a cosmological
touch.   This meant a certain enrichment of the God-
conception, expressed especially in the attributes of
Wisdom, emphasized by Ezekiel as the *criterion* of
divinity wherever he alludes to cosmogonic myths

(XXVIII, 2-7.12.17). But the return to the doctrine of angels annulled in part this enrichment of the God-conception. *Creative Power* cannot mean a real criterion of divinity as long as there are in existence, alongside of the creator, eternal angels, carrying out certain functions in the creation of the world.

Indeed, on this conception of God Ezekiel depends in his entire Weltanschauung and historic orientation:

A marked *reaction* we perceive in the conception of *prophecy*. To be sure, like Jeremiah, Ezekiel, too, preaches against false prophets and the lower mantical forms, especially against its feminine branch (XII, 24; ch. XIII; v. 17 f. against the prophetesses; XXI, 26-29; XXII 25.29), but his own conception of prophecy goes back to that of the old period. He sees God in the anthropomorphic Mercabah vision. Ezekiel has, as we will see later on, a very definite notion of the distinction between *spirit* (רוח) and *flesh* (בשר). However, even spirit appears to him in a very tangible vision. "Ruah", as used by Ezekiel, denotes, as with almost all biblical writers, now "spirit", now "wind"; Ezekiel's contribution to this double meaning consisting in establishing a closer interrelation betwen the two (cf. especially ch. XXXVII). In his prophetic visions he not only sees Mercabah and angels, but he also experiences the immediate influence of the "Ruah" which "comes unto him", "seizes him and carries him away", or also: the hand of JHVH seizes him or rests upon him (II, 2.9.10; III, 12.14.22.24; VIII, 3; XI, 1.5.24; XLIII, 5.6). Jeremiah gives added expression to his purified idea of prophecy by

abhorring in very strong accents the word "Massa"
(משא), then in vogue for the designation of a divine
revelation, considering that word as degrading to
true prophecy: They should not ask: "What was
the 'Massa' of JHVH?", but: "What is it that JHVH
said?", or: "What was it that JHVH spoke?"
"Massa" seemed to him to emphasize too much the
element of phantasy which he insisted on having
removed from the word of JHVH (Jer. XXIII,
33-39; cf. 2 Ki. IX, 25—by the way, the only time
the word (משא) in the meaning of divine revelation
occurs in pre-Deuteronomic literature; the *headings*
in Is. XIII-XXX, as also those of Nahum, Habakkuk
and Zechariah, evidently having been attached at the
final redaction of the Bible).   Ezekiel returns to this
old designation of prophecy (XII, 10; the text,
however, being quite uncertain).   On the other hand,
again, it must be said that as far as the conception
of the *calling* of the prophet as a teacher of religion
and morality goes, Ezekiel not only yields nothing
to Jeremiah but even surpasses him in clearness and
definiteness of formulation and expression (cf. especially chaps. XII; XIII; XIV; XVIII; XXXIII).
As against the old view that the sinner is to be denied
the benefits of prophecy, a view corresponding to
the lower conception of prophecy as a mere mantical
device (cf. 1 Sam. XXVIII, 6.15), Ezekiel progresses
to the conviction that it is just the sinfulness of the
people that calls for the ministrations of the prophet,
the teacher (XIV, 2-11; XX, 3-31); and this duty of
the prophet becomes the greater and the more urgent,
the more the people recognize him as such, thus

expecting of him guidance, instruction and admonition. In this case the prophet's position is like that of the *watch on the tower* in time of war (XXXIII, 2-20; cf. III, 17-21).

Added orientation permits us the further insight that the notion of "Ruah" holds a central position in Ezekiel's trend of thought: It is the unifying "Ruah" who preserves the monotheistic idea in the multimorphic Mercabah (I, 12.20.21; X, 17), and it is He who inspires the prophet in the hour of revelation (cf. above). The same "Ruah" is the all-absorbing feature in the vision of *resurrection* (XXXVII, 1-14). The Ruah of prophecy leads the prophet into the valley (v. 1), and it is the same Ruah which is described as the *vitalizing substance* in contradistinction of the *bones* (body; vv. 5-10; 14). The idea of resurrection is here merely symbolic of the political conditions of the time; nevertheless, the idea is here. And little as we are entitled to think that Ezekiel advanced the idea of resurrection, the fact stands out clearly that he employed the old Jewish idea of the independent existence of the soul in a more outspoken way than did any prophet or writer before him. It is again the same "Ruah" whom God "gives into the heart" of a nation or an individual for *betterment*, and also on this occasion the Ruah is contrasted with the flesh (בשר; XI, 19; XXXVI, 25-27).

This, the help of God to moral betterment, involves, of course, (as has already been observed by the Talmudists), a restriction of *freedom of will*; an attitude which is felt also in the opposite direction, i. e. that of limiting man's ability to mend his ways

(XIV, 9; XXIV, 13). And yet, in spite of this oscillatory attitude in the question of man's free will, Ezekiel is the prophet who, more than any one of his predecessors, tries to clarify the doctrine of *retribution* as such and, especially, in its interdependence with the doctrine of *repentance* (cf. below). And even the idea of the new "Ruah" which brings about a betterment of the heart, appears once expressed in the sense of freedom of will (XVIII, 31: "And fashion ye unto yourselves a new heart and a new Ruah"). This testifies to the intimate connection between the conceptions of God and Soul in the speculation of Ezekiel, as also to the interdependence between the questions of prophecy, freedom of will and retribution and those conceptions, and between each other. The cosmological element in his God-conception led Ezekiel to a deeper realization of the concept of the individual soul, and, like Jeremiah, he, too, was impelled by the circumstances of his time to submit the principle of national retribution to a rigid examination as to its tenability (XVIII, 2 f.). Ezekiel, however, had not the efficient expedient of the monotheistic theory of creation by which Jeremiah was able to allay all doubts and perplexities; Ezekiel's theory of creation not being sufficiently monotheistic to fulfill that task. For this reason the *contradictions* concerning the freedom of will with Ezekiel are even more disturbing than those with Jeremiah, although Jeremiah left these problems as much unsolved as did Ezekiel.

But if Ezekiel does not show much of a conscious effort to clear up the question of free will, his speculation is intently active around the question of *retribution*.

The question of why the righteous suffers while the wicked prospers, already troubled Jeremiah and other prophets (Jer. XII, 1 f.; cf. Hab. ch. I), but never before had this question been so thoroughly discussed and its solution so earnestly attempted as by Ezekiel.

The thoughts of Ezekiel on this question, as restricted, complemented and illumined by each other, may be outlined in the following summary:

In spite of the more liberal utilization of the soul-idea in its eschatological conception (ch. XXXVII), Ezekiel was as little ready to employ the idea of retribution in the *hereafter* in order to solve, or at least to mitigate, thereby the perplexities of the principle of retribution, as was any one of his predecessors. He rather tries hard to solve this problem in a *this-wordly* fashion. We remember the contention of Ezekiel's contemporaries against the "Ways of JHVH" as expressed in the formula of Thirteen, that these were not good inasmuch as they led to the suffering of the just (for the sins of their fathers) and the prosperity of the wicked (for the merits of their fathers; cf. XVIII, 2.25.29.30; XXXIII, 17.20). Some of the prophet's contemporaries went even further in their attack on the "Ways of God". From the injustice they believed to perceive in the world, they jumped to the conclusion that there was no providence, JHVH having left the land (or the earth?) altogether (VIII, 12; IX, 9). To ward off

these attacks the prophet tries to fortify the principle
of retribution with the following theory:

The idea of *individual responsibility* is the un-
alterable principle of the Jewish doctrine of retribution. The attribute of "Visiting the sins of the
fathers", thus the entire principle of national retribution, is given up (XVIII, 2-20). With this principle Ezekiel relinquishes also the very efficient explanation which it furnished through the ages in
the defense of justice, suggesting that the seeming
injustice of the suffering of the righteous and the
prosperity of the wicked is balanced up, respectively,
by the sins or the merits of past generations. Instead
of the principle of national retribution it is now a
stronger emphasis laid upon the principle of *free will*
which is made to serve in the defense of justice.
Man is free in both directions, for good as well as
for evil. And this possibility of complete change of
heart (without displaying it to the outside world)
explains all difficulties about justice. The wicked
surely suffers for his sins, but only if he fails to repent
and to resolve to mend his ways. In the moment,
however, that he repents in his heart and resolves to
reform, his sins are blotted out, and then it well may
happen that he be prosperous. The righteous, again,
is prosperous only if he *remains* righteous, in the
case, however, that he *return* from his righteousness
by committing some actual sins, while remaining
righteous in general, or by becoming wavering in his
love for righteousness even though in his thoughts
only, he may suffer, either for those actual sins committed during the period of his righteousness, or for

the abandoning of the principle of righteousness. Sins for which one has repented, count as little as good actions which one disavows, as it were, by his later conduct.   Later sin extinguishes previous merit, as later merit extinguishes previous sin (III, 17-21; XVIII, 21-28; XXXIII, 9-20).   And to what length the prophet was determined to go in his emphasis upon individual responsibility, is best seen in his insistence on the theory that even in the case of a general disaster that overtakes a land, it is only the sinful who are hit, while the righteous, and were there only three, or even only one, in the entire population of a land, will surely be saved in some way from the general destruction (XIV, 13-20).   As applied to the situation of the nation, the prophet draws the con- clusion from his theory that it is not for the sins of their fathers but for their own sins that the people suffer, and that the *innocent remnant* will be saved (XIV, 21-23 and all passages quoted above about the "Ways of JHVH").   On the other hand, however, Ezekiel maintains that *one* righteous individual may save a whole nation by interposing betwixt God and his people, as teacher and exhorter, making the people realize their sinfulness and arousing them to mend their ways, as also by praying for them to God for forgiveness and mercy (IV, 4-6; XXII, 30.31).

It is justified to say that the rejection of the principle of national retribution was ather a step backward, inasmuch as the principle of the absolutely individual account in life cannot be upheld before either reason or experience.   Nevertheless, it was even this one-sidedness of Ezekiel that led up to a marked progress in the question of retribution. This question, while not a new one, having been taken up and vigorously treated by Ezekiel's predecessors and contemporaries, had never before received anything like a tangible solution beyond the suggestions of the formula of Thirteen. What prophets like Jeremiah and Habakuk offered to the troubled soul of the believer in the way of allaying his doubts and perplexities not appeased by the then unappealing attribute of national retribution, was not a real answer, but a declaration of a regained confidence in God the Creator that His ways surely are perfect even though we mortals cannot fully comprehend them (cf. Is. III, 11.12; XXXIX, 15; Zeph. I, 12 f.; III, 5 f.; Hab. ch. I: question, and ch. II, answer; cf. Mal. II, 17; III, 14-18). And then, too, the object of their query was chiefly the nation, the state, even though their language often suggests the individual. And even Jeremiah who takes up the question from the aspect of an individual case (ch. XII), ultimately acquiesces in the thought that somehow individual and national responsibility obtain together, without attempting to solve specifically the more obstinate questions evolving from the idea of individual responsibility. For what the reduction of the apparent incongruities of a difficult individual case to the principle of national retribution (accounting for the suffering of the just by the sins, or the prosperity of the wicked by the merits, of his fathers) really means, is not the explanation, but rather the abandonment of the principle of personal retribution.

It was here that the one-sidedness of Ezekiel was of great help to the further development.

By his complete rejection of the principle of national retribution, putting everything upon the freedom of change in the individual, he called attention to the just claims of the principle of individual responsibility and caused the development to turn toward a harmonization of the two principles in a conception of retribution which tries to determine the function of each one of them as *one of the factors* which shape the lot of the individual. Ezekiel, therefore, may be considered as the exponent of the doctrine of individual responsibility in Judaism. And although he did not yet develop this doctrine into individual retribution in the hereafter, he nevertheless influenced the development in this direction also, not only through the motive power of the individualistic principle as such, but also more directly by his conception of "Ruah" and through the eschatological elements of his vision of resurrection (ch. XXXVII; the concepts of "Sheol" and "Bor" employed by Ezekiel in his prophecies against *Egypt*, chaps. XXXI and XXXII, are not meant to express the views of the prophet, but to give to his prophecies *local color*, addressing himself as he does to the Egyptians in notions and terms of their own theology; cf. above and Tholodoth I, p. 153 f.).

Like the development of the theoretical principles, the *higher forms of cultural life*, too, were lastingly influenced by Ezekiel. If the great antagonist of art, Jeremiah (comparable to Plato among the Greeks), has not carried the day and the prohibition of the plastic arts not only was never completely observed in practice, but, on the contrary, has so much narrowed down through later authoritative (including the halachic) interpretation that in the ultimate only sculptural and relief presentation of the human face in its natural unaltered features were affected by it; if thus the prohibition of images was so much restricted in its applicability that to a certain extent plastic and ornamental arts continued to be cultivated and developed—this must be credited mainly to the influence of Ezekiel. He denounced the unlawful worship of images as zealously as did Jeremiah. Like the latter Ezekiel, too, believed that the unlawful worship of images calls down the wrath of JHVH upon the people in the same measure as the greatest moral crimes (V, 11; ch. VI; VIII, 14-17; XIV, 3-7; XVI, 17; XVIII, 6.12; XX, 7.28-32.39; XXII, 4; XXIII, 7.39; XLIII, 8.9). And even against the secular forms in which the people were gratifying their artistic sense, the prophet directed his reproving word wherever he had reason to believe art to be detrimental to moral life. So particularly when he denounces *wall-painting*, most likely recently introduced into Palestine from Babylonia, because of the *erotic* purpose which it was made to serve (XXIII, 14-16; cf. above). Yet, great as was his abhorrence of unlawful image-worship and unclean art, so was his enthusiasm for the lawful image-worship, and so his love for art clean and pure. The religious forms of expression conceived by Ezekiel are borne by a high artistic decorative ideal. His Mercabah-visions, rooting as they were in the doctrine of angels, condensed in his mind to the postulate that in the temple of the future the *pair of cherubs*, removed by the rigid monotheists from the first temple before its destruction, be replaced by a reproduction of the *whole Mercabah* as he saw it on the river of Chebar. This he saw in the vision in which the idea of the future temple was revealed to him (XLI, 21; cf. above). In this vision plan and construction of the whole edifice as well as all of the interior equipment are in accord with the artistic Mercabah-idea, the cherub-motif being affectionately employed also outside of the Mercabah in the holy of holies (XL, 1-XLIV, 5; XLVI, 19-XLVII, 2; as to the cherub-motif, cf. XLI, 18-20). The temple as conceived by Ezekiel is a *religious art-palace* in which the predominant Mercabah-idea is an indispensable condition (XLIII, 10-12: "the form of the house", (צורת הבית), is the term expressing the Mercabah-idea). Later on we will see how these contending influences of Jeremiah and Ezekiel made themselves felt in the development growing out from the contact of Judaism with Greek culture.

About *music* in the temple there is nothing in Ezekiel, either. Nevertheless it was indubitably the artistic spirit of Ezekiel that furthered the later development of temple-music (cf. XXXIII, 32: a rather far from flattering allusion to the musical efforts of his contemporaries).

Also in the development of Jewish *literature* the influence of Ezekiel falls chiefly in the direction of the artistic shaping of the material at hand. We have seen how Ezekiel employed the motif of attributes, as found in its manifold manifestations in the older literature, and fashioned it into a highly suggestive scheme in which he framed his thoughts. If we look

away from the historic books which have their
natural chronological frame, the mode in which
Ezekiel develops his thoughts, signifies a degree of
perfection in systematic arrangement and aesthetic-
ally pleasing literary presentation which never before
had been achieved in Hebrew literature.   Ezekiel
as a writer has become the protagonist of a new
literary movement which continued throughout the
entire Graeco-Jewish period and lasted in its effect
far into the philosophic literature of the Middle Ages.
In point of literary material Ezekiel, as it was shown
in the preceding and will be given added illumination
in the following, took hold of all the *themes* which
were treated before him; his own contribution consisting in his, above characterized, attempt of solving
the difficulty inherent in the principle of individual
responsibility.   This we will see particularly at the
analysis of the book of *Job*.   If the basic thoughts of
Job come from *Jeremiah*, the arguments for individual
responsibility it advances, go back to Ezekiel.   And
if we think of the *Testament of Job* in Graeco-Jewish
literature, and further think of the arguments for
individual responsibility in talmudic literature which
are taken from the Book of Job and enlarged upon;
and especially if we consider the fact that some
Jewish philosophers of the Middle Ages (notably
Maimuni and Gersonides) found their thoughts on
providence and responsibility preformed in that book,
we can readily appreciate how far-reaching the
influence of Ezekiel really was (alongside that of
Jeremiah).
     In *legislation* the influence of Ezekiel was more
effective than that of any other single prophet known

to us by name. There is hardly any law question which he has not drawn into his sphere of interest, at least as far as the underlying principle is concerned (XVI, 40.41; XVIII, 5-18; XX, 11-31; XXII, 6-12. 25-29; XXIII, 37-47; XXIV, 16-23; XXXIII, 15.25.26; (XXXIX, 12-17.18-20); all chapters and passages treating of the plan and ritual of the sanctuary, especially: XLII, 13.14; XLIII, 18-27; XLVI, 7-31; XLV, 9-28; XLVI, 1-18). Characteristic of Ezekiel's legislative activity is, in the first line, the added attention he pays to ritual commands in general and to the ritual of bloody sacrifices in particular.   Not as if the attitude of Ezekiel, the priest-prophet, would justify to any extent the presumption that there was any real contradiction between the priestly Torah and the prophetic Torah (cf. above), but it is to be admitted that Ezekiel, at times at least, does speak of the ritual laws in such a way as to suggest that in his esteem ritual laws rank as high as ethical laws.   Characteristical of his attitude are especially the following special laws. The *Sabbath* in its social aspect assumes in the view of Ezekiel the significance of a *Sign of the Covenant* (XX, 11-21). We will see in the following that this became afterwards one of the essential views of his school.   And also *circumcision* has assumed in the view of Ezekiel almost the significance of a sign of the covenant (XLIV, 7-9). *Capital punishment* appears more established with Ezekiel, the champion of the idea of mediation in the doctrine of angels (XVI, 40.41; XXXIII, 47), than in Deuteronomy (cf. above), an element of development which we will yet have to consider (cf. below).   Still clearer is the attitude of Ezekiel on the principle involved in the question of the *guilt-offering*. It is with him that we find for the first time the guilt-offering as a legally regulated established institution (XL, 39; XLII, 13; XLIII, 18 f.; XLIV, 6-31; XLV, 18; XLVI, 19 f.). The guilt-offering, until then mentioned by no code, and merely tolerated as a private institution (cf. above), is not only postulated by Ezekiel as a full-fledged legal institution, but is, moreover, elevated to the highest rank in the order of sacrifices. The guilt-offering is the "most holy" sacrifice on which only the priests, the *Zadokites*, are permitted to do service, while the Levites are admitted to service on the other sacrifices only, mostly in the nature of a free-will-offering (XLIV, 13-15.27.29; cf. XLIII, 19-26). Nothing short of the principle of extreme individual responsibility is sufficient as an adequate explanation of the radical change in the view about worth and position of the guilt-offering. It is the outspoken tendency toward the principle of *jus talionis* which presses to the fore in the establishment of the guilt-offering as well as of capital punishment; this being an element of development of which we will hear more later on.

The *universalistic-messianic idea* is continually losing ground in the time of Ezekiel. Already with Jeremiah we find the idea that the messianic time will bring about the national restoration of Israel to the terror and horror of all other nations (XXXIII, 7-9), although he never had given up the hope of the nations, or at least some of them, *joining* Judaism (cf. above). With Ezekiel, however, the universalistic messianic idea is entirely drowned in the idea of national restoration of Israel. To be sure, Ezekiel devotes his service also to other nations. To them, too, he addresses elaborate messages and warnings. The key-note of his messages, however, is the coming of the great sweeping judgment, in one instance only giving room to the possible prevailing of mercy to a nation other than Israel (XXIX, 13: Egypt). True to his prophetic ideal, Ezekiel was desirous to serve the *stranger* dwelling in the midst of his people with the same ardor as his own people (XIV, 7). Moreover, in his charitable treatment of the stranger, Ezekiel as legislator went so far as to proclaim full equality of the stranger who has produced issue in the land, giving the stranger equal opportunity on the occasion of public land-distribution (XLVII, 22.23). However, the conditions were, religiously and politically, so desolate and hopeless that Ezekiel fell back wholly upon the national hope. His prophetic message addresses itself primarily to his own, the *chosen* people (III, 5 f.; XX, 5). The prophet longs for a *new* covenant (XIV, 59-62; XX, 37; XXXIV, 25; XXXVII, 26; XLIV, 7). Israel shall be restored before the eyes of the nations to whom this sanctification and glorification of the name of JHVH shall be a source of amazement and terror (XX, 9-41; XXII, 16; XXVIII, 25.26; XXXIV, 30; XXXVI, 21-27; XXXVII, 28; XXXVIII, 23; XXXIX, 7.21-23.27.28). It is the trend of the times which Ezekiel partly follows and partly promotes. Similar thoughts we find also with other prophets of that period (so most likely Mi. IV, 5:

as a protest against IV, 1-3 and VII, 16.17).   It was
at that time when the idea was advanced that the
hosts of the heavens have been "assigned" to the
nations for worship (Deut. IV, 19; XXIX, 5—later
additions; cf. also Jer. X, 2.16; LI, 19).   One of the
contemporary prophets goes so far as to conceive an
apocalyptic vision diametrically opposed to the great
universalistic-messianic vision of Isaiah and Micah
(Is. II, 2-4; Mi. IV, 1-3): All nations should prepare
war.   "Beat your plowshares into swords and your
pruninghooks into spears;" (Is. says: "And they shall
beat their swords into plowshares and their spears
into pruninghooks")—"Let the nations wake up and
come to the valley of Jehoshaphat ('JHVH will
judge' "—Is. calls the nations to Zion) "for there will
I sit to judge *all the* nations" (Is. says: "And He will
judge *between* the nations.") "round about" (Joel IV,
9-12; the last two chapters of the book of Joel belong
to the early exilic period).   Through Ezekiel, however, these thoughts received added significance by
his comprehensive conception of world and history
which serve them as setting.   If even with his own
chosen Israel JHVH communicates through the
mediation of angels only, it is quite plausible that the
final divine intention may be to have the nations
placed under the dominion of the hosts of heaven (a
view which we find with some Talmudists and even
with some medieval philosophers.)

In his *conception of history* Ezekiel alludes to the
Canaanitic origin of a part of Israel more clearly than
any other prophet (chaps. XVI and XXIII; cf. XX,
5).   But also the hope for the re-uniting of both

kingdoms under the scepter of a Davidide rings
through the prophecies of Ezekiel more forcefully
than through those of any other prophet. The on-
rushing national disaster was calling for a more
comprehensive national orientation which included
also Israel, now a religious dependency of Judah.
In addition, Ezekiel was, in his views, nearer to old
Israel than Jeremiah or any other prophet of the
last generations. And also the *personal contact* with
the leading spirits of the old *IsraelitishGolah* may have
contributed much to the shaping of Ezekiel's religious
views (XIV, 7; XX, 1). To him Israel once again
was, both religiously and politically, a living force,
and a stronger reclamation of the Israelitish element
was bound to bring new succor to his conservative
ideas in religion and culture; a hope which really
came true. Here we touch upon the very source of
that swaying longing of Ezekiel's for the re-union
of Israel and Juda (XI, 15; XX, 40; XXII, 6; XXV,
3; XXVII, 17; XXXIV, 12-24 (David); XXXVI, 10;
XXXVII, 16-28 (David); XXXIX, 23-25; cf. Echa
II, 1-5; Nah. II, 1-3; Zech. VIII, 13; X, 6). And
also these growing national aspirations were bound
to tone down the universalistic-messianic hopes.

3.   JEREMIAH AND EZEKIEL: TWO SCHOOLS

Jeremiah and Ezekiel, the two great opponents in
world-conception, historic view and outlook into the
future, became the two great central figures on which
the following ages oriented themselves. The only
personality of the past who was still measurably com-
peting with these two heroes in the domination over
the minds of the age, was *Isaiah*. Since, however, the

ideas of Isaiah, as far as they touch upon the opposing views concerned, were absorbed by the one or the other of these two leading prophets, the direct influence of Isaiah was limited to linguistic phrases and expressive combinations of conceptions. All prophets and writers referred to here use motifs and elements of both camps, but gradually there develop two distinct *schools* contending with each other in questions of principle. These will henceforth be referred to as the *Schools of Jeremiah and Ezekiel*, respectively.

The literature of this formative period comprises the following literary units, complete writings or parts of such — Jeremiah, chaps. L and LI; Echa; Isaiah XL-LXVI; Job; Is. XIII, 1-XIV, 23; chaps. XXIV-XXVII; Jonah; Ruth; Zech. chap. IX; X; XII and XIII, 1-6; Haggai; Zech. chaps. I-VIII; Malachi (and parts of Ezra and Nehemiah). With the exception of the three latter prophets, all these prophets and writers were working and writing in the exile, detached from the land of their hope. Yet, that land, the state to be created therein, the new Covenant with God which was to become the foundation of that new state, and the principles which were to serve as the basis of that covenant—all of these were living issues which formed the themes of all spiritual work and all literary activity. These contentions and controversies cover the period between the destruction of the Temple and the Esra-covenant (586-444 B.C.— Modern critics shift the date of Esra down about a full century; but this question is of no importance for the object of our investigation). About this time both camps were preparing for the great event, the *new covenant*, so much longed for, but postponed again and again by untoward circumstances. And when the time, so fervently hoped for, was approaching, there were two parties facing each other, each one of them with its Book in hand, claiming that its book should be made the foundation of the new covenant, the *Book of the Covenant*. But before we proceed to the discussion of these two documents which absorbed the whole previous development and determined the course of the future, we propose to select from the series of literary units mentioned above *three* which we consider as most adequately characterizing the progressing movement of that period, and which also illumine the essential points of difference in the center of that great controversy. We mean *Isaiah* XL.-XLVIII, *Job*, and *Jonah*. These three writings by no means cover the whole field of the controversy, yet they discuss the most essential points, and will furnish us a fair conception of that most complex development. The writers of this period were, in spite of their general allegiance to one of the two schools, strong individualities who were going their own ways in certain questions of detail so as to seemingly bring about a change of front in some of the points. This is especially true of the three writers just mentioned. Nevertheless, the analysis of their writings will prepare us for an adequate understanding of the two prospective Books of the Covenant, which, for that matter, also go their own ways, deviating in certain non-essentials from what we would expect as consistent with the general attitude of their respective schools. The rest of the literary units of this period will be referred to on apt occasions (for a more detailed analysis cf. Geschichte der jued.   Philosophie II, 1, chaps. 2, 3 and 4).

a. DEUTERO-ISAIAH:

This great prophet of the exile deepened the thought of monotheistic creation, but this did not prevent him from embodying Ezekielian elements in his sermons to the extent of their compatibility with the principles of his own school.   Thus be expatiates on the idea of holiness as one of the essential divine attributes; an idea which indeed is in no contradiction with the doctrine of monotheistic creation, but rather complementary to it in its ultimate purport.   In his messages devoted to the announcement of the oncoming liberation, this prophet addresses himself not only against Bel-Marduk (XLVI, 1), but even more so against the more systematically Persian Dualism based on the *Two Principles* of *Light* and *Darkness* or *Good* and *Evil*.   And the need of taking a definite stand against the basic principle of the Persian religion was all the more pressing as the prophet addressed Cyrus as the "anointed" of JHVH, whom JHVH had chosen to liberate His people and to restore His Temple.   This distinction of the heathen king was fraught with danger to the spiritual independence of the Jews, and any tendencies to yield to the religious authority of this "anointed" that may have been pressing to the fore, demanded a vigorous challenge from the prophet most responsible for that distinction (note the trend of thought in XLV, 1-7!).   The line of argumentation followed by this prophet is mostly cosmological in character.   More clearly than with

Jeremiah (cf. Jer. V, 20-22; X, 12 (L. 1, 15); XXIII, 24) there appear in the arguments of this prophet, for the first time in the world-literature, the definite contours of the *Cosmological Proof* for the existence of God. A look at the "star-lit heavens above us" (almost in the language of Kant!), and into the eternal immutable order and the infallibility with which each and every one of the heavenly bodies pursues its course, convey to us the certainty of God's reality with a force overwhelming and irresistible (XL, 26). The stricter logical way of this prophet's reasoning receives its expression also in the systematic frame into which he sets the ethico-cosmological world-conception of Judaism. Originally Judaism began with the idea of *ethical* creation: God created Israel as a *nation* (Hos. VIII, 14), from this sprang up the idea of the ethical-providential creation of the invidual (Is. XVII, 7; cf. Theldoth p. 65), to reach its climax in the general cosmological idea of creation when the conditions of the time favored the development of this doctrine. Now our prophet in his systematic presentation reverses this order: God the creator of heaven and earth is also the creator of the soul of man and the creator of the nation in the ethical meaning of the term (XLII, 5-6). By this the prophet endeavors to establish the unity of the creative power in Nature, both in good and evil, and in History; the idea upon which he lays so much stress as against Persian *dualism* (XLV, 6, 7, 12, 18; XLVIII, 13).

In the metaphysical profundity of his spiritual God-conception our prophet goes beyond Isaiah: God is the *first* and the *last*, the other gods are *nothing* (אפס). The terms in which this prophet expresses

the aboslute unity of God are distinguished by sub-
tility of conception and metaphysical pregnancy of
language (cf. XL, 18. 26; XLI, 4; XLII, 5; XLIII,
10; XLIV, 6, 8, 24; XLV, 5, 6, 14, 21, 22; XLVII, 12).
Jeremiah's theory of the selection of Israel being a part
of the original plan of creation, even more deeply conceived by this prophet, is made the basis of all of his
great promises for the future (XL, 12, 21, 26, 28;
XLI, 4, 20; XLII. 5. 9; XLIII, 1-7; XLIV, 2. 24;
XLV, 7, 9, 10, 12, 18; XLVIII, 7, 13). His independence of both, Jeremiah and Ezekiel, this prophet
manifests in his decidedly favorable attitude to the
Thirteen Attributes. With this formula he opens his
prophecies (XL, 1-5), and with it he closes them
(XLVIII, 3 f.). Like Jeremiah this prophet, too,
sets to rest all doubts in the question of providence by
the thought that man must have confidence in God
the creator who certainly will not overreach his
creatures (XL, 12-14, 27-28; XLV, 11-12, 18-24; cf.
LI, 13). In this question, however, it is the book of
Job in which we find the decisive progress in the
development.

b. THE BOOK OF JOB (RUTH AND ESTHER).

The friends of Job defend, each one of them under a
particular point of view, the theory of the Thirteen
Attributes: God is just, He does not afflict wantonly;
on the contrary, He is merciful, often forgiving the
sinner, or long-sufferingly waiting for his remorse and
repentance. By their arguments Job is driven to
utterances the sting of which is directed against the
entire system underlying the theory of the Thirteen

Attributes. This is in the plan of the writer: The formula of Thirteen is to be attacked. It is to be shown that the mere ethical conception of the divine attributes is not able to cope with difficult situations. True, the formula of Thirteen can be supported by different arguments, and it is admitted that those arguments explain very much, yet it is just the most perplexing cases for the explanation of which the old theory proves utterly insufficient.

The solution of the most perplexing rest of the problem is introduced in the divine revelation in the storm, this solution being: the *monotheistic theory of creation* (chaps. XXXVIII-XLI). In this Job aquiesces—Man cannot comprehend the way of God (XLII, 1-6). It is in accordance with this plan that the author of this book never uses the name of JHVH before the revelation on the idea of creation (XXXVIII, 1; the name JHVH in the first two chapters occurs only in later interpolations; also XII, 9-13 is one of the later Wisdom-interpolations, as easily recognized, verse nine being suspicious enough by the very fact of its being the only time where JHVH occurs in the body of the book before the revelation (chaps. III-XXXVII; the divine names preferably used in this book are the singular אלוה, evidently introduced by this writer, and שדי). Thus the progress in the discussion of the problem of justice in this book, over and beyond Jeremiah and Deutero-Isaiah, is signified by the fact that this writer accepts the monotheistic idea of creation as a solution of the most difficult rest of the problem only, otherwise grappling sincerely with the different aspects of the profound problem. especially with that involved in the relationship of individual responsibility and family-responsibility. This writer draws on Ezekiel, but surpasses him in volume and depth of argumentation:

The *three friends* of Job (the speech of Elihu, chaps. XXXII-XXXVII is a later addition, cf. below), all of them, profess the rigid conception of individual responsibility: God punishes the sinner and rewards the righteous. Phenomena seemingly contradicting this principle do not prove much, for as a rule the prosperity of the sinner as well as the suffering of the righteous is of a *passing* character. The *end* of the wicked is as a rule bitter, just as the end of the righteous is happy as a rule. This principle the friends of Job emphasize especially in their *first* turns, but also in the second and third (Eliphaz: IV, 7-12; XV. 28-34; XXII, 5 f. 12 f.; Bildad: VIII, 4, 5, 13, 20, 21; XVIII, 5-15; Zophar XI, 4-14; XX, 5 f.; the *third* speech of Zophar is submerged somewhere in the long speech of Job in chaps. XXVII-XXVIII). Thus this writer availed himself of the great achievement of Ezekiel, of the more rigid conception of the idea of individual responsibility, avoiding, however, that prophet's radicalism which, ignoring the real facts of life, recognizes individual responsibility as the *only* factor determining the fate of man (leaving the fate of a nation to be decided by the conduct of the majority, or by that of the leaders). Our author has the debatants rather admit that the determination of the fate of the individual by his own conduct is but the *general rule* from which there are many exceptions calling for special explanations. Of such explanations the author offers *three* in the main. These distributed upon the three friends, the dialogue is so arranged that each one of them, although in general availing himself of all of the three explanations, emphasizes *one* of them as his *specific* line of argument. This specific view-point of his each one of them formulates chiefly and directly in his *second* speech, after he has treated the general principle of individual responsibility in his first speech in a way preparing an opening wedge into the trend of his specific argument; leaving the *third* speech to additional remarks intended to meet some particular counter-arguments of Job's. Of these three explanations *Eliphaz* is entrusted with the one which tries to keep up the principle of individual responsi-bility as the decisive factor in the fate of man even in such cases which, superficially observed, appear to be outside of the sphere of individual account; thus limiting the necessity to look for other explanations to some very rare cases. In the first line the thought is advanced that no man can ever be free of sin altogether, even the *angels* cannot. If, then, a righteous man suffers, it is evident that that righteous one is righteous in appearance only (hinted at in V, 17, expatiated on in XV, 14-15; cf. Bildad XXV, 2-6). This is the answer to Job's assurance that he felt free from guilt. But when Job, in the course of his answer to the words of Eliphaz and to those of others, repudiated the thought of his possible guilt, Eliphaz goes on less sparingly: The personal feeling is very deceptive; indeed, one moves within the confines of common law, and this makes him think that he was righteous. Especially there is no reason for the outsider to place

much confidence in the assurances of the allegedly
innocent sufferer and to permit himself to be shaken
by them in his belief in individual responsibility. On
the contrary, there is all reason to believe that the
afflicted in question was righteous only speciously while
in reality engaged in exploiting and oppressing the
weak, arranging it so cleverly as to have them believe
he was their benefactor or at least that he was not
depriving them of their rights. And as to his conscience, his fear of God? That "righteous" does not
believe in divine *omniscience* and *providence* (XXII,
5f., 12f.). This much for the explanation of the
suffering of the "righteous," the really righteous man
suffers only very seldom, if at all. As regards the
prosperity of the wicked, it is to be admitted that the
argument of the secretly righteous is not well applicable. There is, however, another explanation not
applicable in the case of the suffering righteous: You
cannot possibly explain the suffering of the righteous
to be only simulated or illusory. The cases of real
suffering of the righteous, suffering of an easily discern-
ible nature, are too frequent as to be denied. But you
may declare the happiness of the wicked to be simulated and illusory. The really wicked knows no
tranquillity of mind nor peace of heart; remorse
tortures him, and he lives in terror and anguish all
his days, notably in sleepless nights and bad dreams
(XV, 20-27; cf. Zophar XX, 20).

Of course, rare as they may be, there are such cases
to which none of the explanations offered in the
preceding would apply, but there are other ways of
meeting difficult cases. Foremost among these is the

return to the principle underlying the *Thirteen Attributes*, the principle of the account of merit and guilt running through the generations, which was given up entirely by Ezekiel but taken up again by the author of the book of Job.   The task to defend this principle is allotted to *Bildad*, who tries to explain by it those cases in which the other explanations would not work (hinted at VIII, 7; expatiated on in the *second* speech: XVIII, 17-21; cf. Eliphaz V, 4-25; Zophar XX, 10; Is. XIV, 21).

For the explanation of still other cases to which the principle of the tribal or family account may not apply, the author falls back upon another principle underlying the Thirteen Attributes: *Repentance* and *Mercy*. This is the specific line of argument which *Zophar* is made to represent: If a righteous man suffers, this may have for its purpose the warning in time of that otherwise righteous man against certain evil inclinations which begin to take hold of him, in order that he might search his ways and purify them, so that his affliction would render him even more worthy of the divine graciousness and mercy than he was before. And also the happiness of the wicked finds an easy explanation in one of the attributes of mercy, in the attribute of *long-suffering*. By way of mercy the wicked is given a chance to repent and to mend his ways. Only when the sinner so graciously spared lets this opportunity pass by without availing himself of the respite for doing penance, the penalty incurred overtakes him inevitably.   And then it overtakes not only him himself, but also his issue, and that not only on account of tribal or family responsibility, but also, and especially, on account of the circumstance that the issue of the unreclaimable sinner usually walk in the ways of their parents and, like them, they are caught in the net of individual responsibility; an argument by which the counter-argument of *heredity* as reducing the responsibility is very perceptibly touched upon (XI, 12-15; XX, 10; cf. Eliphaz V, 18; XXII, 27).

It is this argument, specifically expounded by Zophar, that *Elihu* enlarges upon, adding color to it by the intimation that the suffering of the righteous in itself may be considered a means to make him worthy of more divine grace, just as the prosperity of the wicked in itself may be but the forerunner, nay, the producer of coming disaster: The righteous is often *tried* by suffering, and when he stands the test his later prosperity is all the greater. Likewise the sinner would often be tried by prosperity, and when he fails to stand the test, his downfall will be the more crushing, the higher he has climbed upon the ladder of happiness (XXXVI, 5f.).

The answers of the friends of Job, we have seen in the preceding, are directed against the question of why the righteous suffers and the wicked prospers, raised by Isaiah, Jeremiah, Ezekiel, Habakkuk, and Deutero-Isaiah (cf. also Mal. III, 13-21). And essentially it is the same question in the discussion of which the author of the book engages Job and his friends. But this writer extends his task in that he goes beyond those immediate problems of justice, taking up the comprehensive discussion of the entire problem of God and Providence. The contemporaries of some of the prophets who were less firm in their faith, never doubt-

ed the existence of God, and even God's might was not
subject to any doubt.   Some of them would doubt the
justice of God inasmuch as they doubted the justice
of the principle of national responsibility; others again
doubted God's *knowledge* of what was going on in
Palestine, because they doubted, not His omniscience
in itself, but His interest in Israel and his land, saying:
"JHVH abandons the land, JHVH considers us not"
(Ez. VIII, 12; IX, 9; cf. Is. XXIX, 15; Zeph. I, 12;
Is. XL, 27-28; XLVII, 10; cf. Echa III, 1-17; the
national complaint in the sense of the problem of Job;
to which complaint verses 18-66 are the answer in the
sense of Zophar and Elihu; especially in the verses
25-39; verses 37 and 38 emphasize in this connection
that even *misfortune* comes from God; cf. I, 18-22).
The author of the book of Job, on the other hand, is
bent on refuting the more radical attacks on the
doctrines of Judaism about God and His ways.   The
figure of Job amid the circumstances as conceived by
the author, answers this purpose.   The arguments of
the friends, especially their insistence on the principle
of individual responsibility, evoke in the terribly
suffering hero who feels deeply hurt in his consciousness
of absolute innocence, an irritated state of mind in
which he would permit himself to be carried away and
to give utterance to thoughts otherwise foreign to
that pious man.   And in this, too, the object of the
author is to drive it home to the reader that even the
most pious man, unless he has the conviction of
monotheistic creation, is exposed to the most radical
doubts in difficult situations.   Thus Job in the
waverings of his mind is representative of all possible

attitudes in our problem. He considers in passing even the idea of *Fatum* (III, 8; VII, 1; XIV, 4). *Prophecy* to which Eliphaz refers for the support of the principle of individual responsibility (IV, 13; cf. XXXIII, 1), has but little authority with him (VI, 6: vagary of dreams?) The attributes of mercy of the Formula of Thirteen are hardly perceptible in the workings of reality; at any rate, not in his own case (VI, 10; VII, 21; IX, 13; X, 14; XIII, 15 (דרביו); XIV, 17; XVI, 13). It is rather the attributes of rigid justice which are constantly in evidence. And in this God goes so far as to destroy even the wholly innocent, simply because *He* is the *almighty*, and nobody has the power to prevent him from gratifying His *whims* (IX, 22; XVI, 9-17; XIX, 6, 11, 21, 22; XXI, 22-26; XXIII, 12; ch. XXIV: the world is full of the most cruel injustices). Nor does equalization in the course of generations (as suggested by one of the thirteen attributes) make itself felt in the workings of reality. For aside from the fact that there is no knowledge after death about what the fate of one's offspring was (XIV, 21-22; cf. below), experience rather suggests the rule of the posterity of the righteous suffering and that of the wicked being prosperous (XVII, 5; XXII, 9). He goes so far as to intimate that it is the wicked who have all the evidence on their side; those who rely upon their own power and their own circumspection, not wishing to have anything to do with God, thus repudiating not only the idea of providence, but the idea of God's existence as well (XXI, 13-14). With this the skepticism of Job reaches its climax, and although he immediately gives the assurance that "the counsel (view) of the ungodly is remote from him" (XXI, 16), he is most violently attacked therefor by Eliphaz in his immediately following third speech. Eliphaz does not go so far as to accuse Job of denial of the existence of God, but he professes to suspect him that he does not believe in divine providence so that nothing prevents him from practicing injustice in secret (XX, 12f; cf. above). The situation built up by the author permits the hero to be inconsistent in his views and utterances. And so we often find Job in the mood of seeing things in the same light as his friends, and often even of surpassing the latter in his confidence in the omnipotence, omniscience and extreme justice of God (some of the passages referred to, especially in ch. XXVII, may, of course, have belonged originally to the friends). So the author of the book of Job created the figure of a hero who in his wavering attitudes represents all tendencies current in his time, from the most radical views of the godless to the most intense confidence in God of the really pious and God-fearing souls in the land. The friends are meant by the author to defend the old views, even though with new, or, at least, improved, weapons, while Job is to represent no definite attitude, but rather the different and conflicting tendencies of the age.

It is in accordance with this character of the hero that also the eschatological attempts at solving the problem of justice are put by the author in the mouth of Job. This explanation, known from of old, had been strenuously kept back by all the previous prophets and writers. But at the time when the book of Job was written, a wave of eschatological excitement seems to have been going very high among the people.   The political conditions favored the development of the politico-eschatological apocalypse of messianic redemption (cf. Ez. chaps. XXXVI-XXXIX; Is. chaps. XXIII-XXVII; LIX, 17-LXVI, 24; Zech. XII, 1-XIII, 6; ch. XIV), while the general cosmological tendencies of the age were favoring also the development of individual eschatology.   This could be also of a this worldy nature, (cf. Mal. III, 17-21), but more than for such that age was longing for a hereafter-eschatology.   The author of this book which tries to carry its Judaism rather incognito, naturally could not consider political eschatology, thus he concentrates his interest on individual exchatology.   But he puts this, in the literature of that time, entirely new suggestion for the solution of the problem of justice, not in the mouths of Job's friends, the respresentatives of the old view, but in that of Job himself, the representative of the general tendencies of that age.

The general view of the author on the soul as a substance seems to be identical with that of Ezekiel. "Ruah JHVH" designates an emanation of the divine substance as contradistinctive of the flesh (בשר), the corporeal (cf. X, 4).   This "Ruah" is also the "Ruah" of prophecy as understood by Ezekiel (Eliphaz IV, 16; Zophar XX, 3).   And also the identity of this "Ruah" with wind or storm observed at times in Ezekiel, is perceivable here (comp. IV, 6 with XXXVIII, 1; cf. also XXXVII, 9).   This latter idea seems to be meant as the platform common to all persons in the cast. But when it comes to the particular question of the

individual soul-substance, the author assigns to the
friends, the representatives of the old view, an attitude
of silence; moreover at times where this veil of silence
seems rather lifted for a while, the author puts in the
mouths of the friends now the plaint, now the confession, that man is or turns into "clay," "earth," or
"dust" and "vermin," and perishes forever (Eliphaz
IV, 19-21; Bildad XXV, 6). Job on the other hand is
pictured as wavering between this attitude and a
pesitive eschatological hope. Now he considers the
"Sheol" which in our book connotes the general idea
of the unknown beyond, as the end of all things when
man resolves wholly into clay, earth, dust or vermin;
only in order to speak immediately of the individual
soul as of an independent spirtual substance, giving
utterance to more or less definite eschatological hopes
(VII, 8f, 21; X, 9, 12, 21, 22; XII. 10; this definite contrast between נפש and בשר seems to be a later
interpolation; XIV. 11-22, XVI, 22; XVII, 13-16;
XXI, 26; XXVII, 3: "as long as my נשמה is in me,
and the רוח אלוה in my nostrils;" cf. XXX, 19-23;
Is. LVII, 16: God as creator of the soul from the
"Ruah;" to the idea of immortality cf. also Is. XXV,
8: obscure; XXVI, 14, 19: resurrection, but for Jews
only; the text however seems to have undergone a
revision, the original suggesting rather metaphorically
political resurrection). And while in most of his
utterances Job appears inclined to believe that the
existence of the individual reaches its goal in the
moment of his death, yet his eschatological hope goes
at times so high as to give once room to a thought
which has been through the ages and still is very

important as an element of development in the positive trend of the eschatological hope for immortality: "If there be life after death? All the days of my destiny would I look forward to the coming of my turn. Thou wilt call, and I will respond Thee. Thou wilt long for Thy handiwork." This would reconcile him to his lot, being assured that God is not upon the watch to get man in the net of sin thrown out by His revengeful omnipotence (XIV, 13-16). These words of highest hopes follow upon and are followed upon by such of deepest despair (10-12; 17-22). This is corresponding to the wavering mood of the age to which the figure of Job is to lend expression. In the age not too far remote from this (most likely before the Esra Covenant, that which produced the speech of Elihu), the concept of the spiritual substance of the individual soul expressed by Job solidifies, as also the definite hope that the soul, coming as she does from God, will surely return to Him (XXXII, 8; XXXIII, 4; XXXIV, 14, 15).

Thus Job and his friends have discussed the problem of justice from all sides, attempting to establish the doctrine of divine justice ruling the world on the ground of the ethical attributes of God. Not that the cosmological aspect of the question was never touched upon in the discussion between Job and his friends. On the contrary, the author in his endeavor to give a faithful picture of all the currents characterizing the age in which he lived, often creates occasion for Job and his friends to avail themselves also of cosmological arguments in vogue. The greatness, the wisdom and the omnipotence of God are incomprehensible to man (of passages of this nature there

remain enough even after due deduction of those
"wisdom"-passages which most likely were interpolated in the Greek period; cf. Geschichte d. jued. Phil.
II, 1, p. 148f and 156f.). Still, the author in his very
wise economy reserved for the great climax of his
philosophic drama *two* new features of prime importance:

First: The views on creation expressed by Job and
his friends, especially those expressed by the formei aś
the representative of his time, are based on Ezekiel's
cosmogony and his doctrines of Mercabah and angels
(Eliphaz IV, 16-18; Job. VI, 10; God is called קדיש;
IX, 5-13: Thiamath-myth (cultivated under the new
Babylonian influence; cf. Tholdoth p. 86); XII, 7f:
XXV, 7f; specially v. 8: Mercabah and v. 12: Thiamath-myth; Bildad: XXV, 3; doctrine of angels, the
same Elihu XXXIII, 23). As against these currents
of his age the author of the book of Job proposes to lay
emphasis on the monotheistic theory of creation in the
spirit of Jeremiah. The author of the book, too,
seems to believe in angels, but in his opinion they are
creations of God, not eternal beings as they were conceived of in previous times, and as it was still believed
by the adherents of the Ezekielian school in the age
of the author (XXXVIII, 7; Is. XXIV, 21;
LXIII, 9; Zech. chap. I-VII; XII, 8; (Mal. III, I
evidently refers to Esra); and also the passages on
Satan, in Job. chaps. I-II and Zech. III, 1, 2). This
was an anticipation of the compromise carried out by
authoritative Judaism in a later period.

Second: The author insists that while the arguments advanced by the friends explain much, the effect
of it all is not the one desired for, namely acquiescence

in the justice of God, but rather a wavering attitude exposed to the spurs and whims of the moment. The friends, that is the idea the author evidently wants to convey to us, even though they do allude to cosmological aspects now and then, yet they lay the chief emphasis upon those arguments which developed within the sphere of ethical speculation; while what is absolutely necessary is to balance the weight of the argument to the cosmological aspect. All the arguments advanced by Job and his friends may at best be able to ward off the attacks upon the idea of God and His justice, but anything like a *positive proof* for the reality of God and His justice must be sought for under the cosmological aspect, and only after this had been done there is a possibility to find positive indications of the reality of divine justice also within the sphere of the ethical:

He who orients himself in the whole of God's creation, learning to admire the harmony in the plan of the universe which embraces all things, great and small, and who perceives the divine loving care for all that lives and feels in the entire realm of nature in its growth and becoming; particularly he who recognizes the divine source not only of the omnipotence manifest in living nature, but especially also of the cognitive powers of understanding as awakened in the wonderful organism of man—he will never doubt God's existence, His justice, His love, and His mercy; he will never despair of his own higher nature, nor consider death as the end of all things (XXXVIII, 17). And to this recognition the author helps the reader by the explication of the cosmological proof for the existence of God and His justice. This proof was first introduced by Jeremiah and further developed by Deutero-Isaiah in his appeal to man to look at the eternal immutable order of heavens, but the author of Job heightens the power of the cosmological argument by a grand picture of nature comprehending all the realms of becoming and all the sources of energy, life, and intellect (chap. XXXVIII-XLI: XXXVIII, 4-12: cosmological; vv. 13-15: rigid justice; vv. 16-38: cosmological; XXXVIII, 39-XXXIX, 30: the cosmological and ethical love of God embracing all living nature; the same repeated in chaps. XL and XLI.).

Thus the God-conception and the principle of retribution receive a thorough discussion in the book of Job, and also the question of soul and immortality appears perceptibly furthered in connection with these two principles. Of the other theoretical principles that of *free will* is implicitly contained in the principle of retribution, and appears to be directly attacked only in the idea of Fatum, indirectly of course also through the attacks on the God-idea altogether (An allusion to the idea of determinism we find in Is. XLVIII, 8, but this prophet appeased all doubts with the reassurance that the workings of the Creator are unsearchable; cf. above). Also the principle of *prophecy* appears as the object of a direct attack. Evidently there were those who have taken a hesitating attitude towards the belief that God reveals himself to man. To this attitude expression is given in Job's answer to Eliphaz' first speech in which the latter refers to a prophetical

revelation (VI, 7; cf. above); only to reconsider it soon
and to come back to his own standpoint according
to which there is no denying of the prophetic character
and thus of the reliability of the "words of the Holy
One" (v. 10). In fact, Job concludes his argument
with the prayer, God may deign to privilege him with
a revelation (XXXI, 35). And this petition was
granted him (XXXVIII, 1-XL, 1-6): This prophetic
revelation conveys to Job and to the world at large
the cosmological proof for the existence of God and
his just and merciful providence over his creation.
With the cosmological God-conception, the author
means to say, prophecy has reached its highest
degree. The author denies in no wise the prophetic
dignity of the ethical God-conception as defended
by the friends of Job, but the new, the cosmological,
God-conception is to him *the* prophetic God-conception. This we can easily concede to the author:
The completion of the God-conception from the cosmological aspect as conceived by Jeremiah, signifies
indeed the height of the prophets' achievement in
their effort to establish the theoretical principles of
Judaism. Nevertheless, the book of Job gives us
definite information about the reaction in the notion
of prophecy. Let us recall that the last report of a
revelation in a dream is the prophetic dream of
King Solomon. Now the first prophetic dream
reported of post-Deuteronomic times is the one in
which Eliphaz is reassured of the truth of the principle of individual responsibility (IV, 12-21). And
Elihu, too, scolds Job for his negating attitude
towards the possibility of a divine revelation, be it

for the purpose of composing theoretical doubts, be it for the purpose of bringing about help in distress, insisting that dreams are the most excellent means for divine revelations (XXXIII, 13f). And the way how in these two passages dreams are introduced as a medium of revelation, shows clearly that there was the realization of the novelty of that feature. In fact, it was something new, it was the reawakening and relegitimatizing of an old idea long ago given up in the circles of legitimate prophets; a change brought about through the new contact with the Neo-Babylonians (cf. Joel III, 2, but also Is. XLVII, 9f; LIX, 21; cf. also above as to Deuteronomy and Ezekiel; Is. LXI, 1f. and Zech. X, 2). Thus the book of Job on the one hand signifies progress in the conception of prophecy in its function: Prophecy conveys not only practical postulates and ethical guidance, but over and beyond this it aids man through the revelation of a deeper insight into the coherence of things and events, serving the great purpose of appeasing doubts and solving perplexities besetting the religious mind (cf. Hab. II, 1-8: there the Job-problem of Ch. 1 is answered in a prophetic vision). On the other hand, however, the book of Job is indicative of a reaction in the conception of the medium of revelation. This may account for the sentiment of the prophet who foresees the time coming when one would be ashamed to confess to having had a prophetic vision (Zech. XIII, 2-6; as to הזינו in v. 4, this word seems to have become at that time synonymous with "dream;" cf. Job IV, 13; XX, 8; XXXIII, 14; Joel III, 1; also Zech. I, 8;

IV, 1; the prophetic visions of Zechariah remind one very strikingly of Ezekiel: "The Man," "The speaking Angel," "The Scroll" V, 1f; "The Mercabah" VI, 1f; in general Zechariah appears to have been one of the most decided representatives of the Ezekielan school; cf. also Echa II, 9, 14; IV, 13).   However, at the decisive final revelation the author of the book of Job omits the dream, thus, perhaps, also in this question signifying his allegiance to the principles of Jeremiah.

And also about the higher expressions of cultural life of the age we can derive some valuable information from the book of Job.

The author of the book of Job subdues his Judaism to a stage of incognito, and for this, if for no other reason, we hardly can look to the book for any direct information about specific Jewish religious cultural life. In addition, this book, as the entire series of literary units of this period mentioned above, was written in the exile where the cultural entity of the Jews was very much reduced, as they were necessarily following the advice of Jeremiah to cultivate a certain cultural communion with the Babylonians.   So, for instance, we find in the book of Job a reference to a new musical instrument named 'Ugab (XXI, 12; XXX, 31: עוגב), never mentioned in the literary products of preceding periods.   Evidently this instrument was adopted by the Jews in the exile from their environment.   To this points also the fact that all nominal and verbal forms of this root (עגב) occur in Jeremiah and Ezekiel only, as, indeed, the instrument itself is mentioned (aside from the late Psalm CL, 4) by one more writer only, who is also otherwise specifically known for his Babylonian connaissances (J₂ Gen. IV, 21). This, however, is all that is found in this book of references to art in the technical sense of the word. The author betrays his Judaism, aside from the entire trend of his speculation, based as it is on the previous development of the problem by the prophets, in several allusions to the first Book of the Covenant and Deuteronomy. But in the actions praised by him as good or blamed as evil we find no allusion to idolatry. And this is all the more significiant in sight of the fact that the other prophets and writers of that period complain so much of idolatry, and forbidden image-worship and speak even much of a very intense cultivation of the unlawful plastic arts (Is. XL, 19-20; XLI, 5-7; XLIV, 9-20: a lively picture of a very brisk industry in drawing, crayon and carving-work, verse 13; XLV, 20; XLVI, 1, 6, 7; XLIX, 16: Tatooing; LVII, 5-8; LXV, 3-7, 11; LXVII, 3, 17; Zech. XIII, 2). Of course, we could account for this by the supposition that the book of Job was written at a time when, under the influence of the monotheistic theory of creation, idolatry had entirely disappeared, namely in the time after the Esra-Covenant (cf. below). But, there are various reasons which do not permit to date the book too late, especially the original book of Job which may not have had the final revelation. This original seems to have been written simply as a defense of justice as expressed in the formula of Thirteen. The final redactor of the book (still without the Satan-story, at the beginning and the reward at the end) changed many particulars so as to adopt it to his plan, namely to use what was originally a final defense of justice as partial defense only, leaving room for the new feature introduced by him, namely the revelation in storm of the cosmological proof of the monotheistic theory of creation as the final answer to all vexing queries which the realities of life thrust upon the believer in God and His justice. This process of literary development given due consideration, it becomes clear that the book cannot be dated too late, and that the original book of Job preceded the Esra-Covenant, or at least, was written at a time close to it (this especially if we consider the late dating of Esra in vogue in our days). The absence of all allusion to idolatry in the book of Job is therefore best explained out of the general spirit of the book which clearly suggests that the question of idolatry was entirely outside of the sphere of interest of the author of the book.

This leads us to an appreciation of the book of Job in its significance as a literary product and in its conception of Judaism as a world-religion; the latter aspect comprising the questions of religious laws and universalism.

For force of language in poetry and prophecy, as also for masterful historic prose, the preceding period has been designated as the classic period of Hebrew literature. And this holds true also as to the conceiving of new religious and artistic motifs. Our period, as, indeed, all the later ages up to our own day, in spite of the very brilliant new creations in language, form and thought, draws largely on the inexhaustible funds of that classic period. Yet, regarding the systematic arrangement of details and their elaboration into an ensemble, the development in Hebrew literature is moving in an ascending line. Not considering the historic writings whose systematic arrangement is determined by the chronological sequence, we do find prophecies of a very high artistic polish in pre-Deuteronomic times, but only small units, the sketching of which while requiring great literary mastery of form, by no means requires great powers of conception and composition. In fact Deuteronomy with its systematic arrangement of theoretical principles and the corresponding practical laws derived from those principles (cf. above), signifies a very perceptible progress in this direction. A more advanced phase of development is represented by the book of Ezekiel with its masterly woven motif of attributes. Our period, however, goes in the perfection of the art of literary composition far beyond the stage reached in the book of Ezekiel. The author of the book of Job borrows its motifs of attributes from the book of Ezekiel modifying them in accordance with his purposes. There the divine names of Shadday and Adonay JHVH are the fore-stages, JHVH the reached goal, The same is the case in Job, only that here the temporary name Adonay JHVH is supplanted by the name Eloha (singular of Elohim). In Ezekiel we find visions of angels and Mercabah, and so also in Job, except that in the latter the angels and the Mercabah are but fore-stages, representing the views current in the age of the author, while he himself argues the case of the monotheistic theory of creation after the fashion of Jeremiah. As in Ezekiel so also in Job the inquiry into the justice of the ways of God

is the central problem.   Only that in the book of Job
the problem is entered into more deeply, Ezekiel's
one-sidedness ·in the emphasis laid upon individual
responsibility and the dogmatism regarding the full
solvability of the problem put on a broader basis, a
fact which finds expression also in the extension of the
discussion from the problems of justice to the problems of God and the human soul.   This broadening
and endeepment of the problem called for the display
of greater skill in composition, such as this author
actually had at his command.   This manifests itself
especially in the variegated sequel of the dialogue as
also in the subordination of all particulars to the
main aspect of the book.   The principle followed in
the structure of the dialogue has already been described in the preceding.   And also the subordination
of all details to the main aspect was established in our
analysis above.   Still there are two points to be added
which are characteristic of the book of Job as a literary
product.

First, the original author of the book (including the
revelation in the storm) considered his task done with
the introduction of the cosmological proof.   He did
not feel the need of restoring Job to health and
prosperity.   On the contrary, it is in keeping with the
main issue of his work that the case of his hero should
be explained by no mere ethical consideration, such as
the restoration at the end undoubtedly suggests.
This case should rather stand as an example of a
situation which can be explained, or, rather, as a case
which can be comprehended, only in the light of the
cosmologico-ethical proof.   It was a pure theoretical

drama that the author of the book saw and conceived. And even though we are unable to fix the exact date of the book, everything points to the assumption that this is the oldest dramatic narrative in Hebrew literature. Accordingly, the dramatic narrative in Hebrew literature sprang forth from and grew on pure theoretical soil. Thus the reaction against the historical literary motif which is dominating in all older biblical writings, also in the prophetical including Ezekiel, was of a very radical nature. The book of Job with the short story of the misfortune of the hero as an introduction, was a drama with almost no action. Evidently, however, this was the radical step of one strong individual genius. The general trend of literature in that period tends rather to a blending of the old preference for historical actions and events with the new theoretical interest. This new interest, most likely gradually growing (in literary attempts now lost), was developed by the author of Job to the highest degree it was ever to attain in Hebrew literature. This we see right in the additions to the book of Job, itself. The originally theoretical drama receives a back ground richer in action. The beginnings of the action are traced to their origin in heaven where Satan appears as the real originator of the drama. And as in the beginning so also at the end, later writers felt a lack of adequate action which would bring the whole drama to an harmonious conclusion. These considerations, as much as the desire to give support to the attitude of Elihu that suffering may be a trial preparatory to and productive of greater happiness, seem to be responsible for the "pleasing end," the story of the restoration of Job after the patiently endured trial, when his blessing in prosperity and posterity was much greater than ever before.

This tendency toward the problem drama manifest itself in the fact that of four dramatic narratives of biblical literature in the following period not less than three are problem dramas, viz. Jonah, Ruth and Esther, while the fourth, the Song of Songs, anyhow treats a very important ethical, even though not theological, problem; namely the conflict between the two great world powers, the power of love and the power of the King, or rather: the power of love and the power of all those other passions and ambitions combined which are bound to seduce the heart of the lover to faithlessness. Of these four writings we have selected the book of Jonah for special discussion. As regards the Song of Songs it will be sufficient for our purpose here to point out that even this book, the only one in biblical literature which does not display any thoelogical interest, and which has the sexual motive as its central motif, treats of a deep ethical problem and gives eloquent testimony of how intensely the universal human interest was clutivated in biblical literary spheres. It is known how much endeavor it took Rabbi 'Akiba to retain the Song of Songs in the canon. This makes it appear very likely that other literary products of the literary genre of the Song of Songs were actually kept out of or excluded from the canon causing their traceless perdition.

This touches upon the second point which, as mentioned above, we have to add to the characterization

of the book of Job. This point will develop into
the main aspect for the books of Ruth and Esther
to be discussed here incidentally.

The subordination of all particular features to the
main aspect in the book of Job signifies not only a
literary contrivance of high dignity and perfection,
but beyond this a new aspect of high ethical value.
The book of Job is the only one in biblical literature
and most likely in all Semitic, nay in the world-
literature of antiquity, in which the problem of
justice is treated free from all and any national
aspect. It would be possible to venture an explanation of this circumstance out of pure literary motives.
And we have to admit that to a certain extent it was
with an eye to the literary harmoniousness of his
work that the author avoided to infuse national motives
into the evolving dialogue: The author achieved his
object first by the supple interweaving of all intrinsi-
cally coherent motives, but, secondly, also by careful
exclusion of all motives suggesting themselves through
precedence and habit, but not lending themselves to
be brought into an intimate organic interdependence
with the basic thoughts of the book. And yet, we are
inclined to assume that the decisive motive in this
case was not of a pure literary, but rather of an
ethico-religious, nature. And herewith we come to
discuss the book of Job from the aspects of legislation
and universalism. It is a definite attitude in these
great questions of culture which the author of the book
wishes to emphasize through this rather negative way
of expression. All the previous prophets and writers
believed, and prayed for, that the attributes of mercy
be efficient for Israel, as a nation, to a higher degree

than for other nations.   Only as to individuals there
was no difference between Israelites, proselytes or
even heathen (Ez. XIV, 6, 14, 20).   Now in the book
of Job no cognizance is taken of the existence of different nationalities and for this very reason the principle
of national responsibility is replaced by that of family
responsibility.   Man, plain and simple, is spoken of
in this book: In a discreet literary form, yet fully
consciously and intentionally, the author draws before
us his prophetic ideal of one suffering humanity with
one problem of suffering and one solution thereof:
The acting figures bear names outspokenly non-
Jewish (Elihu not belonging to the original draft of the
book).   As his hero he takes the son of a land against
which there was a much justified grudge in the hearts
of the Jews, the son of a nation (Edom) that, for her
political malignity, was a target of hatred to the Jews
(Ob. ch. I; Mal. I, 3,4; Ps. CXXXVII, 7; Echa IV, 21,
22).   The laws referred to in the book do betray, in
content and language, their Jewish origin, but in
themselves they are of a pure ethical nature.   It
certainly would be wrong to say the author was an
opponent of all ritual piety.   For not only is the
guilt-offering spoken of in the introduction (I, 5: a
guilt-offering out of doubt—an element of development pointing to the future; cf. below to the Priestly
Code), and this in a passage which according to all
evidence must be ascribed to the original author,
but, also in the dialogue itself Elpihaz gives Job the
advice to pay off his vows (XII, 27—again pointing to
the future; cf. below to Jona), which phrase is idiomatic
for paying off a vow to bring a thank-offering.   Never-

theless, it remains a fact that the law largely at the bottom of the concept of merit and guilt in the book of Job is not only international, which holds true also of the sacrifices, but also purely ethical.   And they are ethical to the extent of raising humane postulates even beyond the laws of Deuteronomy, to say nothing of Ezekiel's list of merits and sins (cf. especially Job chaps. XXIX-XXXI; also the list of sins in Deut. XXVII and the Scroll of Curse in Zach. V).

Coming with this ideal postulate in mind to examine the other literature of that period we soon perceive that while the author of the book of Job stands by no means entirely alone in his high ideal, none of the prophets and writers we know of goes as far as he goes; and further that the circumstances prevailing in that age hardly favored that ideal, even in its somewhat reduced shape in which it is found with the other writers.

The author of the book of Ruth for instance, has mapped out for himself the task of fighting that radical particularism which went to the length of excluding from marriage with a Jew even such non-Jewish women as would sincerely join the Jewish religion and the Jewish nation (cf. Mal. II, 11f; Esra chaps. IX and X; Neh. IX, 2; X, 31; XIII, 1, 23-30). The author defends his attitude that such women may well be received into the Jewish fold, by telling the story of Ruth which testifies to the claim in vogue that the great revered dynasty of David descended from a Moabitic woman.   This is the central motif around which the author weaves other motifs in a most skillful manner: the motif of divine justice (the

Job problem) and that of sexual love in connection with
the problem of *Love* and *Law*.   With this he links the
further intention of drawing an idyllic scene of
Palestinian still-life in the time of the Judges.   All
of which he achieves in a short but masterly sketch:

Famine is reigning in the land, a national disaster
by which of course also the individual is hard hit.
Elimelech, accompanied by his wife Naomi and his
two sons, emigrates from Palestine to Moab.   Elimelech dies, evidently in punishment for his indifference
to the national disaster manifested in his leaving the
land and his attempt to escape for himself and his
family the workings of national responsibility.   He
then gets his share by the workings of the principle
of individual retribution, he dies (cf. the alternative
in 2 Sam. XXIV, 13 and 2 Chr. XXI, 12; the death
of Elimelech was a case of individual Debher; cf. in
the following to the Priestly Code: Khareth-individual
Magguepha).   Thereupon the two sons of Elimelech
marry non-Jewish wives.   For the emigration
Elimelech alone was responsible, but for the mixed
marriage with foreign women who failed to embrace
Judaism, the sons themselves were responsible.   They
were so to say outside of the sphere of the workings of
the principle of national retribution, but then also
outside of its protective influence.   Hence the
individual Debher by which they are overtaken, both
die.   Naomi, the innocent, remains alone in her grief
and affliction, like Job (Ruth I, 1-5).   But this hard
tried heroine never falters in her faith in the divine
attributes of mercy.   She resolves to return to
Palestine, and in bidding her daughters-in-law

good-bye she commits them to the mercy of JHVH
(1, 8).   The daughters-in-law refuse to leave her, but
only Ruth is persistent enough to join religion and
nationality of Judaism: "Thy people is my people,
and thy God is my God" (I, 16).   Upon her arrival in
Bethlehem Naomi tells the townspeople of her fate,
her name should now be rather Marah (the bitter,
afflicted) than Naomi (the sweet, happy).   And also
the name of God should in this connection be rather
Shadday, the Almighty, the dispenser of rigid justice,
than JHVH, the Merciful (I, 20, 21; cf. Ezekiel, Job,
and the Priestly Code).   Ruth becomes then a frequent visitor in the fields of Boaz, the very man upon
whom she has certain legal levirate claims (II, 1-20).
Upon the advice of this her benefactor she follows the
maid harvesters (comp. II, 8, 9, 15 with II, 21-23).
Clearly the chasteness of the Moabitic woman is to
be emphasized.   One recalls at once the story which
presents the "daughters of Moab" in quite a different
light (Gen. XIX, 30-38).   That famous story purports
to refute the claim of the peoples of Ammon and Moab
upon divine origin and to brand them rather as the
offspring of incest (cf. Gen. VI, 1-4 and my article
"The Monotheistic Redaction etc. in "Hatoren,"
New York, I, p. 146-47).   And, to give color to his
view that also a Moabitic woman can be chaste, the
author construes a situation similar in all details to that
in the famous story, differing only in the result, in that
in this case the Moabitic woman deports herself most
chastely, although according to her view of the
situation she was the legal wife of Boaz.   And here
the author is not remiss in having the Judean patriarch

give testimony to the Moabitic heroine that he noted her chasteness long ago, suggesting that she may have given up the chance to marry some rich man out of consideration to the requirements of Judean law (III, 1-10).   The dramatic development reaches its climax in the main motif: From the alliance of this Jewish patriarch with this Moabitic woman is to come the Jewish dynasty.   Anything tending to mar this alliance tends to mar the birth of that dynasty. And this alliance is about to be marred, there being a legal obstacle in its way: According to Jewish law an other man comes in as first consideration for the levirate-marriage with Ruth.   Boaz is now the hero in the side-motif of the narrative.   From this struggle he emerges victorious.   Law triumphs over Love (III, 11-18).   Fortunately the first to the title resigns from the levirate with all the rights and duties involved therein.   The tension is relieved, the situation saved, the drama reaches a pleasing solution in all its motifs. In the main issue: The Jewish dynasty is to spring forth from the intermarriage of the Judean patriarch with the Moabitic woman.   This is the victory of universalism.   In the side-issues it is rather particularism that is victorious.   The Moabitic woman joins Jewish religion and nationality.   Within the province of the sexual motif chasteness is the indispensable condition.   In the collision between Love and Law, the latter is victorious.   In the end also love is victorious, but only that chaste love that respects law and submits to its biddings.   It is the love that respects law and justice, the rights of others, that is victorious in the end.   This touches upon the most important side-issue of the narrative, on the question of justice. The righteous is victorious in the end, and also in our book this is the case: Naomi, the innocently suffering heroine in the background, is vindicated, she is happy like Job after the restoration (IV, 1-11, 13-17; comp. גאל in verse 14 with Job XIX, 25, and the "seven sons" in verse 15 with Job XLII, 13).   A later age tried to delve even more deeply into the main historic motif by adding the interesting detail that also Boaz, the grandfather of King David, on his own part, is the offspring of a highly objectionable marriage, namely that of Juda-Thamar (Ruth IV, 12, 18-22 as compared with Gen. chap. XXXVIII).   And also the motif of justice appears intensely deepened by this addition. The workings of God are manifest in history, and what appears to man to be a sin provoking divine vengeance (the case of Judah-Thamar), or the suffering of the just (the case of Namoi—Ruth), is oftentimes but the fulfillment of the great plan of the God of History who in the shaping of the destinies of his chosen people assigned an important part also to the nations.

Similar to the book of Ruth in its motifs is the book of Esther (belonging to the following period), otherwise so different in character.   In the center of the interest is here the particularism of the Jews which, attacked by a representative of the nations, emerges victorious from the struggle.   Next in importance is the motif of justice.   No divine name is used in this book; the just guidance of history through divine providence reveals itself in the course of events.   The Jews are spared and the right upon Jewish particular-

ism is granted, owing to the mixed marriage of King
Ahaswer and a Jewess coming from the first dynasty
of the Kingdom of Israel.   The motif of love in the
book of Esther is in all details a pendant to that of the
book of Ruth.   In the latter a Jewish man and a non-
Jewish woman lay the foundations of the Judean
dynasty of the future, in the former a non-Jewish man
and a Jewish woman of the Israelitish dynasty of the
past help to sustain Jewish particularism.   And also
in other ways this author makes non-Jews work in
favor of Jewish particularism (Hathach, Harbonah).
Common to both is the idea: Jewish particularism is
the natural supposition, but this should not obstruct
the farther reaching outlook into unity of mankind,
moreover, even intermarriage is not to be rejected
entirely, being, as it may, sometimes a part of the
great workings of God destined to bring about the
greatest changes in history.   In the book of Ruth the
aim is that of bringing about the dynasty of David,
hence the recommendation of intermarriage under the
condition of conversion of the non-Jewish woman
(the conversion of a man to the religion of the woman
was not thought of in those days).   In the book of
Esther, on the other hand, the aim is that of bringing
about a royal act of grace through the influence of a
Jewish woman, hence the toleration only of intermarriage, the Jewess retaining her relegion and
nationality.   The books of Ruth and Esther as compared with each other, represent two currents which
have their sources in different conditions of the times,
and which address themselves to different classes of
people.   The book of Ruth, written at a time when

the hope for full national restoration with the help of a non-Jewish Power was about to be fulfilled, aims at a full national life in Palestine with the universalistic idea of the unity of mankind in the background. In the book of Esther, on the other hand, written at a time when alongside of the national center there was already what may be called a permanent diaspora, an ideal is being pursued very much similar to that of the so-called Assimilationists of our own time: The Jew is not distinguishable from his environment as far as external appearances go, he is not found out if he does not display color himself (Esth. II, 10, 20; III, 4, 5, V, 8; VII, 3). Evidently, the Jews were different from their surroundings neither in language nor in dress (cf. Zeph. I, 9). We move here in a cosmopolitan atmosphere. The names of the leading Jewish figures, Modrechai and Esther, are non-Jewish, nay emphatically pagan, and even reminiscent of a pagan religious motif: Marduk and Ishtar, the very motif with which Judaism in its struggle for life had to cope so much from its very beginnings to the time of Jeremiah. The Jews put in an effort to be good and loyal citizens, at times manifesting also personal loyalty to the king without calling attention to their merit for due recognition (II, 21-23), but at the same time they are always ready to accept due recognition and rank-elevation, and to devote the best that is in them to the service of king and country (VI, 1-11; VIII, 15). Mordechai climbs high up, to the position of Vice-Roy of the Perso-Median World-Empire. The only thing insisted upon is religious separatism. In the first half of Haman's accusation lies the program of the

author: "There is a people scattered and dispersed
among the peoples in all the states of the Kingdom,
and whose laws are different from (those of) any other
people" (III, 8).   Only the addition: "and the laws of
the king they obey not" is being disputed.   On the
contrary, it is asserted, the differences concern religion
only.   Against any attack upon this religious liberty,
granted them by king and constitution, they are ready
to defend themselves, if need be, with arms in their
hands.   Not all the fellow-citizens, so the author wants
to have it understood, have a desire to destroy the
Jews, it being rather only a small minority of "Jew-
haters" (IX, 1, 5), led by Haman, the offspring of
the old arch-enemy of Israel, of the tribe of Agag whose
emnity toward Israel goes back to the days of Moses
and Samuel (Amalek-Agag).   By this the author
desires to arrest our attention on the account of sin
going through history.   Saul and Agag faced each
other in emnity in the time of Samuel, and now, after
many centuries, their direct descendants are facing
each other with the same emnity.   And this is the
only historic reminiscence in this book; there being
otherwise no reference to existing or expected national
conditions in Palestine: Jewish religion, cultivation of
reminiscences of the glorious past, and the eternal
struggle with the small minority of Jew-haters, but
no national hopes of their own—this is the program
of the author, the program of the permanent diaspora.

Also other prophets and writers of this period
meditate on the question of the relationship between
the Jews and the nations.   Their aspirations do not
go as high as those of the author of the book of Job

who in questions of justice refuses entirely to take cognizance of any difference between nation and nation, The attitude of those writers is generally that of the books of Ruth and Esther: The Jewish nation and her religion remain in their separation, and also as regards justice the Jews are God's chosen people, being governed by the attributes of mercy to a greater extent than are the other nations. But with some of the prophets of this period there developed a peculiar notion of mercy and selection: The beginnings of this development we find with Ezekiel who assigns to the prophet the task of saving the sinful community (cf. above). With Ezekiel the meaning of it is rather that the prophet would bring on the betterment of the community through his warnings, and also that he would effect a delay of judgment through his prayer appealing to the attribute of long-suffering. Of the idea that the righteous could save the guilty through his own righteousness, there is but a slight hint in Ezekiel, although this thought is found in an older source, in the prayer of Abraham for the doomed cities; where, however, the thought is given the restricting bent that the general disaster may be averted in order that the innocent should not be destroyed together with the guilty, leaving the possibility of the punishment to be meted out to each sinner individually (Gen. XVIII, 23-32; notably verses 23, 31, 32; this entire passage, however, may not be any older than the book of Job). This thought entered a combination with the idea of the suffering of the just as a trial with the purpose of bringing about the sufferer's own purification and his own increased happiness, as set forth, especially by Elihu, in the book of Job.   This produced the idea that an individual is able to save others, even a whole people, through his righteousness, as also, and most especially so, through his suffering.   Another step in this direction led up to the bold idea that one individual nation expiates through her righteousness and her suffering the sins of the entire world community of nations. This is a new explanation of the suffering of the righteous, individual or nation, involving also a new conception of the selection of Israel.   The righteous suffers not only as part of the whole, by virtue of the principle of national retribution, but also for the whole community.   Israël suffers rot only as part of humanity, by virtue of the general principle of retribution, but also *for* humanity.   Notably this thought is developed by that great prophet of the exile to whom the middle chapters of Deutero-Isaiah are ascribed (XLIX-LIX).   The christological idea of the "Servant of JHVH", the "Ebed JHVH," suffering as "vicarious expiator," developed and solidified on the soil of the Job-problem in its combination with the problem "Israel and the nations" (Is. XL, 2; XLII, 1-4, 19-22; XLIV, 21; XLVIII, 20; XLIX, 1-7; LII, 13-LIII, 12; LIV, 17).   This led to a reawakening of the idea of messianic universalism. Israel, the prophet of JHVH, will lead all peoples to JHVH. However, this universalism is marked by an admixture of a national-religious element.   The later prophets of this period take the same attitude toward religious ritual in general, and particularly toward bloody sacrifices, as Jeremiah and Ezekiel in this, and their predecessors in the preceding period. They reject the sacrifices, even when they are intended for JHVH, as long as they are not offered with pure hands (ethical purity) and a pure heart (purity of religious beliefs). But they considered the sacrifices, and this again in agreement with the older prophets, as very important inasmuch as they serve as an activation of one's religious beliefs, and they point to the regular flow of religious national life as to a great divine blessing. These latter prophets, however, go beyond their predecessors, including Jeremiah and Ezekiel, in that they bring the national religious idea, as expressed in the sacrificial and general religious ritual, in close connection with the universalistic idea. The nations, led to JHVH by Israel, will not only confess JHVH (cf. Jeremiah), but they will also have to perform certain rituals. Individuals embracing Judaism are forbidden to enter the sanctuary unless they observe the laws of circumcision, Sabbath and Levitical purity (cf. Ezekiel). Nations who wish to confess JHVH will have to bring Him their sacrifices. Some even demand taht the proselytic nations pilgrim to Jerusalem to celebrate there the Sabbath, the New Moon, and the Succoth Festival (Hab. II, 14; Is. XIV, 1; XXIV, 13-15; XXV, 3f; XLII, 4, 6, 10, 11; XLIII, 23; XLIV, 28-XLV, 8; in connection with the idea of creation, as often; XLV, 14-25: the same; chap. XLIX: the same; LI, 4-11: the same; LII, 1: circumcision and Levitical purity; LV, 4, 5; LVI, 1-8: the proselytes: Sabbath, circumcision and sacrifices; LVIII, 1-14: against ritual without justice, but even with justice the Sabbath remains an indispensable

condition; LX, 1-7: universalism, with the understanding, however, that the nations will sacrifice in
Jerusalem; LXI, 5-9: universalism, and: no sacrifice
at the expense of justice; LXII, 2; LXV, 11: accusation of neglect of the Temple; LXVI, 1-4: against
sacrifices where injustice prevails, in connection with
the idea of creation; LXVI, 12-24: against violation of
the dietary laws; universalism, but the nations are
expected to observe Sabbath and New Moon; Zech.
VI, 15; VIII, 20f: conversion to Judaism in multitudes;
XIV, 9: universalism; verses 16-21: universalism, but
the nations are expected to celebrate the Succoth;
Mal. 1, 6-14: the Jews are admonished to see to it that
the sacrifices they bring, be without blemish, as indeed
all the nations everywhere bring only such to the name
of JHVH; II, 12-15: no sacrifice at the expense of
justice; cf. Zech. VIII, 9-17; III, 1-12: justice is the
demand, but also a purified sort of sacrifice and other
ritual exercises as a reward for which, so the promise
goes, God will accept the sacrifice graciously, and all
the nations of the earth will recognize Israel and his
God; as to the strengthening of the ritual postulates in
this period cf. also Hag. II, 11-14: a *halachic* interpretation of one of the laws of Levitical purity).

National seclusion on the one hand and a universal
outlook on the other—this is the characteristical mark
of the latter half of this period. National seclusion
was the resultant of political conditions. Amid the
then prevailing conditions there was no hope for
monotheistic conquests among the nations. The
universalistic outlook again was consequent to the
cosmological interest which at that time was intense

in both schools as interpreted by Jeremiah and Ezekiel respectively. The school of Ezekiel was interested in the primitive history on account of the doctrine of angels with which it is so deeply interwoven. The school of Jeremiah on its part was interested in the history of the beginnings on account of their idea that the entire development of creation and history was directed toward the selection of Israel. This may account for the relatively numerous allusions to primitive history found in the few prophecies concerned (Ob. I, 10, 18; Is. XLI, 8, 9; XLIII, 1, 2, 7; XLIV, 1-5, 21; XLV, 3, 4; XLVI, 9f.; XLIX, 6: note the frequent use in these chapters of the names: Jacob-Yisroel; LI, 1, 2, 9, 10: elements of Babylonian cosmogony; LII, 4 (cf. Gen. XLVII, 4; Deut. XXVI, 5); LIV, 9; LXIII, 7f., especially verse 16: Abraham and Yisroel (as Deities?) renounced; Zech. X, 11; Mal. 1, 2; II, 8, 10). This interest in the primitive history and the common origin of humanity (cf. Mal. II, 10) induced prophets and writers to conceive the relationship between Israel and the nations in a rather universalistic vein.

All of these questions, in addition to the questions of creation and sacrificial cult which are not treated of in the books of Ruth and Esther, are discussed in the small, yet brilliantly written book of Jonah.

c. THE BOOK OF JONAH:

This pearl of biblical narratives is on the whole an apology in the defense of the attributes of mercy especially of the much attacked attribute of *long-suffering*. The author is an adherent of the old school to which the Formula of Thirteen was the essential definition of God, although he evidently confesses the monotheistic theory of creation (cf. below). He builds his narrative in the *evolutionary motif.* He himself uses right from the start the divine name of JHVH, but in relation to non-Jews the name of God is Elohim (I, 6, III, 3, 8-10), except for the passage describing the catastrophe when the people of the ship pray to the God of Jonah, to JHVH. Jonah is meant to be a representative of that group which opposes the attribute of long-suffering as well as the whole principle of non-individual retribution, and also the idea of universalism. According to their view it takes the whole apparatus of sanctuary and sacrifice in Jerusalem to bring down divine mercy. The author of this book fights this view even more decidedly than the authors of the books of Job, Ruth and Esther. He achieves his aim by reducing the prophet Jonah, the representative of his group, *ad absurdum*:

The non-Jewish city of Niniveh, declared ripe for judgment already by former prophets (Zeph. III, 13-15; Nah. chaps. II and III), has brought her measure of sin to overflow, and the prophet receives the command to warn her. But he tries to deny himself to the high calling of the prophet which consists in warning, instructing and bringing about betterment (cf. Ezekiel), persuaded, as he evidently is, that the only task of the prophet was the announcement of the immediately pending inadvertible judgment. Why not destroy the sinful city, which is non-Jewish at that, instantly? Why this long-suffering? Jonah goes on board a ship bound for

Tharshish to escape God. How absurd! As if
JHVH was only the God of Palestine, and not "the God
of Heaven," "who created the sea and the dry land
as well," as the prophet himself afterwards formulated
his confession of faith (I, 9). That is just it, the
attitude of this prophet in the question of mercy is in
contradiction with his confession of faith. Now the
prophet is soon to be led to a very efficient realization
of God's universality which he almost denied through
his action. God throws a storm over the sea, the
boat is in peril. All pray to their gods, the prophet
alone trying to oversleep his guilty conscience until
the "others," the non-Jews, awakened him to the
grim realities around him. It is just this the author
wants to say: The overemphasis of the principle of
individual retribution leads to fatalistic cruelty:
The prophet was caught in the delusion that each
individual bears his own guilt. Now the non-Jewish
fellow-passengers correct his view. They lay down the
principle representing the view of the author, that in
cases where the lot of the individual is bound up with
that of the whole, it is the communal principle of
retribution which governs, so that all may suffer for
the sins of one of their number. The only thing left
is to find out by lot who is the guilty one. The lot
points to the prophet (I, 7; the author thus admits the
lot as a legitimate mantical means which may at
times be successful even though cast by non-Jews;
but the passage about the lot may be a later interpolation; cf. Tholdoth I. p. 94-106). Jonah now
declares his proud national religious confession of
faith: "A Hebrew am I, and the God of Heaven do I

worship who created the sea and also the dry land!"
(I, 9). He also confesses his guilt, but recognizes
neither the principle of general retribution nor that of
long-suffering, refusing the suggestion to pray for
mercy, and rather insisting that his lot be isolated
from that of the others.   He drives his extreme theory
to the limit of self-destruction advancing the suggestion that he be thrown over board.   This done, the
sea subsides.   Then the non-Jewish inmates of the
ship sacrifice thanks-offerings (I, 10-16; cf. II, 10);
by which the author evidently takes a stand against
the sacrifices as an instrument of mercy, as also
against the view that the thanks-offerings of non-Jews
were not acceptable to God as much as those of Jews.
Instruments of mercy there are indeed, but such are
relinquishment of the evil way, consciousness of guilt
and moral improvement, and these exclusively
(III, 8).   This can be done without a sanctuary and
without being a member of the Jewish race.   Now the
prophet surely deserved it to be treated in accordance
with his own theory, but the narrator's mind is set
upon beating this theory with the undeserved delivery
of the prophet.   God *is* long-suffering, He sends the
drowning prophet a large fish (or: a little ark).
Jonah is saved (from the more than deserved individual flood), and, getting a new chance to abandon his
evil way and to carry out the mission assigned to him,
he experiences on his own body and on his own soul
the great benefit of the attribute of long-suffering
(II, 1-III, 2).   The dull Ninivites, by no means a
chosen people, find, unaided by either sanctuary or
sacrifices according to the Jewish ritual, the right way

how to secure the efficiency of the attributes of mercy (III, 3-10; comp. verses 9 and 10 with Ex. XXXII, 14 and parallels). It is the prophet who remains obdurate: "Did I not know it well," he reproachfully addresses God, "That Thou art a God gracious and merciful, long-suffering, full of kindness and reconsidering the decree of judgment!" The Formula of Thirteen which he thus quotes, evokes his dislike, but, unwilling to relinquish this theory in spite of all the experiences he had gone through, life no more holds any charm for him (IV, 1-4). But God is extremely long-suffering, and He brings it tangibly before the eyes of the prophet how indispensable the attribute of long-suffering is, and that the entire feeling nature is in need of it (IV, 5-11; cf. Job at the end). This latter point deserves our special attention. Already in the description of the repentance carried out by the Ninivites the author emphasizes the principle of universal retribution, first in that he marks the act of repentance as an important affair of state carried out by the king and his leading ministers, and secondly by extending the workings of that principle from the community of man upon the community of all animate beings.

These were the main currents of thought and the main issues which absorbed the interest of prophets and writers in the time immediately preceding the Esra-Covenant. So far we had to deal with the free production of literary personalities, i. e. with such that advanced no claim to official authority. This seems to account for the fact that we found among them no extreme representatives of the opposing

two schools. This changes when we come to those
writings which were launched with the claim to assume
authority as Books of the Covenant, the Priestly
Code and the Book of Holiness. These books, too,
combine, each one of them in its own manner, Jeremian and Ezekielian elements into one system, but
this only in subordinate questions and external
features. Where, however, there is a question of
principles, these two books face each other in un-
mitigated opposition.

d. PRIESTLY CODE.

The Priestly Code raises the monotheistic doctrine
of creation in connection with the idea of Israel's
selection into a well rounded system: Creation,
History, Sanctuary and Law form parallel individual
systems the constituent parts of which cover and
mutually condition each other. The idea of creation
carries everything, it accounts for the course of
history and for the postulates of the law. The first
chapter of the book of Genesis, the account of creation,
is the foundation upon which everything is immovably
established. On the occasion of some particular laws
such as Sabbath and the inalienability of inherited
ground, this stands out even more boldly through
the emphatic contrast with the Book of Holiness where
those laws are based rather on the attribute of holiness
or on the historic argument of the exodus from Egypt,
respectively (Tholdoth I, p. 117-118). The Priestly
Code is a Book of Laws, of the laws of history and of
human conduct. There are no theological discussions
as we have them in Deuteronomy and in the Book of

Holiness. The theory is kept rather in the background, in the book itself there are presented results and postulates only. Divine Justice and Might manifest themselves in the course of history and give the law its binding power, inasmuch as they are the same attributes which express God's creative power. God is the source of wisdom, the wisdom of creation, revealing itself to man in the weak reflection of it with which he himself was endowed. This is most evident in this document's description of the erection of the Tabernacle and of prophecy (Ex. XXXI, 3; XXXV, 31f; XXXVI, 1f; Deut. XXXIV, 9). The spirituality of God is simply taken for granted, it being understood that the essence of God is identical with the spirit of wisdom (רוח חכמה); the same Spirit who called creation into being and organized it; the same who inspires the prophets; the same who evokes and sustains the spirit in the flesh (comp. Gen. I, 2 with the passages quoted above and Gen. I, 27 (verse 26 evidently belonging to B. H.); V, 1 and IX, 6: creation of man in the divine image—cf. below; Num. XVI, 22; XXVII, 16). The attribute of holiness is barely intimated (Lev. X, 3; Num. XVI, 3; XX, 12, 13; XXVIII, 11; Deut. XXXII, 51). In the idea of unity P. C. completely follows Deuteronomv and Jeremiah: angels are never mentioned, for him they do not exist at all (the passages about the Cherubs in the tabernacle were not in the original P. C.; cf. Tholdoth I, p. 89ff). The revelation at Sinai goes on without thunder, lightning and fire, only the *Cabhod* appears "like fire" (Ex. XXIX, 15-18; cf. below and Tholdoth p. 80). The lower mantical forms, especially necromancy, are most rigidly forbidden (Lev. XX, 6; cf. below and to the law of Khareth); which prohibition corresponds to the above mentioned fact that the prophets of this period frequently accuse the people of these illicit practices.   The divine revelations to Moses are carried on by the *Voice* which sounds to him from out of the Tabernacle, or from out of the Holy of Holies over the Ark (Ex. XXV, 22; Lev. I, 1; Num. VII, 89).   The dream as an instrumentality of a divine revelation never occurs, what in the case of the Priestly Code which usually in theoretical controversies takes his attitude by silence rather than by express statements, means that he rejects that means of prophecy.

The spiritual conception of the *human soul* in the Priestly Code as pointed out above, involves the concept of *immortality,* but, like Deuteronomy, also this document observes eloquent silence about the whole question.   The attitude of the Priestly Code in the question of retribution is, as we will see soon, different from that of Deuteronomy, but the eschatological superstitions and practices among the people were the same in both periods, and so the Priestly Code, too, found it advisable to suppress all escahtological hopes, or, at least, not to emphasize them, in the authoritative document, the Book of the Covenant.

Man's *freedom of will* is simply taken for granted (the passages in Ex. VII-XIV telling of the hardening of the heart of Pharo, and thus contradicting to a certain extent the principle of free will, were not a part of the original Priestly Code; cf. Tholdoth I, p. 87-88).

But most expressively the theoretical standpoint of the Priestly Code mirrors itself in its conception of history and in its practical postulates in cult and law.   Not that the Priestly Code avoids everything which he finds with the opponents of his school.   On the contrary, the Priestly Code signifies the highest literary and artistic finish in the employment of the motif of attribute of Ezekielan fashion as a motif of literary composition.   What he could not take from his own master (Jeremiah), he took, with the sovereign liberty of the artist, from the master's great opponent. And not only the book of Ezekiel, but also the entire literary treasure of the past was drawn upon for forms of expression and elements of literary organization.   However, all the free use of elements and motifs conceived and developed in the opposing school notwithstanding, as far as the principles go the Priestly Code remained the most radical representative of the school of Jeremiah.

The Priestly Code carries the entire historical development into the plan of creation.   The primitive history of mankind and its continuation in the history of Israel still belong, in a measure, to the act of creation which but with the erection and dedication of the Tabernacle in the desert has received its last finishing touches.

The following is its conception of the course of history:

God creates the world and rules it by His attribute of rigid justice, the principle on the basis of which all of creation is organized and established.   Everything goes well on the ground of this principle, until the generation of the flood is reached (this is the first sin in the conception of this author, who eliminates the stories of the Paradise, Cain and Abel, and the Tower—which, no doubt, were known to him). In accordance with this conception the Priestly Code in the early chapters uses exclusively the divine name of *Elohim*, the name that stands for rigid justice, and which was then the only one revealed to man. Then came the corruption of man, mankind violated the principle of justice, it indulged in violence (חמס). And the answer of Elohim was the only one to be expected under the reigning attribute—the destruction of all flesh, the flood.   Mercy is not considered at all, one, Noah with his family, is saved, only because he was "perfectly just" (Gen. VI, 9f; comp. Ez. XIV, 14, 20).   Then follows the Covenant with Noah, as the symbol of mercy, and the Rainbow in the Cloud, as the sign of the Covenant, appears in the distant sky (Gen. IX, 9-17; comp. Ez. I, 28 and Is. LIV, 7-10).   Going on with broad outlines of the period intervening between Noah and Abraham the Priestly Code reaches the special tribal history of Israel.

Now, how does the Priestly Code dispose of those stories in the tribal history of Israel which were eliminated by Deuteronomy, the second Book of the Covenant?   The radical way of Deuteronomy was not open to the Priestly Code.   In the first place, because the attempt of Deuteronomy to cut away the entire pre-Egyptian history has not proved successful, and secondly because the doctrine of monotheistic creation adopted by the Priestly Code required one continued narrative of early history from creation to the dedication of the Tabernacle in the wilderness.

Thus the Priestly Code takes a middle track between those of EJ and Deuteronomy: He relates all essential events of the tribal history of Israel, inclusive of the woman-figures, but eliminates all those involving stories which in any way may be suggestive of ideas subversive of his principles.   Notably he avoids very carefully all traces of angels and sexual motifs (except for the Dinah story Gen. XXXIV which is related in a few words, evidently because of the emphasis it lays on circumcision and the prohibition of intermarriage).   God makes a new Covenant with Abraham, instituting circumcision as the sign of the Covenant.   This marks a further step leading up to the final revelation of the attributes of mercy, wherefore Elohim reveals another name of His, Shadday (שרי), an intermediate attribute between "Elohim", which is rigid justice, and "JHVH" which is mercy (Gen. ch. XVII; comp. Ez. I at the end).   The requirement of being "perfectly just" (תמים) as a condition for achieving divine grace, is still valid (Gen. XVII, 1).   It was only after these intermediary stages that the great name of JHVH was revealed to the greatest prophet, to Moses (In this the P C effects a compromise between the older sources E and J.   In E the name Elohim is the only one known to the patriarchs, Moses receiving the name JHVH.   In J Abraham already is acquainted with the name JHVH. P. C. then follows E in delaying the introduction of the name JHVH until the time of Moses, but folows J, that the patriarch Abraham received a new divine name, but this was not the final great name JHVH, but El Shadday, a name evidently introduced first by Ezekiel). From now on the Priestly Code uses exclusively the name JHVH. In conjunction with the revelation of the great name the *Cabhod*, the halo, or the Rainbow in the Cloud, which in the time of Noah appeared on the firmament as a sign of the promise of mercy for a distant future, appears now on Mount Sinai, that the entire Congregation might realize the righness of divine mercy (Ex. XXIV, 15-18). And we have to understand it so that it was the reflex of this Cabhod which, according to this source, was visible on the countenance of Moses. The great prophet to whom the great name, the ideogram of mercy, was first revealed, embodied in his appearance also the sign of mercy, the halo, the Cabhod (Ex. XXXIV, 29-35). So the appearance of the sign of mercy is in close connection with the act of creation of which the rainbow is an integral part. Creation and History are bound up in mutual penetration, and both of them have one course, one goal, the bringing about of the reign of mercy. But the time for revealing the formula of mercy has not come yet, this is to be the crowning phase of creation, which was not yet finished so long as the Tabernacle has not been erected and dedicated. And so the Priestly Code relates of the erection of the Tabernacle in the wilderness. This is a new feature with him, the older sources knowing nothing of such a tabernacle (although there are some intimations of the existence of some modest tent as a place of shelter for the Ark). The Priestly Code takes his picture of the Tabernacle from Ezekiel's vision of the sanctuary of the future, and, carrying out certain changes required by his principles and as suggested by certain old traditions, he transplants it from the future back into the past, and from the holy land to the wilderness. What Ezekiel in his vision saw as the improved model to restore the destroyed Temple of Solomon, the Priestly Code conceives of as the original heavenly model according to which also the Temple of Solomon was patterned. Now follow the prescriptions about the Tabernacle and the holy service (Ex. chap. XXVff). Then, after the dedication of the Tabernacle, and then only, the time has come for the Priestly Code to introduce its new formula of attributes of mercy (Num. VI, 23-VII, 1f):

"JHVH bless thee, and keep thee

JHVH make his countenance shine upon thee and
      be gracious unto Thee

JHVH lift up His countenance upon Thee and
      give thee Peace".

This is the Formula of Attributes in the Priestly Code, to which the explanation is added:

"And they shall put My name upon the children
      of Israel, and I will bless them."

The name of JHVH now stands as the ideogram of the new formula of attributes in the Priestly Code, as it stands for the old formula in the older sources. After the revelation of the new formula of attributes, the Priestly blessing, the Cabhod (the Rainbow in the Cloud) appears over the Tabernacle, visible to the whole community (Lev. IX, 22-24; comp. Ex. XI., 35). The revelation of the formula of mercy brought mercy within the reach of the people.

The suggestion that the Priestly Blessing is the formula of attributes in the Priestly Code as against the old formula of Thirteen of the older sources,

becomes at once clear in its meaning and verified in
its contention, when we look into the reasons which
might have caused the Priestly Code to replace the
old formula by a new one. This leads us to the
following conclusions:

The Priestly Code introduces a new formula of
attributes, because he rejects the old formula
of Thirteen on principle. He is opposed to the
attribute of Long-suffering (wherefore he always
uses קצף: immediate outburst of the storm, instead
of חרון אף which still admits of ארך אפים), to the
responsibility of later generations for the sins
of the fathers (wherefore the word פקד in the P C
never has the meaning of "visiting sin"), and notably
to the attribute "forgiving sin" (wherefore P C
never uses the phrase נשא עון in the sense of "forgiving sin" applying to God as in the Thirteen and
in the older sources in general, but rather, and exclusively, in the sense of "bearing sin", applied to
the sinner.)   The forgiving of sin in the Priestly Code
is taken out from the workings of the free divine
mercy and framed into a legal institution.   Remorse
and repentance are not in themselves a sufficient
means to achieve forgiveness (as maintained in
Deuteronomy), but it takes the prescribed legal
sacrifice. The key-note in the new formula of
attributes is "Peace", "Shalom", a word which already
in older sources often connotes mercy (cf. Jud. VI, 24;
Is. IX, 5).   Scattered elements of the Priestly Blessing may be found in older (as in younger) writings,
but the Priestly Code, in its opposition to the old
formula of attributes more radical than any of the

writers or literary units preceding it, signifies the linguistic formulation of the opposition.

In the Priestly Code the principle of individual responsibility appears most strongly accentuated. The principle of national responsibility is not relinquished altogether, but it is confined to national sins. The permanent institution of sanctuary and sacrificial cult to the sustinance of which all contribute their share, protects the people from the reign of rigid justice, from the Magguepha (plague), in that the constant efficiency of the attributes of mercy are assured by the regularly offered prescribed sacrifices. But in the case of sins committed against God's plan of salvation with Israel, the Magguepha would set in, mercy expressing itself only in the limitation placed upon the sway of the scourge as to time and numbers. Instances of this sort we find in the stories of the Spies, of the Band of Korah, and of Ba'al-Peor, when also some not directly involved have been drawn into the thrown out net of the scourge (comp. Josh. XXII, 17-20). In the case of Korah, Aaron, the Highpriest, stops the Magguepha, using incense as a means of grace; in the case of Ba'al-Peor it is again a hereditary priest, *Pinehas*, who by prompt and resolute action stops the Magguepha. He wielded the power of the attribute "zealous God" (El Kanna" —in older sources attached to the "Angel of JHVH") and he was rewarded with the "Covenant of Peace", the "Berith-Shalom", or the "Covenant of Mercy" (Num. XXV, 11-13; "Shalom" here is the same which we find as the key-note of the Priestly Blessing; cf. Jud. VI, 23, 24; 1 Ki. XIX, 10-14). Also the

inaccessibility of the sanctuary to such as have there
no function to perform, is considered as being of public
concern, so that the violation of the pertaining laws
may cause the Magguepha to rage among the people.
And even of these sins of a public character there is
no account of sin running through the generations,
only the present generation incurring the punishment. The principle of national retribution is thus
reduced to a minimum, and all stress laid upon the
principle of individual responsibility, notably for
sins which are in no direct connection with public
affairs.

In the question of the *guilt-offering* the Priestly
Code takes a compromising attitude. Previously
this institution, as far as it enjoyed, or claimed, official
recognition, included also deliberate sins. The opponents of the institution rejected it altogether.
The Priestly Code then brings about a compromise
between the two extreme positions, recognizing the
guilt-offering for unknowingly committed sins, but
rejecting it as a means of expiation for knowingly
and wilfully committed sins; with one exception,
namely in the case of sin against property where the
damage done can be made good. There is only one
kind of expiation for wilful sins—*Khareth* (כרת),
eradication through the hand of God (Lev. chapts.
IV and V; Num. XV, 22-31). Khareth is really
nothing else than individual Magguepha.

Thus the party represented by the Priestly Code
drew the most radical consequences from the basic
principle of the School of Jeremiah. What we have
recognized in Deuteronomy as a slightly surging

tendency to limit the workings of the law of capital punishment, condensed within the party of the Priestly Code in the postulate to abolish capital punishment altogether. And even in the only instance exempt from this postulate, the crime of murder, the power of the court is greatly limited. The court is to prosecute the accused and bring him to trial. But when found guilty, the court shall by no means execute the murderer, or even deliver him into the hands of the blood-revenger, as Deuteronomy has it. The only decree the court may give out, is to withdraw from the convict the protection of the law from the blood-revenger. It is for this latter to get the murderer and to overpower him at the risk of his own life. In all other cases of capital crimes (and there are quite a number —perhaps 28—of them in the Priestly Code) the court is not called upon to carry out the execution of the sinner. This is the most radical consequence drawn from the principle of rigid monotheism, which rejects the angels and all intermediation between God and the world. God Himself, and He alone, rules the world in justice; and it is not given to the court, to human intermediation, to decide on life and death of a human being in an irreparable way. There is always the possibility of error on the side of man, while on the side of God there is the absolute surety that, no matter what happens, justice will be done in the ultimate (cf. as to all what was said in the preceding and also as to what will be said in the following, about the Priestly Code, in the pertaining chapter in Geschichte der juedischen Philosophie II, 1, text and notes).

This touches already the chief aspect under which the Priestly Code is to be considered as to its influence upon *cult* and *life*, the aspect of *legislation*. It would be altogether amiss to draw inferences from the Priestly Code as to what the actual conditions in religion and culture were like at the time of its completion and redaction. In the first place, the law-code in P C has been compiled in the exile on the ground of older elements, and was calculated to serve as the *Constitution* of the future state in Palestine, And secondly, what we have to deal with here is a radical theory which bravely attempts to impress its spirit upon life by bringing about a radical change rather than to reflect the conditions as they actually were at that time. From the Priestly Code we learn the ideal of the spiritual leaders of one party rather than a reflex of life itself, even though at times some such reflex pierces perceptibly through the carefully polished surface.

The attitude of the Priestly Code to *art* is much more conciliatory than that of Deuteronomy, to say nothing of Jeremiah. It accepts the absolute prohibition of images, but it insists on the employment of the highest decorative art at the erection of the Tabernacle. In this it shows the influence of Ezekiel (of which much remains even if we accept the very plausible suggestion that much of the grandeur in the description of the Tabernacle and the multifarious sacrifices was not in the original P C). It was the trend of the age: Sacrifice and Ritual were then very much in vogue (cf. above), and the Jeremian party could not help make concessions to the ritualistic tendencies of the age. This accounts also for the Khareth-punishment for ritual sins, notably for such committed in connection with the sanctuary. The Priestly Code is the first, and the only, code in the Pentateuch which puts capital punishment (Khareth) on ritual crimes. The first Book of the Covenant and Deuteronomy know nothing of capital punishment for ritual crimes, even not for the desecration of Sabbath (for which the Book of Holiness has exceution by the court; even though otherwise knowing nothing of capital punishment for ritual crimes).

As to capital punishment for incest which we find for the first time in the Priestly Code (the older sources knowing nothing about it while the Book of Holiness has placed upon it capital punishment through the court), it suggests perhaps that the Babylonian environment necessitated stricter measures. This may also account for the rigid stand of the Priestly Code against intermarriage. In a book of Laws, as the Priestly Code essentially is, we cannot expect any messianic-universalistic sermons. Their absence in itself would, therefore, not indicate any opposition on the part of the Priestly Code to such ideas. But the Priestly Code bears altogether the unmistakable stamp of the national-ritualistic tendencies of its age.

In its totality the Priestly Code represents a finished blend of the highest speculative elements of rigid monotheism with elements of extreme national ritualism. It also contains a new speculative element which seems to be out of all connection with the preceding development, but which was destined to achieve great importance in the future. It is the elements of the *Theory of Ideas* which in the Priestly Code appear for the first time covered by responsible authority. This originally Babylonian theory which later was taken up and elaborated upon by Plato in his own way, is not entirely new in biblical literature. Some traces of it we find in the book of Job, and even further back in Jeremiah, and, notably, in Ezekiel's "model of the house" (cf. above). But in its definite expression, as this theorem appears in the Priestly Code, it is a new element in biblical literature at large: Man is created in the *image* of God, and the Tabernacle that the Israelites were to erect in the desert, is shown to Moses on Mount Sinai in a heavenly pattern covering the minutest details. It is evident that the Priestly Code, otherwise disinclined to mystical elements, admitted this theorem for the great power of moral persuasion it wields. But the fact remains that with this theorem an element is introduced into biblical literature which, more than any other, helped Jewish thought on its way toward philosophic development, and which evoked in its midst the great spiritual struggle in the history of religion, resulting in Christianity.

e.   THE BOOK OF HOLINESS.

The *Book of Holiness*, in the main a collection of laws with a *Thochaha*, or Admonition, at the end (Lev. XVII-XXVI; some sections, however, notably the laws about Khareth, belonging to P C), in the shape in which it was offered as Book of the Covenant, is a compilation lacking in literary unity.

In the collection of laws embodied in this book those points are especially elaborated upon in which the adherents of this party differed with their opponents of the Priestly Code.   As Book of the Covenant it must have had a historic introduction.   Indeed, all tends to confirm the assumption that the Book of Holiness contained the early history of the tribes in the fashion of EJ.   In other words, the story of EJ was given as the introduction to the collection of laws which in the main make up what there is of new material found in the Pentateuch and traced to this source.   Furthermore,   it   seems   that   the   tribal history, as taken from EJ, was complemented by that sketch of primitive history which we find in the beginning of the Pentateuch and which is called the second report of creation (Gen. chaps. II-XI, minus the elements belonging to P C).   Thus the Book of Holiness in the shape in which it was presented by its promoters with the claim to be made the Book of the (new) Covenant, stood in all questions of principle, inclusive of the question of angels, on the ground of old, pre-Jeremian Judaism.   At the same time, however, it contained some new elements which are absent in the pre-Jeremian sources.   First of all the modified report of creation which we believe to have opened the original Book of Holiness, is in reality nothing else than a more monotheistic elaboration of that Babylonian cosmogony elements of which we find in Ezekiel (ch. I).   Also in the present shape this second report of creation dwells much on the important functions of the angels in the act of creation, yet it is all but evident that the older sources from which

the second report of creation was drawn, contained
some more cosmogonic elements of such a nature that
even the Ezekielian school found them objectionable.

The Book of Holiness, considered as a whole,
inclusive of the assumed introduction consisting of
the second report of creation, or J₂ (—younger J),
and the tribal history of EJ, presents itself in the
following setting:

The author of the narrative, evidently because
of his belief in angels, from the very start uses the
combined name JHVH-Elohim, but only where he
himself is speaking, using Elohim alone wherever
the creatures speak of God (Gen. III, 1, 3, 5).   Clearly
the creatures do not know of the name JHVH as yet.
The first sin (Gen. III, the sin about the Tree of
Knowledge) winds up without mercy.   And, mark,
it is the angels, the Cherubs with the sword, who bar
the first pair of humans from the Paradise (Gen.
III, 2, 4; comp. Josh. V, 13, 14; 2 Sam. XXIV, 16,
17, as comp. with 1 Chr. XXI, 16; Ez. ch. IX).
Then comes the second sin: *Cain*.   This sinner does
appeal to the (old) formula of attributes of mercy
(IV, 13), nay, God himself suggests to him the possibility of mercy blotting out sin (IV, 7).   In this
chapter the author uses exclusively the name JHVH:
to mark the solemn occasion of the introduction of the
attributes of mercy.   The mortals, however, as yet
do not know the name JHVH.   There is only given a
sign of mercy, on the body of the one who is to receive
it, the, so thoroughly misunderstood, *sign of Cain* (on
his forehead, comp. Ez. IX, 4, 6; Ex. XXVIII, 36).
This sign is a parallel to signs given to Noah, Abraham
and Moses in the other sources (Rainbow, Circumcision,

conversion of staff into serpent and the reconversion of serpent into staff). In E and PC the name of JHVH and the attributes of mercy are revealed to Moses, in J to Abraham, but here, in BH, the name of JHVH is revealed in the time of *Sheth* (Gen. IV, 26). And from now on the author, too, uses exclusively the name JHVH. A higher grade of mercy is reached by the sacrifices offered by Noah after the flood (Gen. VIII, 20-22), and still higher powers of mercy are suggested by Sinai and Tabernacle. The same Cherubs which barred the first humans from the Paradise, are now carrying out the functions of mediators of mercy in the Tabernacle (comp. Ez. VIII, 2, 3; IX, 3f; Zech. III, 1f; IV, 1f: Ps. LXXX, 2f, and Tholdoth I, where it is shown that the passages in Exodus about the Cherubs in the Tabernacle can by no means be attributed to PC, and that they rather belong to the same source as the Cherubs before the Paradise).

The *God-conception* of the Book of Holiness, in spite of the cosmological interest shown in the (second) report of creation, has remained essentially the same as in pre-Deuteronomic times. But there is some new emphasis laid in the Book of Holiness upon the idea of divine *holiness* which we know from Ezekiel (BH in Lev. XI, 44, 45; XVIII, 21; XIX, 1, 8, 12; XX, 3, 7, 8, 26; XXI, 8, 15, 23; XX, 2, 9, 10, 32). It is safe to assume that the strong emphasis laid on the divine attribute of holiness in the Ezekielian school was meant to counteract the anticipated harmful influence of the stories based on motifs of angels and their sexual relations to humans, stories which the Book of Holiness may have contained to a larger extent than now ascertainable.   But the fact remains, the Ezekielian school must be given credit for the clear expression given to this high ethical idea which signifies such a decisive progress in the development of the God-conception.   This emphasis laid on the idea of holiness by the Book of Holiness (whence its name), is polemically directed against the emphasis laid in the Priestly Code on the monotheistic theory of creation.   So, for instance, in the different reasons given by these two sources for Sabbath (BH in Ex. XXXI, 13-15: the attribute of holiness; PC Ex. XXXI, 16-17: creation; comp. Ex. XX, 11; Ez. XX, 12-24).   The same controversy we find with regard to the inalienability of land property in the land of Israel.   As against the Priestly Code which takes the reason from the monotheistic theory of creation: "for Mine is the earth!" (Lev. XXV, 23), the Book of Holiness simply refers to the ethical God-conception: "for I am JHVH, your Elohim!" (ibid 17).   Indeed, this controversy is not confined to the two commandments mentioned, but extends to the reason for all commandments: According to the Priestly Code the binding force of the Torah rests on the idea of monotheistic creation, according to the Book of Holiness it rests on the ethical God-idea.   And yet, this controversy was merely concomitant to the historical conditions under which the issues and side-issues between the two main schools evolved.   In itself the idea of extreme holiness contained nothing which the school of Jeremiah had to antagonize. On the contrary, this school rejected the old popular conception of primitive history just because they deemed it harmful to the realisation of holiness in life; their only concern having been to have the laws of holiness based on the cosmological God-conception, considering it, as they did, as the only basis solid enough to support a life-system of holiness.

In all other theoretical questions, such as *prophecy*, *freedom of will* and *retribution*, the Book of Holiness stands on the ground of the older, pre-Deuteronomic, sources, which is natural, considering the fact, that, following their founder and leader, the Ezekielian school never recognized the Deuteronomic Covenant. But this holds true only as regards the general trend of ideas, in detail there are some qualifications.

First of all there opens a new aspect in the question of *immortality*. As to the *substantiality of the soul*, the second report of creation (which we assume to have been embodied in the introduction of BH) stands on the ground common to all biblical writers. This stand appears especially emphasized here in the specific act of creation of man's soul on which this writer elaborately expatiates (Gen. II, 7). This account, however, goes beyond all other sources in its direct treatment of the question whether there was any possibility for man to acquire eternal life (Paradise story). True, the amount of the pertaining story in its present shape is a negative one; yet there is ample reason to believe that in its origin, or in one of its phases in the course of time, this story had a more pleasing end (in later products, of the Graeco-Jewish period, there is sufficient evidence that the end of the story at one time was the promise of immortality at the "end of all things"—comp. The Life of Adam and Eve, and similar writings). And in connection with the question of eternal life also the problem of *free will* is touched in the Paradise story in a very peculiar way. It has already been mentioned above, that the misgivings ascribed to God in the second account of creation: "Lest man take from the Tree of life and live eternally" (Gen. III, 26), really means divine fear of man's free will and the attempt to prevent him from exacting this great power of his. This is quite in keeping with what we remember of similar tendencies in older pre-Deuteronomic sources on which the Book of Holiness drew for its historical introduction. But here we find quite an elaborate view on the question of free will:

Man was endowed with free will from his very origin. When the command came to him not to eat of the Tree of Knowledge, he had the power to obey or to disobey. Originally, however, Adam was inclined to use his power of freedom in the direction of the divine command (which, of course, means a certain limitation of his freedom). This inclination to obey, this source designates as the inability to distinguish between Good and Evil. And from the whole context the intention of the story in its present shape seems to be that of conveying the following idea: Adam was possessed of free will, but before the awakening of the sexual impulse in him, man was in a state of child-like innocence, always inclined to obey (comp. Is. VII, 16 and Jon. IV, 11, as also 2 Sam. XIX, 36, and further Is. VIII, 4 and Babli-Ber. 40a bottom). By the creation of Eve the possibility of losing this child-like innocence was increased, yet they have remained in this state even after the awakening of the sexual impulse and its gratification.

In this state the humans would have remained eternally, had they not eaten from the Tree of Knowledge and had not acquired the power of distinguishing between Good and Evil, originally an exclusive possession of the divine (and even the angels go wrong if they follow the sexual impulse from which they are not entirely free, according to an old inferior conception of the divine preserved in this source, Gen. VI, 1f). And had the humans remained in this state, they never would have thought of reaching out after the Tree of Life. But now, after their awakening, God had to take His measures to bar man from the possibility of achieving eternal life in the flesh (comp. Gen. VI, 3: nevertheless, in the case of Enoch the possibility of immortality in the flesh seems not to have been entirely out of the question, V, 24). The question of immortality of the soul outside the body is not touched here, although the doctrines and legends of Babylonian and Egyptian eschatology cannot have remained unfamiliar to this writer. Either he imposed upon himself the same restraint as the other biblical writers, or the pertaining elements, if ever there were such in the original account, have been effectively "hidden away", or eliminated. And then, too, the distinction between the corporeal and the spiritual in the entire Ezekielian school was not exactly insisted upon as it was in the Jeremian school (notably not in the conception of things as we find them in the source J_2 in Gen. chaps. II-XI, and as especially evident from Gen. VI, 1f, where the angels are brought into sexual relation with the "daughters of Adam").

The influence of these mythological conceptions is quite perceptible also in the forms of *prophetical revelations* found in the constituent parts of the Book of Holiness. Adam and Eve see with their own eyes of flesh the Cherubs with the sword which bar them from the Paradise. God Himself does not appear in human form in the present conception of the Paradise-Legend. But another passage, one which most likely was embodied in the historical introduction of the Book of Holiness, admits the revelation of God Himself in human forms: The prayer of Moses to be permitted to see the Cabhod of God, is answered with the restriction that the living man (in the flesh) can see only the *back*, but not the *face* of God (Ex. XXXIII, 20-23; comp. Ez. ch. I and parallels.)

As to the *practical consequences* from the theoretical principles it is, as has already been mentioned, safe to assume that the Cherubs in the Tabernacle were a postulate of the Book of Holiness (which may be said also of many an other element of the ornamental pomp and of the wasteful abundance of sacrifices, wrongly ascribed to PC). Thus we may consider the party represented by the Book of Holiness as adherents of Ezekiel also by reason of their more favorable attitude toward the plastic and decorative arts within the limits of lawfulness. And this is quite in accordance with the almost scientific interest that this source takes in the origins of human civilization as to the primitive development of arts and crafts, as also in the general mental evolution of man: The Paradise legend explains the origin of man's recognition of Good and Evil; the names of the founders of cities and of tents and herd-camps, as also those of the inventors of musical instruments and of the first artificers in brass and iron-work, are registered (Gen. IV, 17-22); the origin of the *Giants* is explained (VI, 1-4); Noah is mentioned as the first *vine-planter* (IX, 20f), and Nimrod as the first hunter (X, 8f). But the most noteworthy of all is the attempt to explain the difference of *language*, as found in the legend of the Tower (XI, 1-9).

In the sphere of the principle of responsibility and retribution it had already been mentioned that the Book of Holiness, as representative of the old formula of attributes and of the doctrine of angels, defends the institution of capital punishment and increases the number of capital crimes. In the question of *guilt-offerings* we may, there being no reliable data on the subject, well assume, that the Book of Holiness in its original form stood on the ground prepared by Ezekiel.

f. THE COMPROMISE.

Thus in those days, so decisive for the future shaping of Judaism, in the days immediately preceding the Covenant of Esra, two parties faced each other, each one of them advancing the claim that the book prepared by it for the purpose be recognized as the Book of the Covenant and be made the basis of Judaism in all of its manifestations; in the conception of the past, in the God-conception, as also in all theoretical principles and practical postulates in the legislative, religious and cultural shaping of

life in the State to be restored and rebuilt.   Neither
of the two parties was strong enough to carry out
its own program to the complete exclusion of the
opposing program.   And so it came to what is
usually the course in cases like this, they came to a
mutual understanding, they entered a *compromise*.
And a thorough orientation in Bible and Talmud
(especially in the Mishnah) convinces us almost
beyond any reasonable doubt that the Book of the
Covenant of the Esra-Covenant consisted of the
Priestly Code and the Law-Code in the original Book
of Holiness (Lev. chaps. XVII-XXVI and some
other passages; to this and to all that follows cf.
Tholdoth I, p. 113-125, and Geschichte der jued.
Phil. II, 1, p. 122-138).   To the attentive reader of
this Book of the Covenant, the enlarged Priestly
Code, the evidence, confirmed also from other aspects,
continually grows that the school of Jeremiah under
the leadership of Esra was represented by a group
small in numbers but strong in spirit, while the school
of Ezekiel consisted of the overwhelming numbers,
the large masses of the people, silently but surely and
determinedly following their leaders in the defence
of their old Judaism with theories, stories and forms
of worship so dear to their hearts.   And this determined the character of the compromise: The Jere-
mians were victorious in the principles, while in
practical questions, directly touching upon the daily
life of the people, they had to make concessions to
the Ezekielians.   The new Book of the Covenant
received its report of creation and its conception of
the tribal history from the original Priestly Code.
This took care of the God-conception and of all other

theoretical principles involved. They were established and confirmed in the fashion they received in the Jeremian school. As to the Law-Code of the Book of Holiness and its concluding Admonition which were admitted to the combined Book of the Covenant, it is true that they rest on the basis of the old formula of attributes which the Jeremian school rejected. But the dissention on this score was not so much one of principle as rather one evolving out of the peculiar circumstances accompanying the controversy. For taken for themselves there is no contradiction on principle between the ethical and the cosmological God-conception, as indeed, not only later Judaism, but to a certain extent already Jeremiah himself formulated the ethico-cosmological God-conception (cf. above). Of course, there is the vital difference on the question of national retribution as expressed in the attribute of "visiting the sins of fathers upon the children" which was rejected by the Priestly Code. But in this question the Priestly Code party evidently had to give in to a certain extent. The unacceptable attribute does not occur in the sections admitted into the combined Book of the Covenant, but certain passages which are based on the old formula in general were allowed to remain in the portions embodied. Thus Priestly Code and Book of Holiness in combination present the cosmologico-ethical God-conception: God is the creator and the ethical ideal of man. Nay, He is the latter because He is the former.

In the question of *angels*, as in all other theoretical questions, the original Priestly Code has impressed its seal upon the combined Book of the Covenant.

The accounts of creation and early tribal history of the Book of Holiness were entirely eliminated. And also from the laws of the Holiness-Code evidently all passages were removed which alluded to principles opposed to those of the Priestly Code, at least wherever they were of an irreconcilable nature. What has been retained of the principles of the Ezekiel school, is the emphatic appeal to the idea of divine Holiness which, taken by itself, is not only reconcilable with the basic idea of the Priestly Code, but in the ultimate, even as much insisted upon by the latter as by the original Book of Holiness. Indeed, this controversy, too, was due more to the peculiar circumstances concomitant to the historical development than to a real contradiction in the principles themselves.

And also in those practical questions in which the theoretical principles are immediately involved, the Jeremian party succeeded in prevailing upon their opponents: The absolute prohibition of images has become the recognized law. In the Second Temple there was neither Ark nor Cherubs, nor any other of the relics guarded in the First Temple. As to the employment of decorative arts in the sanctuary there was probably no serious difference between the two schools, as also the Priestly Code insists on a certain amount of display in the decoration of the sanctuary and in the elaboration of its service; an attitude which must have made it impossible to be too rigid in these questions in their application to private life.

Of the concessions to the Ezekiel school indubitably the most important is that made in the question of *capital punishment*. This institution was retained,

but the Jeremian party succeeded in enacting also
their institution of Khareth in certain cases, especially
in those ritual crimes on which the Book of Holiness
places no death penalty at all.   In other cases the
compromise resulted in a combination of both
judicial execution and Khareth: The same case appears in two places, once under the injunction of
judicial execution and once under that of the Khareth
penalty.   On the surface it seems to be a flat contradiction, but Tradition harmonizes them: The judicial
execution should be carried out only where the
evidence of the crime is above all reasonable doubt,
while where there is the slightest shadow of a doubt
the court should leave the case to the workings of
divine providence through Khareth.   And also the
interpretation of Khareth underwent a change, consequent to the compromise effected in its application:
Originally Khareth must have meant more than mere
intimation that the sinner would suffer "death at
the hands of Heaven".   It most likely implied a trial
to find out the guilt and, if he was found guilty, the
"ban" of the accussed.   The word "Khareth" as
used in the original Priestly Code is evidently a
technical term expressing some sort of a proceeding
leading up to acquittal of the accused or to his indict-
ment with some practical consequences which marked
the convict as one who has forfeited his life to heaven
(wherefore PC never uses כרת in the usual meaning
of "making a covenant", using הקם instead).   But
on the occasion of its being welded together with the
institution of judicial execution, the practical features
of the Khareth institution, now applicable to lighter,

or to dubious, cases only, have been considerably extenuated and mitigated, even though never entirely eliminated.

In this harmonizing interpretation we strike the roots of *Oral Tradition*. For not only in questions of principle, as that of capital punishment, but also in many other legal and ritual questions, there were differences between the two Books of the Covenant. And they were important and far-reaching enough, even if they did not touch directly upon the very principles themselves. Contradictory injunctions of that kind were retained at their respective places, or, at times, alongside each other, leaving it to oral interpretation to determine how the contradictory injunctions may be correspondingly applied to differently constituted cases. This was a step forward in the development of the principle of oral tradiction over and beyond the status reached in Deuteronomic times. The law-code of Deuteronomy represents the law of the first Book of the Covenant, enlarged and elaborated upon so as to adapt it to changed conditions. In other words, what has developed in the time intervening between Sinai and Deuteronomy as oral interpretation, has then, by the proclamation of the Deuteronomic law, been converted into written law. This, of course, is the beginnings of the development of the principle of oral tradition. But oral tradition in its proper, technical, sense means *oral interpretation* of the *written* law. And this has its very origin in the circumstances evolving from the compromise between the two codes of laws of the two opposing Books of the Covenant. In certain cases the compromise consisted in just this, both injunctions were retained, with the understanding that the harmonization in their application is left to oral interpretation; a procedure which in the course of its natural evolution led up to the formulation of some *rules of interpretation*, some of which are already indicated in the very text of this product of the compromise, the third and last Book of the Covenant.

And there is another question of some import in which the Jeremian school prevailed. This concerns the attitudes of the two schools toward the second, the Deuteronomic, Book of the Covenant. The Jeremian school surely had valid reasons to prepare a new Book of the Covenant to supersede Deuteronomy. Deuteronomy did not suffice them any more, from many aspects. They had the doctrine of creation to take care of over and beyond the theoretical interest of Deuteronomy, and, in consequence of this, they wanted to have in their document a certain conception of the early history of the tribe which is missing in Deuteronomy. The same may be said of the more developed sacrificial ritual and the decorative art in the sanctuary. And there certainly are many other such ritual laws as to which the Jeremian school felt the need of a formulation better adapted to the new conditions of life. Nevertheless, there was practically no difference on principle between the original Priestly Code and Deuteronomy, except the one concerning the principle of national retribution through the generations still retained by Deuteronomy, but which the Priestly Code retains only in cases of national sins, and only for the adults of the present generation. Considering, however, that any punishment exacted on any generation would, most of the time, necessarily involve later generations in its natural consequences, the difference between the Priestly Code and Deuteronomy in this question is reduced to the very few cases where a punishment carries no natural consequences to the following generations, and to cases of private sins where the Priestly Code rejects the principle of national retribution retained by Deuteronomy.

Quite different from this was the relation between the original Book of Holiness and Deuteronomy. The only point in which these two documents agreed, was just the one in which the original Priestly Code differed with Deuteronomy. As against this only point of agreement there obtained between the two not only the differences which obtained between Deuteronomy and Priestly Code, and which we have found to be different attitudes not irreconcilable in themselves, but also all those differences on principle which divided the Priestly Code from the Book of Holiness. Acordingly, the party of the Priestly Code had no reason to wish the complete abolition of Deuteronomy as part of the national document. They most likely would have changed in Deuteronomy the only point in which they differed, had they not had to submit to a compromise. Not so the party of the Book of Holiness. Had they prevailed, they would have ousted Deuteronomy from its authoritative position altogether. As it was, the Priestly Code having prevailed in all questions of principle, Deuteronomy has retained a certain position of authority alongside the new Book of the Covenant, the Priestly Code as combined with some parts from the Book of Holiness. Deuteronomy was not considered a part of the Book of the Covenant, but it still was considered a part of the "Torah," under the name of "Repetition of Thora" (=Deuteronomy), covered by the idea that Moses before his death addressed the Israelites giving them an outline of the "Torah" as embodied in the new Book of the Covenant which is the real "Torah." The promoters of the Esra Covenant had no difficulty in accrediting this theory to the people. And before their own conscience, too, they could be perfectly satisfied that their Book of the Covenant is exactly what Moses wanted to be the Constitution of the Jewish State. More than this they do not claim. The idea that Moses himself wrote the entire Torah, inclusive of the historical account, is asserted neither in the Torah itself, where Moses is spoken of in the third person, nor elsewhere in the Bible. This idea is a late product evolved out of the struggle against rising Christianity (cf. Tholdoth II, the chapter on "Torah from Heaven").

This, of course, necessitated new endeavors at harmonization, as there were, and still are, certain discrepancies, and even contradictions, also between Deuteronomy and the enlarged Priestly Code. And this again could be achieved only through interpretation, thus enhancing the principle of oral tradition the small beginnings of which we perceived in the new orientation necessitated by the compromise.

Fourth Chapter

THE POST-ESRANIC PERIOD.

THE development of Judaism in the time which is covered hereby the admittedly wage designation "post-Esranic period," evolves its features in very much complicated formations. On the one hand this time still belongs to the biblical period, especially so, when we consider that the task of the final close of the Canon had not been taken up before the days of the schools of *Hillel* and *Shammai* (about 65 C. E.), and was not completely finished until the time of R. Akiba (second quarter of second century). On the other hand, however, right the immediately post-Esranic time (notably if we shift the date of Esra down by a century—cf. above) signifies the coming into visibility of heretofore latent currents which, while having their wellspring in biblical thought, are already well in the thick of interrelation with new historical agencies, and manifest themselves in new forms of expression. And if we consider the individual movements in their characteristic tendencies, we may say that in the time immediately following the period of Esra, our attention is claimed by *three* distinct *lines* of development.

As the *first* we may address that element in the general development of the time which is evidently the continued activation of biblical thought and biblical literary form. As "biblical" goes here that perceptibly isolated current in the literary activities of the time which is mainly oriented on biblical

writings and biblical themes, possibly still fighting
Semitic paganism, or, at any rate, against the Persian
influence of the late biblical period, a struggle full o
victories, but also of concessions. For a certain
length of time this line of development is the only
one visible above the surface, and, apparently
absorbs the entire fund of spiritual and cultura
forces active in the field. For was it not their all
absorbing task to lay the foundations of the new
rejuvenated state on solid biblical ground and to
guard it against legions of politico-religious adversa
ries among whom the blood-related Samaritans were
the most dangerous, just because they claimed racia
and religious unity with the Jewish people?

Soon, however, a new element distinctly differenti-
ates from the general biblical background, New
formations surge through the foldings in the old strata
and new colors blend with the old ones to a new form
of expression which bears witness to a new spring o
thought and energy, not easily definable. In the light
of the later, fully matured, formations of these incipient
elements, we call this new form of thought and energy
the *talmudical line* of development. What is generally
called the *Sopheric period*, really sets in immediately
after the Esra-Covenant, and signifies nothing else but
just the beginnings of Talmudical Judaism. One surely
feels the potent touch of Talmudic Judaism in the late
biblical writings: There lives already the distinc
consciousness of a *written past*, as it were, which is to
be developed in oral tradition and converted into new
realities. This new spirit has its origin, as it has
already been pointed out, in the fusion of the origina

Priestly Code and the original Book of Holiness with a view to harmonizing the discrepencies by oral interpretation according to certain rules.   Here and there we still find attempts at taking an independent attitude, on the whole, however, the prevailing attitude is that of harmonizing eclecticism.   For new great developments there was rather a lack of the necessary factor of friction.   Semitic paganism had been completely overcome, the contact with the Persians had soon spent its movent power.   At this juncture came the *Greek influence.*   This influence, intensely perceptible already in the latest products of canonical biblical literature, imparts also to Sopheric-Talmudical thought a certain coloration characteristical of the entire talmudical period.

But alongside of this the contact with the Greek world evolved a new trend of thought which we may call the *Alexandrian line* of development (beginning at the end of the third century B. C.).   It is Alexandrian even though its beginnings go back to Palestine, because this trend of thought had to recede in Palestine before the strong Sopheric-Talmudic spirit, and it was only in Alexandria that it reached its highest degree of efficiency and developed into a powerful entity all of its own.   The difference between these two lines of development is essentially this: The talmudical line represents the development of biblical Judaism under Greek (Platonic) influence, while the Alexandrian line represents a Greek (Platonic) conception of biblical Judaism as a finished product under the aspect of eternity.   This line of thought found expression in *Graeco-Jewish Literature.*

From the preceding it is clear that the post-Esranic period of biblical thought cannot be presented in an exposition entirely isolated from the other lines of development. Rather will it be necessary at times to extend our presentation on phenomena and features which properly belong into the spheres of the two aforesaid trends of development. In general the chronological limit could be set at the time of the Maccabean Wars, or, which is the same, at the time when the Book of *Daniel* was written (about 168-167 B. C). But now and then it will be necessary to consider even such features which, in their consequences, point far beyond this time.

The literary units representing this period are *Psalms, Proverbs, Chronicles,* inclusive of *Esra and Nehemia, Koheleth* and *Daniel* (Esther and Song of Songs whose final redaction falls in this period, have been considered in connection with the book of Job).

1. THE FINAL REDACTION OF THE TORAH:

The fusion of Priestly Code and Book of Holiness into one Book of the Covenant on the ground of the compromise characterized above, was a renewal of the attempt at complete ousting of the narrating sources E and J, and of the first Book of the Covenant, undertaken long ago by Deuteronomy. And, on the whole, this attempt was much more successful now than it was the first time. The "Torah," consisting of the enlarged Priestly Code and Deuteronomy, was for quite a while after the Esra Covenant the authoritative document of Judaism. The rigorous *weltanschaung* of the Priestly Code prevailed among the people.

The prevailing doctrine of attributes was that advanced by the Priestly Code, a doctrine which knows nothing of forgiving of deliberate sins or of long-suffering, and which even for unwilful sins knows of forgiving only by means of the prescribed sacrifice of expiation. This produced that fear of sin and rigorosity of conscience which at all times have been the distinguishing marks of genuine Judaism. But as a matter of fact, the old literature was not ousted. For not only the masses of the people, but also some of the prominent leaders, poets and writers were cleaving to the old narratives and to the ideas they expressed with tenacious love and enthusiastic conviction. And also the general conditions of that age were rather favorable to the conservative bent of mind. The movement which sets in soon after the Esra Covenant, and which is already essentially Sopheric, to wit, the movement for the *popularization* of Judaism's Doctrine and Law, necessitated certain concessions to the popular mind. We know that the endeavor at popularisation brought about the change from the ancient Hebrew script (retained by the Samaritans) to the easier and more modern square script in use since. But more than for such external measures, the situation called for concessions to *popular beliefs* and popular conceptions of things. In addition to this there was the *Persian* influence. One of the most prominent doctrines of Parsism was that of the important position of angels in the relation between heaven and earth. This enhanced the adherents of the doctrine of angels in Judaism. And also the opponents of that doctrine, the authoritative

circles, could well afford to be less rigid in their
negative attitude, now that the theory of monotheistic
creation took firm roots even in the hearts of many,
if not of all, adherents of the doctrine of angels.
Against angels as *creatures* of God even the most
rigid opponents could afford to show less implacable
opposition (in olden times the angels were considered
eternal like God Himself).   And then, too, at that
time they have already begun authoritative collection
and preservation of the literary monuments of the past.
And among the old writers and prophets there were
such as stood on the ground of the doctrine of angels
and of the old conception of national history.   All of
which evidently so strengthened the position of the
conservatives that their demand for a new redaction
of the national religious document, the "Torah,"so as
to have their views represented therein, to a certain
extent at least, could not well be ignored, or even
successfully repressed, any longer.   And so, according
to all the evidence at hand, about a century after the
Esra Covenant, the new, and essentially the final,
redaction of the Torah took place.   The enlarged
Priestly Code was combined with the narrative of
E J—inclusive of the first book of the Covenant,
into one presentation, to which was added the Book
of Deuteronomy as the "Repetition of the Torah"
(משנה תורה), a position which this document held
since the days of the Esra Covenant (the addition of
the second report of creation, Gen. II-XI, as of many
another mythological element, most likely took place
at a much later date).

   This event most likely took place at a time of
gathering and restoration after a longer period of

political upheaval and general interruption of regulated communal and political life under any form of established authority. As they gathered the remnants of former organizations and started the work of reconstruction and reorganization, the time was extremely favorable for the carrying out of the change in the complexion of the national document and for replacing the old "Torah" by the new document without the people at large noticing much of what has taken place. In fact, the old "Torah" was little known among the people, only the final product, with the popular elements in it, having appealed to the heart of the people and gradually become popular as the national document. And even with respect to those initiated, there was no serious difficulty about the change. As has been mentioned already, at that time there existed no such notion of a Torah written down literally by Moses himself, with historical narratives, law-codes, and all (to say nothing of the notion of a "Torah" as a sort of heavenly entity): Moses is spoken of in the third person, thus avowing implicitly and explicitly that the Torah is not the product of Moses in a literary sense.

The idea of angels being created by God is not expressly stated in the Torah, it is, however, implicitly suggested. And as so many another question, this, too, was left to oral interpretation. And in general, with the final redaction of the Torah on the ground of the *new compromise*, the sphere of influence of the institution of oral interpretation was greatly and essentially enlarged. The oral interpretations which have become necessary after the first compromise under Esra, for the harmonization of the contradictions in theory and law between Priestly Code and Book of Holiness, as also those between these two and Deuteronomy, have proved insufficient to meet the new situation. For to the old contradictions new ones have been added, and the new were deeper going and farther-reaching than the old: the contradictions between E J (and later also J₂) and the first Book of the Covenant on the one, and between the enlarged Priestly Code and Deuteronomy on the other side. There was a need for new, more precisely defined, rules of interpretation (cf. Tholdoth I, p. 126f.).

The eclectic character of that time, thus represented by the Torah in its present form, even our Pentateuch, mirrors itself also in the biblical writings of that period.

Except for Chronicles which as a book of history presents the workings of justice in history rather indirectly, it may be said that what we have found with regard to the literary units of the preceding period (such as Ezekiel, Job, Ruth, Jona), holds true also of the literary units of this period: Their chief topic is the problem of the "Ways of God," the problem of justice. There is, however, a new feature which gives this period an entirely new hue in the development of thought and in the fashion in which it is being expressed: I mean the Greek influence. The manifestation of this influence is *twofold*. It is *positive*, inasmuch as some writers of this period try to blend Platonic and biblical elements into one harmonious mold. But it is also *negative*, inasmuch as they had to fight certain general Greek, and among them also some specific Platonic, elements which were favored and embodied into Jewish life and letters by the so-called *Hellenists*.

The *positive* Platonic influence which chiefly claims our interest here, may be analyzed into *three features*:

First, the problem of justice, in the center of thought crystalization in biblical speculation of all times, was the strongest congenial feature which the biblical spirit found in the philosophy of Plato (the question whether or not Plato knew anything of the Bible, or was under its influence, directly or indirectly, shall not be considered here). Plato's intense ethical God-consciousness carried so much of a Jewish appeal to the late biblical writers that they were readily induced to weave some leading thoughts of Plato's philosophy into the Jewish system of thought and life. For was not the chief problem of Plato's philosophy the same which from the very beginning has always occupied the center in the biblical world of thought? *What* is justice? and: *Which life* is the *happier*, that of the just, or that of the unjust?—these are the two questions around which swing all the discussions in the writings of Plato (cf. the outline of Plato's philosophy in my Geschichte der juedischen Philosophie II, 1 ch. 3). As a consequence of this influence we find that also in the biblical writings of this period the question of "the defense of justice," as the explanation of facts and phenomena of life subversive of justice is called by Plato, appears in the technical Platonic formulation: Who is happy, of whom may we predicate אשרי? (cf. ibd. p. 305). In connection with this we also notice the emphasis laid on the Platonic *cardinal virtues* of Wisdom, Fortitude, Temperance and (as root and amount of all) Justice, as the core of the ethical God-conception; this, however in harmonious penetration with the Thirteen Attributes of mercy, quite unknown to Plato.

Second, the old biblical thought of "walking in the ways of God" (imitatio dei—the talmudic הדבק במדותיו) entered a fusion with the same element in the philosophv of Plato, the postulate of *resembling God* (homoiosis theo): Individual and state shall be governed *theocratically*. Except for a few isolated passages, it is true of the Bible as well as of Plato that the form of government of the state is a matter of indifference, so long as the state is being ruled theocratically, which means under dominion of the cardinal virtues for Plato and under the dominion of these virtues but combined with the Thirteen for the biblical writers. In fact, it may be said that the biblical writers in their overwhelming majority prefer the theocractically ruling monarch to all other forms of government, as witnessed by the commanding figures of the *ideal rulers* created by *Isaiah* and other prophets, notably in the emphasis laid on the personal element in the ideal figures of *David* and the *Messiah* (cf. ibid. p. 203-208). Corresponding to this is the appearance, in some biblical writings of this period, of the *ideal King* in Platonic fashion and of the, likewise Platonic, thought that the individual is a miniature state which, accordingly, shall be governed under theocratic principles. In this wise biblical ethics assumes a definite trend into the sphere of *political Sophia*, especially in the Proverbs.

Third, the preponderance of the cosmological aspect in the God-conception of the Jeremian school which in principle had conquered the field, as also, and especially, the *theory of ideas* which, in the doctrine of man's creation in the image of God and of the erection of the Tabernacle after an ideal heavenly pattern, had been embodied in the new Book of the Covenant and thus enjoying a certain measure of authoritative recognition, prepared the soil for the metaphysical influence of Plato, quite perceptible in the biblical writings of this period.

Analyzed under the aspects thus circumscribed, the biblical writings of this period unroll before our eyes the following picture of the spiritual and cultural movements of that age:

2. PSALMS AND PROVERBS:

Psalms and Proverbs, different as they are in literary form, have from our point of view much in common which suggest their joint consideration. In the first place, the measure in which they furnish us information on the spiritual and cultural currents in the post-Esra period: Both of these books are compilations of small literary products hailing from widely different times, writers and literary schools. The Psalms for the most part are evidently the product of this period, even though it must be admitted that some of them may be very old, and that others are indubitably of a time preceding the Esra Covenant. This holds true also of the proverbs in the book of Proverbs. But more important than this rather external relation of these two biblical books is their intrinsic spiritual communion of interest. Psalms and Proverbs deal with the same problems and stand, with regard to all positive results, on common ground.

Deducting less than thirty special Psalms[1], it may be said that all the rest of the one hundred and fifty Psalms which make up our collection, have for their sole topic the *problem of justice*: Every one of these more than one hundred and twenty psalms is a "defense of justice" in the technical Platonic meaning of the word, even though some of them may have originated in pre-Platonic times. Again and again it is the defense of the doctrine of the happiness of the just, in spite of all hard facts of real life seemingly pointing to the contrary, what the Psalmists in the pious outpourings of their deeply stirred souls are primarily concerned with. This doctrine appears now in the form of steadfast faith, now in the form of a more or less developed argument, then again in the form of a trembling question addressed to God Himself: how long will reality continue to discord so crudely from the divine moral order, and again in the form of a fervent prayer that divine justice may soon shine forth in all its glory. But in all of these forms of manifestation, be their object historic justice in the life of the nation, or be it every day justice in the life of the individual—in all of them one longing struggles for expression, the longing for the justification of the idea that justice prevails in the world. And the same is to be said of *Proverbs*. The Proverbs present themselves to the reader as a collection of practical rules of life. And such they really are. But in their totality they lend expression to the same doctrine

[1] These are: XV, XVI, XIX, XXIV, XXIX, XXXIII, XLV, LI, LXVII, LXXII, LXXXVIII, XCIII, XCV, C, CIV, CXIII, CXIV, CXVII, CXIX in part, CXXII, CXXXI, CXXXIII, CXXXIV, CXLVII, CXLVIII, CL.

of the happiness of the just as the Psalms. Very
often one proverb, in the center of a string of proverbs
crystallizing around it, would express the basic
thought which is to be brought out, through the proper
arrangement of the individual, originally independent,
proverbs into some sort of a coherent unit. And in
such cases it is almost invariably the above doctrine
which is thus pressed to the fore (cf. II, 7-22, continued
in III, mark v. 12; IV, 18, 19; V, 21; VI, 15; VIII, 35;
ch. X; XI, 31; and all the passages quoted in the
following solutions to the individual problems treated
in Psalms and Proverbs).

In both, Psalms and Proverbs, the whole *God-
conception* is placed under the aspect of the question
of justice. Alongside of such Psalms and proverbs
which deal with the God-problem exclusively under
the ethical aspect, there are also such as treat this
problem under the combined ethico-cosmological
aspect, be it under the influence of Plato (notably
where the doctrine of *Wisdom* and *Logos* is involved,
as in Prov. III, 19, 20; VIII, 21-31; XXX, 1-5; comp.
Job. X, 4f; XI, 2-6, 10-20; XXVIII, 12-19, 20-28—all
being passages which evidently are later interpolations
inserted in our period), be it as a result of the internal
evolution of thought in the Jeremian school (which
applies especially to the Psalms). In the Psalms, the
unjust (רשע) under which term often (notably where
"traitor"---בוגד, זד—is used as synonym) the Epicurean, the Hellenist, may be meant, is often attacked
as the *denier of God*; as one who advances the prosperity
of the wicked as an argument for his attitude, denying
the existence of God altogether, or, at any rate, His

interest in the doings of the world of men (cf. Ps.
X, 4-6, 11-13; XIV, 1, 2; XLII, 4, 11; LIII, 2; LIV, 5
(זדים? comp. LXXXVI, 14); LVIII, 12; LXXIII,
11f.; LXXIV, 22; LXXVIII, 8; XCIV, 7; CXV, 2; the
two postulates discussed in these passages, the
existence of God and His providence for the world,
taken jointly with the postulate of desisting from the
attempt to bribe God by sacrifices and the like, often
met with in the Psalms, have their parallel in Plato's
three theological postulates).   As against these heresies,
the Psalmists lay emphatic stress on the postulates
denied by the unjust, the postulates of God's existence,
His omniscience, omnipresence and eternity; attributes which make up the essence of providence, the
attribute of eternity covering specifically cases of
historical providence.   Some of the Psalmists would
add to their steadfast assurances of faith in the rule
of divine justice, more or less developed arguments
alongside the line of the *cosmological proof* for the
existence of God (cf. VII, 9, 10; VIII; XI, 4, 5; XIV,
2; XXIII; XXXVII, 23; XL, 5f; three postulates;
LXV, 7; LXXIV, 11-18; LXXV, 3-8; LXXVII, 14f;
LXXVIII, 19f.; LXXXIX; XC, 4; eternity = CII,
13, 26-29; XCII; XCIV, 8-11; XCV, 4; CIII, 19f.;
CIV; CXV, 3f.; CXXXV, 6f.; CXXXVI; CXXXIX
(omnipresence); CXLVII; CXLVIII).   In *Proverbs*
where the "fool" (סכל) stands for the unjust and
wicked (זר, רשע), the God-denying attitude of the
opponent attacked does not appear as sharply defined
as in the Psalms, still once it is expressly formulated
(XXX, 19), and it is even more so indicated in such
passages where the opponent is fought, in the same

manner as in Psalms, by the strong emphasis laid upon
the providential attributes of God (Prov. V, 21; XV, 3,
11; XVI, 2, 3, 9, 11, 33; XVII, 3; XIX, 21; XX, 12:
cosmological proof = 24 and 27; XXI, 1, 2, 30, 31).

Another point in the formulation of the God-conception common to both, Psalms and Proverbs, is the
fusion of elements of the old and the new formulas of
attributes, corresponding to the fusion of ethical and
cosmological elements in the God-conception: All
Psalms, inclusive of the few embodied in early biblical
writings, are conceived in the *motif of attributes*.
Psalms are Songs, a genre of literature which in the
whole Bible is almost invariably held in the motif
of attributes. There is hardly a Psalm in which that
motif is entirely missing. In most of them nearly
every verse contains one or more allusions to the old
or the new formula of attributes, if, indeed, not to
both of them. In some of the Psalms, especially in
those of historical conception, the situation presented
in Exodus chapters XXXIII and XXXIV, anent the
revelation of the formula of Thirteen, is very inter-
estingly reflected and varied. In some Psalms there
appear new variations of the formulas of attributes,
recognized and employed as such later in Agadah and
Liturgy (cf. Gesch. d. jued. Philosophic, II, 1. p.
152-156).

Another important point clearly accentuated in the
Psalms is, that in spite of the many temporary names
of God introduced by the ancient prophets, the name
JHVH has remained the unique name of God in the
period after Esra (cf. Zech. XIV, 9). Of course, we
find in the Psalms all divine names, and combinations of

such, used in the rest of the Bible, but *the* name of God is JHVH.   Not less than *a hundred* of the hundred and fifty Psalms are absolute JHVH—Psalms.   *Twenty-seven* Psalms are conceived in the *evolutionary motif*: The Psalmist uses Elohim as a name of God, only in order to introduce the name of JHVH at a suitable moment, a literary device which we know from the older sources.   *Nine* Psalms, while using chiefly the name Elohim, use also the name JHVH, only the *fourteen* remaining being aboslute *Elohim* - Psalms. This unexpected phenomenon, the use of Elohim as the divine name (not met with since the days of J!) is in part accounted for by special situations, as the relation of God to the nations and similar special features required rather the general name of God of justice than the specific Jewish name of the God of justice *and* mercy.   In part, however, the revived usage of the name of Elohim may be explained by the suggestion that on account of prevailing conditions they would rather avoid the use of the great name, out of apprehension that it may be desecrated by the nations of their surroundings, and so they would pronounce it Elohim while still writing JHVH, some of them even writing Elohim (comp. Adonay of the contemporaries of Ezekiel; mark Ps. XLV, 21, where the Psalmist deplores the necessity to suppress the name JHVH; cf. Gesch. d. jued. Philosophic ibid. p. 199-201).

The position of the old formula of Thirteen in our period was also enhanced through the contact of Judaism with Plato.   The rigorous postulates of the Priestly Code as to the means by which to achieve divine grace, were among the congenial elements common to both, Judaism and Platonism. It was, however just this disharmony in the God-conceptions of Judaism and Platonism which led those Graeco-Jewish writers who desired to accentuate the specific Jewish view, to lay much stress on those distinguishing elements of the Jewish God-conception which are embodied in the formula of Thirteen (comp. the Testaments of the twelve Patriarch, the Letter of Aristeas, Philo, de virtutibus, and other Graeco-Jewish writings). Seen thus, we simply find this to be one of the points in which some Psalms are to be considered under the aspect of Graeco-Jewish literature. However, also those Psalmists who show Greek influence are very careful to emphasize the specific Jewish attitude wherever feasible; particularly in the employment of the motif of attributes in the sense of the *theocratical idea*: All of these thoughts, scattered in various Psalms, appear in a concentrated formulation in *two* Psalms which, from this aspect, may be considered a *twin Psalm*: Psalm CXI presents an ethico-cosmological definition of God through the attributes of the Thirteen-formula in combination with the cardinal attributes of Plato (cf. כח, חכמה and יראה in 6-10) set in an alphabetical acrostic (The influence of Plato here can best be perceived by a comparison with the acrostic definition of God in Ps. 145 where the combination of the ethical and cosmological elements show no trace of Platonic influence). As a counterpart to this Psalm which defines the attributes of the *creator*, follows Psalm CXII, likewise an acrostic, in which the attributes of the *creature*, of the "God-fearing man," under the aspect of homoiosis theo, or resembling God, are sung.   The Aleph of the acrostic is represented by אשרי (Happy is the man): the just, the God-fearing, is the happy.   And, as in its individual application, so also in its bearing upon political ethics, the theocratic idea in the Psalms is the consistent reflex of the God-conception as elaborately formulated in the Psalms.   This is evident in the *historical* Psalms in which the argument is advanced that the violation of the theocratic principles has always been productive of national disaster, while obedience to those principles has always meant national greatness and prosperity (cf. Ps. LXXIV, LXXVII, LXXVIII, LXXXI, LXXXIII, LXXXIX, CV: tribal history in the terse style of PC; CVI, and others), and also in those Psalms in which the *ideal King* (Plato's *Philosopher Ruler*) is pictured and sung (Ps. II, XVIII, XX, XXI, XLV, LXI, LXIII, LXXII, LXXXIX, CI, CXXXII; comp. CXXII).

In Proverbs we cannot expect a motif of composition similar to that found in the Psalms, nevertheless there are in individual proverbs as well, as in the manner of their arrangement, many decisive elements of both formulas of attributes, and even new formations of epigrams of attributive definitions (cf. Gesch. d. jued. Philosophie II, 1. p. 156).   And also the general usage of the name JHVH is confirmed by Proverbs as much as, nay much more so than, by the Psalms: The only divine name absolutely used in Proverbs is JHVH.   Considering now that in Proverbs undoubtedly a good deal of popular language has been conserved, it becomes clear that JHVH was the only divine name in vogue among the people (cf. XXX, 9 and Gesch. II, I, p. 197). The theocratic idea in its Platonic sense is the central thought pursued in Proverbs, but also the motif of the Thirteen is accentuated often enough (XIV, 17, 21, 22, 29, 31; XV, 18; XVI, 5, 6, 10-16: ideal king, 32; XVII, 5; XVIII, 10: the name JHVH! XIX, 11, 17; XX, 8: id. k. 22, 26-28: id. k.; XXI, 13, 14, 21; XXII, 11: id. k = XXV, 2-4; XXV, 15; XXVIII, 8, 13, 20; XXIX, 4, 14: id. k. = XXXI, 1-9!).

It may well be said that in the struggle against the destructive elements of Greek culture, as mirrored in Psalms and Proverbs, the Jewish God-idea has become clearer in its conceptual features and has developed more definitely into the practical theocratic ideal for the guidance of state and individual. Indeed, we could say that in Psalms and Proverbs the principles of the Jeremian school appear to hold unchallenged sway. It corresponds, however, to the eclectic character of the age, if here and there we find traces of the belief in angels (Ps. XXXIV, 9; XXXV, 5; LXXXIX, 7, 8, 11: Thiamat-myth; XCI, 11; (XCIX, 1); CIII, 20, 21; CIV, 3, 4; (CXXXII, 8); CXLVIII, 1, 2.—*Prov.* (XVI, 14?); XVII, 11).

A new feature in Proverbs is the *Theory of Ideas* in the form of the doctrine of *Wisdom* or *Logos*. The theory of ideas, in the conception of it in the Priestly Code (cf. above), has nothing in common with the belief in angels. But not so in the Platonic conception of that theory. To the Jews of the Greek period ideas could be conceived of but as a sort of angels. Thus those who believed in angels experienced no difficulty in adopting the theory of ideas. The opponents of angels, however, had to employ the art of interpretation, and the soil for a convenient interpretation was well prepared: The attribute of Wisdom was pressed to the fore by Jeremiah in his monotheistic theory of creation. But Plato's theory of ideas, too, emanated from his conception of the attribute of Wisdom (the cosmological Sophia). Now this common point of view has furnished the starting point of that interpretation. They accepted Plato's Ideas in their *undivided totality*, as it were. The ideas, the components of the attribute of Wisdom, are the organ of creation in Plato's philosophy. The undivided attribute of Wisdom is the organ of creation in the conception of those adherents of the monotheistic theory of creation among the Jews who were influences by Plato, but insisted on the rejection of angels. This theorem was to them all the more acceptable, as the *exemplum presens* of that Wisdom, the *Torah*, was on their hands: Wisdom was soon *identified* with Torah. The Torah, according to this interpretation, is not only the *causa finalis*, but also the *cause movens*, the cause of creation. In the old proverbs the Torah was extolled as the emanation o f divine Wisdom, as found in Isaiah, Deuteronomy, and other old writings. These ethico-theocratical thoughts have now furnished·the point of crystallization which attracted and amalgamated those new elements of the theocratic idea which flowed from the Platonic conception of it. But in the writings of Plato, especially in The State, the theocratic thoughts are developed in intrinsic connection with the cosmologico-metaphysical foundations of the system.

So it happened that not only the poem which had for its purpose the glorification of the monetheistic theory of creation, the book of Job, but also the book which has the theocratic idea for its central thought, the book of Proverbs, has attracted Jewish-Platonic thoughts on creation (Prov. III, 19, 20; VIII, 21-31; XXX, 1-5).   In the Psalms, even in such of a cosmological character, nay even in such in which cosmological thoughts are interwoven with decisively Platonic elements (as in Ps. III), and even where such elements are bound up with theocratic thoughts of Platonic fashion (Ps. 111-112), there is no vestige of the doctrine of Wisdom as Logos (if we do not consider CIV, 24 as such).   This may be explained, perhaps, by the plausible suggestion that the Psalmists were much more careful in adopting Greek elements, and that also later interpolators were less daring in their dealings with the Psalms, because of the place these have been given in *liturgy* at an early period (cf. below).

Of the other theoretical principles, *prophecy* is hardly ever expressly referred to in Proverbs.   This would at any rate, permit the inference that gnomic sages and poets were not much interested in prophecy, a fact which may perhaps be taken as an indication that at the time in the course of which most of the proverbs contained in our collection were conceived, prophecy was no more an actual phenomenon.   Prophecy was then considered as "closed."   In olden times, when prophecy was an actual phenomenon, it, indeed, was made the subject of popular gnomics (I Sam. X, 12; Hos. IX, 7, 8; comp. Jer. XXIX, 26).   And also the Psalms point in the same direction.   Actual prophetic visions are mentioned only as a matter of past ages. Moses, Aaron and Samuel had prophetic visions, God spoke to them through the Cloud (XCIX, 6, 7). The patriarchs are designated as prophets (CV, 20; comp. Gen. XX, 7). God spoke to David in a vision (LXXXIX, 20; comp. above to Zech. XIII, 4). From the plaint of one Psalmist (LXXIV, 7-9) it could be inferred that in his time the view was prevailing that with the destruction of the Temple in Jerusalem prophecy had to cease. It would, then, appear that this Psalm refers to the time preceding the erection of the Second Temple. For the time of the Second Temple the Psalms indicate the presence of a *reduced grade* of prophecy which some of them designate by the phrase "God spake in His Sanctuary" (LX, 8 = CVIII, 8; LXII, 12; LXIII, 3; LXVIII, 2, 5; LXXIII, 17). In the Psalm quoted last (LXXIII, 17) the Psalmist expects the solution of the problem of justice through some sort of a revelation, to which he looks forward at his next visit to the Temple. We have met with this function of prophecy in Ezekiel and, even more so, in Job. This reduced grade of prophecy reminds one of the "Holy Spirit" (רוח הקדש); comp. Ps. LI, 13) described by the Talmudists as the form of prophecy which at the time of the Second Temple supplanted genuine prophecy which had ceased forty years after the Restoration (It is possible, however, that Ps. LXXIV refers to the temporary destruction at the immediately pre-Maccabean time, or, perhaps, to the final destruction through the Romans. If this is the case, the Psalmist deplores the extinction of even this reduced form of prophecy. As to the immediately pre-Maccabean time, there is a parallel information to the same effect: 2 Macc. IV, 46; IX, 27; XIV, 41).

The *free will* of man is the general supposition in the Psalms, and in some of them it is especially emphasized (XXXIV, 13; LXXXI, 13). Nevertheless, some Psalmists display certain waverings which we know from former days: God is petitioned for a new heart (LI, 12; comp. Ezekiel), as also the other way: to lead the unjust from sin to sin (LXIX, 28, comp. Pharao and the sons of Eli). One Psalmist gives, perhaps, some consideration to the suggestion that the unjust are born with their wickedness (LVIII, 4; comp. Is. XLVIII, 8). Another Psalmist tries to alleviate the great weight of human responsibility involved in the freedom of man's will, by the suggestion (later developed by the Talmudists) that God disregards evil thoughts as long as they have not been converted into action, while he pays regard to and answers good thoughts conceived in prayer and devotion (LXVI, 16-20). And also in *Proverbs* the idea of free will is the general supposition (especially emphasized in XIX, 3), but, as is to be expected in gnomic wisdom, the practical suggestion is advanced that the will of man can, and should, be *educated* to choose the good (XX, 11 in conjunction with XXII, 5, 6).

It is, however, the principle of *retribution* which occupies the center of interest in both of these writings. Almost all the Psalms, and also the proverbs in their present arrangement, aim, as has already been pointed out, at the defense of justice. It is, therefore, entirely in accordance with what is to be expected, if we find in these two collections (of Psalms and proverbs,) all attempts at solution of the problem known to us from the older sources, in a more or less developed form:

The *end* of the just is good, is the general basic thought, advanced in Psalms and Proverbs against all the illusions of pretentious reality (especially Ps. I, 3-6; VII, 12f.; XI, 5.6; most especially XXXVIII, 37, 38, and very often; Prov. XII, 13; XVI, 25: the end = XXIII, 17.18 = XXIV, 14.

Responsibility is *not* exclusively *individual*, there being an account of merit and sin going through the generations (Ps. XVII, 14; XXI, 11; XXV, 12; XXXIV, 17; XXXVII, 9.10; 22-28; LII, 7; CIII, 17.18; CIX, 8-15; CXII, 2; CXXVII, 3; CXXVIII, 12; Prov. XII, 5; XIII, 22; XIV, 11; XVII, 5; XX, 7; XXVIII, 8, comp. Job XXVII, 17).

Responsibility is also *national*, the entire nation may suffer for the sins of national leaders or for sins of a national character, and also this national responsibility is controlled by an account of sin and merit going through the ages. This is illustrated most persuasively in the *historic* Psalms. In this connection these Psalmist would refer also to the greatness of the creator, and to the messianic idea— thoughts apt to appease the inquisitiveness of man (cf. especially Ps. LXVIII; LXXIV; LXXVI-LXXXI; LXXXIII; LXXXVII; LXXXIX; XCV; CIII; CV; CVI; CXXXV-CXXXVII). In Proverbs we miss the emphasis on the principle of national responsibility. But in its stead we find the abstract political Sophia which in the ultimate leans upon the idea of national responsibility (VIII, 14-21; XI, 14; XXV, 2.3 and all passages about the *ideal King*).

Then again there is the solution suggested by Elihu in the book of Job: The sufferings of the just are a purification of the afflicted; the divine trial leads man to self-trial and self-test and, subesquently, to greater efforts in the fear of God and in actions of justice (Ps. LI; XC, 3, 15; XCIV, 12, 18; CXVIII, 17, 18; Prov. III, 11, 12).

Then, the righteous is contented with little: The necessaries of life, enjoyed with a good quiet conscience and in the realisation of being in harmony with the time-tested principles of wisdom, justice and the fear of God, render the life of the just happier than can be the life of the unjust with all of his possessions and apparent joys of life which, in reality, are unable to din his inner unrest and anxiety. This idea, expounded by Eliphaz in Job, is the general note in Psalms and Proverbs, at times, however, it is accentuated with special stress (Ps. XVII, 14; XXIII, 1, 2; XXXVII, 1f, 7.16.25; XLIX, 6f.; Prov. III, 23-25; IV, 10-19; XIII, 25; XV, 16.17; XVI, 6.19; XVII, 1; XXIV, 19 (III, 31) = Ps. XXXVII, 1, 2). Particularly in Proverbs this solution is suggested under the aspect of the virtue of *temperance* (Sophrosyne), one of the basic doctrines of the book. Of Plato we are reminded by the proverbs against the *sexual passion* as the greatest passion of man (II, 16f; V, 3f; VI, 25f; VII, 5f; IX, 13f), and by those agianst *wine* (XX, 1; XXI, 17; XXIII, 30; XXXI, 4; comp. Ps. LXXV, 9; LXXVIII, 65; CIV, 15 where the old Jewish attitude is taken that

wine moderately used is commendable. Contradictory utterances o'n the question of wine there are
many in Bible, Plato, Graeco-Jewish and talmudic
literatures.)

The thought of the illusory nature of possession
and enjoyment in this world leads up to the *eschatological solution* of the problem of justice.

As to this question there are many utterances in
the Psalms which seemingly point in different directions. Some seem to negate the *substantiality* of the
soul. They seem to posit a *general spiritual substance* (Ruah) which comes from God to animate the
flesh, or the dust, for a certain period of time, but
this individuality perishes entirely when God withdraws this Ruah (LXXVIII, 39; CIII, 14-16; CIV,
29.30: of animals; CXLIV, 4; CXLVI, 4). Other
Psalms speak of the *Sheol* where man (continues some
shadowy life after death, but) does not praise God
and does not call His name (VI, 6; XXX, 4.10;
LXXXVIII, 4, 7, 11 12; CXV, 27.) However, a
thorough investigation into these utterances in the
light of the basic disposition of these God-intoxicated
Psalmists, and, especially, in the light radiating from
the vast majority of the passages under discussion,
makes it clear, that the above passages are not to be
taken in the heretical, or at least skeptical, sense
indicated. The Sheol is to (or, at any rate may) be
taken in the connotation suggested by the majority
of the passages in which this word occurs: Sheol is
the place where the unjust undergo punishment
after death. There they are banned from before the
countenance of God (mark Ps. LXXXVIII, 4-7

where this is expressly stated). There man does not
praise God for His mercy, because there divine
mercy does not prevail. The prayer of the pious
always urges that his soul be saved from that Sheol
(IX, 18; XXVIII, 1; XXXI, 18; XLIX, 9, 15, 16;
LV, 16, 24; LXIII, 10; LXXXVIII, 4; LXXXIX,
49; CXLIII, 7). Likewise, from the other series of
passages referred to above, we are justified to accept,
as the real amount of the utterances, the idea of the
substantiality of the Ruah; considering the suggested
negation of the individuality of the human Ruah an
extreme self-humiliation of the pious Psalmist. We
are entitled to this interpretation, because the vast
majority of the pertaining passages show an entirely
different face. The substantiality of the soul which,
in addition to Ruah, is sometimes called "heart,"
"soul," "glory" (XXXV, 17: יחידתי "my only one";
CL, 6: נשמה, comp. Ps. XVIII, 16 and Job), is conceived of as remaining in its individuality also after
the death of man. And, however discreet these
Psalmists are in language and picture used in expressing their eschatological hopes, it is an unquenchable
longing of the individual soul after the God of life,
which is reflected in their songs and prayers. It is
but this what they mean when they express their
confident hope for dwelling "in the lands of life,"
"bliss in Thy Right forever," "light of life," "light
of Thy countenance," "fountain of life," "the good,"
and the like (XVI, 8-11; XVII, 14, 15; XXII, 27
(30?); XXV, 12; XXVI, 13; XXXI, 6; XXXV, 17;
XXXVI, 8-10; XLII, 3; L, 14; LXIII, 2, 8; LXXXIII,
25, 26; LXXXIV, 3; CIII, 1-4.14-17; CXVI. 7-9).

Of course, it is easily possible, and even very likely, that the sentences with the negative attitude described, originally *have* expressed a rather pagan view of Sheol and a denying suggestion as to spiritual individual immortality. But the pious Psalmists who employed these old *ready-made* proverbs in their songs and prayers, undoubtedly gave them the interpretation suggested here. This interpretation is also confirmed by contemporary Graeco-Jewish literature.

And in these Psalms, in which the punishment of the unjust in the Sheol (later "Gehinnom") and the reward of the just in the "light of Life" (later "Gan-Eden") are the object of song and prayer, this doctrine appears as the *last trump* in the defense of justice: There is a final account for the individual in a *hereafter:* for the unjust there is judgment and (bodily) punishment in the Sheol, for the just there is spiritual bliss. In *Proverbs* the substantiality of the human soul is once hinted at (XX, 27), of the Sheol it is expressly stated that it is under the providence of God (XV, 11), and the whole theory of the Psalms of the judgment of the unjust in the Sheol and the "way of life upward" of the just, appears confirmed in a number of proverbs (II, 18, 19; V, 5, 6; VII, 27; IX, 18; XIV, 27.32: בחומי?; XV, 24 (comp. Koh. III, 21); XXI, 16).

And also the final answer in the book of Job, the appeal to the doctrine of *monotheistic creation*, is not missing in Psalms and Proverbs: He who contemplates over the work of creation and, in the sense of the cosmological proof, learns from it the reality of the creator in His grace and mercy, will put at rest all his doubts and perplexities, convinced that there is a final equalizing Justice which rules the world. The ways of God are indeed above human comprehension. Who knows? Perhaps there is in store (perhaps in a spiritual soul-life in the "Sanctuary") for us some more enlightenment about the ways of God (Ps. XLIX, 21; LXXIII, 16, 17, 22; XCII, 10; Prov. III, 5-7, 19, 20; VIII, 12-14, 22-31; (XX, 17, 21; XXIV, 12, 13;) XXV, 2, 3; XXX, 2-6).

The individual Psalmists and gnomic poets dwelt on one or the other of these suggested solutions of the problem of justice, following their special inclinations and personal religious experiences, but all of them together bear witness to the fact that exposition and discussion of the problem of justice, as conceived by the author of the book of Job, has found many followers in the schools of Psalmists and gnomic poets. The pious Psalmists and the poets of practical wisdom have converted the deep thoughts of the book of Job, not so much accessible to the people at large, into small currency, as it were. And this furnishes us the connecting link between the theoretical principles and the higher cultural forms in the period represented by the books of Psalms and Proverbs.

Psalms and Proverbs are by no means an altogether new genre of literature in our period. Many a Psalm undoubtedly originated, wholly or in part, in previous times. In Job there appears many a string of proverbs embodied skillfully into the trend of discussion, and the same may be said of Psalms.

A comparison of the parallels in Psalms and Proverbs referred to above, with each other and with their parallels in Job, makes it clear that *aphoristic proverbs* furnished the cells, as it were, out of which Psalms and Proverbs were strung in mosaic construction; the same possibly being true also of older biblical songs. New in our period are *two* features. *First*, the elaboration of, old and new, proverbs into Psalms or strings of proverbs, is the *prevalent literary genre* of our period. *Secondly*, as compared with Job, Psalms and Proverbs are, as has already been mentioned, popular literature. Psalms and units of proverbs would be recited or sung by professional singers in public places. Especially it was the Psalms which soon reached the ranks of the people who soon started employing them as prayers. Psalms and Proverbs proved the most efficient instrumentality for disseminating the doctrines of Judaism among the people at large. But the Psalms are to be rated above the Proverbs, not only because the Psalms, with their fervent religious enthusiasm and intense religious experience, made a deeper impression on those who listened to them, than did the proverbs, but also, and especially, because of the great *historic function* which must be attributed to the Psalms: The Psalms helped prepare that time in which Jewish religion freed itself from the sacrificial ritual. Most likely already in the Babylonian exile, at the time when the Jewish multitudes were attracted by the idolatrous practices in their surroundings, there were pious Jews who satisfied their religious longing by reciting, or singing, Psalms. And this movement, to install prayer instead of

bloody sacrifices, never ceased again even after the
erection of the Second Temple and the restoration
of the sacrificial ritual.   The Covenant of Esra, the
Book on which it was based, with its monotheistic
doctrine of creation and its rigorous doctrine of attributes, influenced the minds of the people deeply
and lastingly.   Nowhere do we find the complaint
that the Jews in the days after Esra have indulged in
idolatry or even in sacrificing outside the Temple.
It is in Deuteronomy where we find the first endeavor
at centralization which meant the prohibition of
sacrificing outside the walls of Jerusalem, the center
of worship in Palestine (This explains the Temples
in *Eelphantine* and *Helippolis*.   By a less rigid interpretation these places could, each in its time,
become the center of worship for *Egypt*, without
ceasing to recognize Jerusalem as the *national*
center and the place of highest authority in matters
national and religious).

But, as many another reform started by Deuteronomy, the centralization of the sacrificial cult was
not realised until the days of the Esra-Covenant.
And so it developed by natural necessity that the
Palestinian Jews living in the "Province" (the
technical name for all Palestine outside Jerusalem)
continued the institution of prayer (as a substitute
for sacrifices) even after the erection of the Second
Temple.   In this they were aided by the Psalmists,
as they in turn have encouraged and furthered the
development of Psalmodic literature.

And here we touch an important characteristic of
our period.   In the Psalms idolatry in Israel's past
(CVI, 35) as also among the other peoples in the

present (XCVI, 5; XCVII, 7; CXV, 5-8; CXXXV, 15-17), is spoken of, but nowhere is there, in Psalms or Proverbs, any trace of accusation or suspicion that the much blamed unjust were guilty of anything in the way of idolatry.   It is, evidently, in connection with this that while we often find, in Psalms and Proverbs, complaints about the undue luxuries indulged in by the unjust, we find nothing about what would disclose the position of Psalmists and gnomic poets as to the extent of the validity of the *prohibition of images* in their time. This question, evidently, was of no actual interest any more. The Second Temple in its imageless equipment marked the admissible measure of decorative art, which in general was observed by the masses of the people. The Hellenistically inclined unjust tried to establish gymnasia and stadia, but nothing of an outspoken idolatrous character. They never renounced the Temple and its worship.   On the contrary, they were ardent in the bringing of copious sacrifices. It was rather the Psalmists and gnomic poets who declared their sacrifices worthless and abominable.   Now the Psalmists certainly were not opposed to the prescribed sacrificial cult.   On the contrary, the sacrificial cult is upheld not only in Psalms in which the national idea is pressed to the fore (X, 16; XLVIII; LXXVI;   LXXXIX,   4:   David   (comp.   ibid. 21.50; CXXII; CXXXII); CXXVII, CXLIV, 7, 8; CXLVII, 19, 20), but also in Psalms of a *universal* character (XLVII; LIX; LXVI, 8; LXVII: mark Elohim = LXVIII, 29-33 = LXXXII, 8; XCVI-XCIX, 2; CI, 1-3: all nations should bring thank-offerings to

JHVH and recognize Him as *Elohim*; CXIII; CXVII; CXXXVIII, 4). No thought of a serious opposition against the sacrificial ritual prescribed in the written Torah can be sustained for the period under discussion. In many Psalms the Torah is already exalted as a closed authoritative document, as the *exemplum presens*, as it were, of a higher heavenly reality (comp. Ps. XIX; CXIX a. o.). Moreover they go beyond the written law and exalt the *Sopheric* institution of *music* as a means of worship in and outside the Temple, with great emphasis (XLIII, 4; XLVII, 6, 7; XLIX, 5; LVII, 9; LXVIII, 26; LXXI, 22; LXXXI, 2, 3; XCII, 4; XCVIII, 5, 6; C, 1; CVIII, 3; CXXXVII, 2, 4; CXLVII, 7; CXLIX, 3; CL, 3-5; comp. below the discussion of Chronicles). Nevertheless, it may be said that some of the Psalms oppose the sacrificial cult to a certain extent. First of all they lay much stress on the thought of the older prophets that only he has a right to come to the sanctuary or to set his foot on the Mountain of the Lord (in order to bring sacrifices!) who is a strict observer of the ethical laws of the Torah (Ps. XV; XXIV). Then, too, some of the Psalmists are against the *sin-offering*, and, in further pursuance of the attitude taken by the writer of the Book of Jonah, they are rather in favor of *thank-offerings* (in contrast to this attitude, deviating as it does, from the stand taken by the Priestly Code in the question of retribution and expiation, we find in some Psalms reminiscences of the Khareth-institution: XXXIV, 17; esp. XXXVII, 9, 22, 28, 34, 38; CI, 8; CIX, 13, 15; comp. Prov. II, 22; otherwise Proverbs are entirely

universalistic, comp. Job). And, finally, some of
the Psalmists prefer prayer and song as a means of
Grace to bloody sacrifices, as indeed the sacrificial
worship derives its worth altogether from the prayer
concomitant to it (Ps. IV, 2; V, 2-4 (comp. LXXII,
5); XXVI, 6, 7; XXVII, 6; XXVIII, 2; XXX, 5;
XXXIV, 6; (XXXVI, 7: reminiscence of Jona,
concluding verse); XXXIX, 13; XL, 2-12 (!); XLII,
5-9; XLIII, 3, 4; XLIX, 8; L (!); LI, 17-21 (!);
LIV, 8; LVI, 13; LXI, 6-9; LXIII, 3-6; LXV, 2-5;
LXVI, 13-20 (!); LXVIII, 30-34; LXIX, 14, 31, 32;
LXXII, 5 (morning and evening prayer?—comp.
Dan. VI, 11, 12: *three* times daily, which is evidently
a *later* development); LXXII, 9-15; LXXVI, 12:
LXXX, 5; LXXXIV, 9-11; XCV, 2; C, 1; CII, 17-32:
note verse 19: Prayer is to be *established* as an *in-
stitution* for later generations; CVI, 44; CVII, 21, 22
(23-32: the situation reminds of Jona!); CIX, 7;
CXVI, 12-19; CXIX, 62, 147, 148 (V, 2-4; LXXII, 5);
CXXII, 1-4; CXXX, 2-6 (V, 2-4; LXXII, 5; CXXXIV,
1); CXXXVIII, 2; CXLI, 1, 2; *Proverbs* XV, 8, 29;
XX, 25; XXI, 3, 27; XXIX, 4).

We touch here an historic formation of great
magnitude which was of decisive import in the
development of Judaism for all times to come:

3. INSTITUTION OF LITURGY: CONFESSION OF FAITH.

Prayer as such is no new phenomenon in our
period. Private prayer, of course in conjunction
with a sacrifice, is an institution common to many
peoples of antiquity (comp. Is. I, 15). And also
certain prescribed prayers for sacrificial functions,

private and public, go back to an early period (comp. Gesch, d. jued. Philosophie II, 1, p. 239-240). The new feature which we learn from the Psalms, is the preponderance of prayer over sacrifice. One cause of this phenomenon we have found in the circumstance that by the rigid insistence on the idea of centralization of the sacrificial cult, the Palestinian Jews were gradually led to consider prayer as *the* divine service; a movement which favored the development of Psalmodic literature, as it in turn was furthered and fostered by this very flourish of the eminently religious literary genre of Psalm and Song. But there also were other factors which greatly favored the development of prayer as an institution.

The new redaction of the Torah obliterated the distinct position of those theoretical principles which were recognised as such by the authoritative representatives of Judaism. Authoritative Judaism could, as has already been pointed out, take a less implacable attitude toward the doctrine of angels, now that the monotheistic theory of creation has deprived it of its most dangerous sting. And yet, this doctrine has remained a constant menace to the purity of the theoretical principles of Judaism.

The conditions of the time called for an institution through which the positive principles of Judaism would be distinguished and marked as such. And also some influences from without were working in the same direction. In the Persian period the principles of Judaism had to be defended against the destructive influences of Parsism, just as in the Greek period against the subversive elements of Hellenism.

Indeed, our very Psalms have been such a defensive measure. The Psalms are, as we have just seen, prayers, in which God is praised and petitioned for help, but in which at the same time also the theoretical principles of Judaism are being defended. When, in the Temple, on the occasion of sacrifices, or in private prayer-meetings, Psalms were recited or sung, these recitals and songs were meant also as a *confession of faith* in the presence of the congregation. And it could not take long before the authoritative representatives of Judaism availed themselves of the opportunity offered them by this progressing form of devotion, to take the new institution under official control and to develop it with a conscious effort to make it serve the best and most vital interests of Judaism. The idea soon suggested itself to introduce, at the Temple in Jerusalem as well as in the private meetings of devotion in the Province, such prayers and songs which would express the principles of Judaism in a more *systematic* and *exhaustive* way than it had been the case in the Psalms. In pursuance with this effort it was natural to arrange the recitals and songs in the Temple in such a way as to exclude from the Temple all prayers and Psalms which possibly express views declined by authoritative Judaism, as, for instance, the doctrine of angels (found in some of the Psalms). In the Province it was sufficient to establish a certain order of prayers, recitals and readings, as *obligatory*, to emphasize certain principles as the authoritative doctrine of Judaism, and thus sufficiently marking all additional, *free*, selections of Psalms and readings as

not authoritative. In the *Temple*, of course, everything had to be under authoritative control. There
nothing could be uttered that could not be accentuated as authoritative doctrine.

Thus in the time comprising the end of the Persian
and the beginning of the Greek periods, there has
developed the fixed institution of *national-religious
Liturgy* at the Temple in Jerusalem and in the prayer-
meetings in the Province, and, by and by, also in the
Diaspora (in the Temple and the private homes of
prayer): They marked certain selections of the
Torah for obligatory, daily or periodical, readings,
and composed short benedictions and prayers to be
read and recited at the Temple in Jerusalem in conjunction with the sacrifices, and in the private houses
of worship at the time of the prescribed daily sacrifices. And these daily prayers and recitals were so
arranged that in their entirety they represented the
full *Creed* of Jewish religion. For Sabbaths and
festivals there was an added scriptural selection expressive of the significance of the day and its special
ritual. This effort to accentuate the creed of Judaism, accounts plausibly for the interesting and instructive fact that in the oldest list preserved in the
Mishna (and contested by other lists contained in
other talmudical sources) all scriptural selections for
recital or reading were taken from those parts of the
Torah which we today have recognised as the enlarged
Priestly Code and Deuteronomy. It was this,
evidently, the time when the Torah assumed its
final proportions of today, but certain parts of it
were deliberately excluded from public recognition.

They rather selected such passages which they wanted to accentuate as expressive of the essentials of Judaism. Moreover, a thorough examination of the pertaining sources, in Bible and Talmud, establishes the fact that at the Temple in Jerusalem the Torah in its present volume never was recognised as the authoritative document of Judaism. From all we can see the inference is urged upon us that the copy, or copies, of the Torah preserved in the Temple up to the time of its destruction through the Romans, comprised no more than the enlarged Priestly Code and Deuteronomy (comp. to the preceding, as also to the following, Tholdoth I, p. 126-144).

The "Order of the Day" in the Maccabean period consisted of the following units:

Benediction of Creation (יוצר אור), Benediction of *Israel's Selection* by *Revelation* (אהבה רבה), the *Decalog*, the *Shema*, as the principle of *Unity*, *Wehayah*: the principle of Retribution, and *Wayyomer*: the principle of *free will*. Then followed the (later so called) "Three First" and "Three Last" benedictions of the "Thephillah," or "the Eighteen Benedictions" (likewise a later designation, after the twelve "intermediate benedictions" had been, by and by, inserted between the "First three" and the "Last three." Later another, the thirteenth, middle-benediction was added, the benediction against the heretics). The "three first" were called: *Aboth* (Fathers) expressive of the idea of the Covenant with the Patriarchs on the ground of the Thirteen Attributes (on which later also the "intermediate benedictions" were built); *Geburoth* (divine might) and

Kedushoth (Holiness), which, together with Aboth, convey a well thought-out definition of the Jewish God-conception. The "three last" were *Abodah* (Worship), a prayer for the favorable acceptance of the sacrifices as a means of achieving divine grace; *Hoda'ah* (Thanks), prayer of thanks and confession of faith in divine providence; and finally *Birchath Chohanim*: the *Priestly Blessing* with the key-note of *Shalom.* Thus the Thephilla unites the old formula of attributes with the new (first half of Thephilla: Thirteen; second half: Priestly Blessing; and also the "intermediary Benedictions" may be analyzed along the same line). In the *Ma'amadoth* (Standing Orders, introduced later in our period, comprising twenty-four lay organizations in as many district-towns in Palestine, corresponding to the twenty-four priest and Levitical organizations in Jerusalem, called Mishmaroth: Watches) they would add every day, at the time of the Morning-offering in the Temple, the corresponding section of the story of creation in the first chapter of the Torah, so accentuating the belief in God as Creator.

Thus the theoretical principles of Judaism were formulated and emphasized, and this was done in the spirit of the old compromise between the principles of the Jeremian school and those doctrines of their opponents which, though opposed by some adherents of the Jeremian school for some special reasons evolved out of concomitant historical developments, could well be harmonized with those principles. In brotherly peace alongside each other rest in this confession of faith the once opposing doctrines of

ethical holiness and cosmological creative power in
the definition of God, as also the *Thirteen* and the
Priestly Blessing

The daily prayers of those days represent the
result of the development of the teachings of the
prophets in the highest degree of philosophic purity.
It is the essential principles of Judaism which were
formulated and accentuated in those prayers and
recitals.   The theory of angels was excluded, as also
those later formulated and sanctioned doctrines
which we call *"historical dogmas"* of Judaism.   In
the chronological order of their later sanction as
dogmas, they are: Bodily *Resurrection*, Spiritual
Immortality in the sense of *Retribution* after death,
Personal *Messiah*, "Thora from Heaven," meaning
the *literal inspiration* of the Torah, and, finally, the
binding power of *Oral Tradition*.   The daily prayer,
as an instrument of confession of faith, was destined
to embody in the future the doctrine of angels as
well as all the historical dogmas just mentioned.
This was done partly by enlarging the, originally
very short, benedictions and prayers, and partly by
added benedictions and prayers some of which were
introduced in early Tannaitic, and still later, times.
The dogma of Resurrection found its place in the
benedictions of Geburoth, that of angels in Kedushoth
(and elsewhere), and that of Messiah in the benediction
of *Geulah* (Redemption) between Shema and Thephillah (and also in the "intermediary benedictions").
The dogma of Immortality has (except for very late
additions) found no direct expression in the "Order
of the Day," for definite reasons (nearly the same as

in olden times: the fear to encourage the people in their desire to establish relations with the dead), but, it was discreetly included in the dogma of Resurrection (comp. Tholdoth and below). The dogma of the "Torah from Heaven" has found accentuation in a *negative* way: At the time when *Christian Antinomism* declared the ritual law abolished, even at the time when, as a measure against just this antinomistic movement, the dogma of "Torah from Heaven" was formulated and sanctioned (comp. Mishna Synh XI, 1), the Decalog was removed from the "Order of the Day," so as not to give support to the antinomistic doctrine that only the laws covered by the authority of the Decalog are binding, to the exclusion of all ritual laws. The *positive* expression for this dogma is contained in the general conception of "Torah" as indicated in some of the prayers, notably in *Ahabha Rabbah* and in the benedictions before and after the reading from the Torah. The dogma of Oral Tradition, in conception and formulation incidental to the dogma of "Torah from Heaven," has found its expression in the *Sopherim Benediction* (Al hat-Tzaddikim).

The development just sketched has, it is true, not entered into the visible horizon of historic actuality until the post-biblical period, but the beginnings of that development go back, as already preceived in the preceding, to the late biblical period, and took place in intimate interrelation with late products of biblical literature. And just as the Psalms, extending as they do over the entire period under discussion, have proved suitable instrumentality for the presentation of the introduction of the "Order of the Day" and its function out of the conditions of the time, so will the biblical books yet to be discussed, and which characterize the very end of the biblical period, furnish us a most suitable instrument for the presentation of the, above sketched, later dogmatical development of prayer as confession of faith, and to understand it out of the spiritual currents of late-biblical times. This method will prove most handy for conception and presentation of the spiritual and cultural currents at the end of the biblical period out of their essential and, for the future development, most decisive witnesses and documents. The historical dogmas stand to the essential ones in the same relation as the oral law to the Torah. Indeed, the historical dogmas are quasi the oral principles of Judaism, while the essential dogmas are quasi its written principles, inasmuch as they represent the very contents of the teachings of the prophets.

Thus our way of looking at the matter brings us in intimate touch with the very well-spring where post-biblical Judaism emanates from the biblical spirit. We have struck the parting of the ways: We have left for some while already the characteristic path of development of biblical Judaism, and are now engaged in orienting ourselves in an outlook upon *two new paths*, in which the old undivided path has split up: the *Alexandrian path* and the *Talmudic path*, reaching out still further with an outlook into a more remote future:

4. CHRONICLES (inclusive of Esra and Nehemia) and DANIEL.

The book of Daniel in its present form is a product of the immediately pre-Maccabean time, the time of the Syrian oppression preceding the Maccabean War. Nevertheless there is hardly room for any reasonable doubt that those sections of the book which treat of the history of the Jews in the exile, are based on elements of older literary documents. The story of Daniel and his three friends fill out that gap which we perceive in Chronicles between destruction and restoration of Jerusalem (2 Chronicles, XXXVI, 20-22). Chronologically the books of Chronicles, Daniel, Esther, Esra and Nehemia present history and pre-history of the Jews from Adam to the Covenant of Esra in broad outlines. This is the avowed purpose of the writers of these books. Critically read, the book of Chronicles (inclusive of Esra and Nehemia) furnishes us valuable information about the time intervening between the Esra-Covenant and the composition of the book. The date of Chronicles cannot be fixed with any degree of exactness, but it is quite certain that the *final* redaction of the book was influenced by Greek thought, preceding, however, the Maccabean War by a few decades. This state of affairs suggest the joint treatment of the books Chronicles and Daniel, so as to use them as documents for the time preceding the Syrian oppression, and to consult the later elements of the book of Daniel as documents for even the time of the Syrian oppression. This picture would not be complete, unless we consult also the book of *Koheleth* whose date most likely is the time immediately preceding that of the Syrian oppression, the time of the Hellenistic movement. Thus Koheleth seems to be older than Daniel in its final redaction, yet because of its older elements the book of Daniel must be treated first.

In *Chronicles* whose author draws on various old sources (cf. above), one perceives the mixed origin of the people of Israel much more definitely than in the other historical books of the Bible. The process of birth of the nation does not appear to have been definitely completed even as late as the time of David and other kings of his dynasty (cf. the first chapters of the book, notably VI, 41; V, 17; IX, 1; XI, 1; comp. 2 Chr. VII, 7 and Esra IV, 3; VI, 18; VIII, 35). The Chronist places the *House of David* in the center of Jewish history. The tribe of Judah with the house of David was the point of crystallization around which the final ethnical formation of the Jewish nation solidified into shape. The relation between the interest in the existence of Old-Israel, and the hope for a final re-union of Israel and Juda, on the one side, and between the inclination to revive and to strengthen the belief in angels and the sundry objectionable doctrines in its wake, on the other side, has already been referred to (cf. Ezekiel). These tendencies, suppressed in the time of the establishment of the Esra-Covenant, revived later, and, as has been presented above, led up to the new, and final, redaction of the Torah. Now it is this spirit of reaction which appears revivified in Chronicles, the spirit, of the last compromise, as mirrored in the Torah in its present shape and volume:

The *God-conception* of Chronicles is the ethico-cosmological, a combination of JE, Deuteronomy and Priestly Code, but with a certain hue radiating from the Platonic thought of the three cardinal virtues as the sum total of all active attributes (cf. 1 Chr. XXVIII, 9; XXIX, 11-12: definition of God with a Platonic shading: 2 Chr. I, 10 (the Platonic element clearly dsitinguishable when compared with 1 Ki. III, 9); II, 5 = VI, 18, 30; XVI, 9; XXXII, 8; Esra V, 11, 12; VI, 9, 10; comp. Dan. II, 11-18-23; IV, 5, 15, 31; V, 11; VI, 21). But the reactionary influence of Babylonian-Persian (and partly also of Greek) culture makes itself felt in the revivification of the doctrine of angels as represented in Chronicles and Daniel. True, Chronicles draws on old sources, but the fact that the author while using the old sources did not care to eliminate the passages about the angels—this fact in itself makes him an adherent of that doctrine. But in addition to that we find that he sometimes uses more intense colors in the presentation of angels than his sources. In the report of the plague in the time of David (1 Chr. ch. XXI) the attribute of Wrath (אף) appears more personified than in its parallel in the book of Samuel (2 Sam. ch. XXIV). With regard to the *Cherubs* he not only embodies in his book the account from the book of Kings (2 Chr., III, 10-14), but reports in addition about a vision in which David saw the Sanctuary in the *Idea*, and on this occasion he marks the Cherubs as the *Idea of Mercabah* (1 Chr. XXVIII,

18, 19; comp. Ezekiel). Now in the Second Temple there were no Cherubs, this strong emphasis is, therefore, to be taken as the *endeavor* to further the cause of a hopeless postulate, defended again and again by the numerous adherents of the doctrine of angels, but just as persistently repressed by the authoritative representatives.

In the book of *Daniel* the old doctrine of *angels* appears more elaborate and more systematically developed. We find here not only the new feature of *names of angels* (Gabriel and Michael), to which there is no parallel in the rest of the Bible (cf. above, first chapter), but also an actual *political organization* of the hosts of heaven. Each (political) nation has its representative in heaven. Wars between the nations, victory and defeat, are decreed in the Counsel of God with His angels, where the heavenly representatives of the nations try to protect the charges entrusted to them. This points to Babylonian-Persian influence, but one is inclined to think in this connection of the parallel heavenly organization in the *Iliad*. And also here there is a marked revivification of the Mercabah (Dan. VII, 9, 10). From here a track leads (over Graeco-Jewish and talmudic developments) to the embodying of the doctrine of angels into the "Order of the Day."

Also in the conception of *prophecy*, from of old in close connection with the doctrine of angels, we indubitably perceive a certain reactionary development. In Chronicles this is expressed by elements drawn from older sources. More intense is the reactionary spirit in Daniel where prophetic visions are equipped with all the mythological features known from early pre-Deuteronomic times, such as *dreams* and angels as a means of revelation.

In the wake of the revived doctrine of angels there appear also some waverings in the doctrine of *free will*. As in the old pre-Deuteronomic sources we find also in Chronicles, alongside of the general supposition of man's will being free, certain utterances tending to restrict freedom of will. And utterances of that kind we find not only in passages drawn from older parts of the Bible (2 Chr. X, 15; XVIII, 19), but also in *additions* which the Chronist may have drawn from other sources, but which most likely are amplifying explanations of his own (2 Chr. XXV, 16; XXXII, 31; XXXV, 21, 22).

In the doctrine of *retribution* as a theoretical principle we find in Chronicles nothing beyond the general idea of God's guidance in History. Very interesting, though, is the frankness in the treatment of the question in Esra, VIII, 21-24: Esra would feel ashamed to ask the king for an escort, as he had told him "The hand of our God is over all those that seek Him for their welfare, but His might and His wrath over those who forsake Him!" And so they prayed to God, and God answered them. Evidently, they were not unaware of the fact that reality often refuses to live up to the best doctrine, and so they considered asking the king for an escort. Upon reconsideration, however, they found that asking the king for protection on their way to fulfill the great mission of Restoration would express distrust in their own doctrine of God as the guide of History in whose name they are about to undertake that great work.   And so they prayed to God, in accordance with their doctrine.   And their prayer was successful, their doctrine triumphed.

More elaborate is the discussion of the principles of retribution in the book of *Daniel*, notably in those elements of it which mirror the strong *eschatological current* in the days immediately preceding the Maccabean War.   But before going into this question we will discuss those elements in Chronicles which permit us a deeper insight into the development of the higher cultural forms of life in the pre-Maccabean period.   And, incidentally, we will strike the very roots of the principle of Oral Tradition as it evolved from the historic conditions of that time.

The spirit of the times as reflected in Chronicles is a blend of the old mythological tendencies and rigid, intellectually tuned, obedience to the law, which we know from the Priestly Code.   Obedience to the law was then a matter of course.   Nobody in those pre-Hellenistic days could think of undertaking anything forbidden by the law.   At the same time, however, the reawakened mythical tendencies called for means of activation and energization.   The more rigid the determination to abide by the law, the more urgent was the need for an outlet for the new energy produced by those reawakened tendencies.   There were two ways: *First*, they conceived the past in mythological equipment to the extent limited only by the possibility to still harmonize it with the unyielding law.   *Secondly*, they tried to realize in practical religious and cultural life as much of their theoretical postulates as they could wrest from the authoritative representatives of Judaism of that time. With respect to practical questions the adherents of the Ezekiel School had, of course, to impose upon themselves more restraint than in the historical conceptions in their literary activity. Of the past, of the Temple of Solomon, the Chronist knows much about Cherubs and Mercabah. But when he comes down to his own time, to the Second Temple, he knows nothing of the kind. No doubt, the party to which the Chronist swore allegiance, would have desired very much to have in the Temple not only *two Cherubs* but rather a *complete Mercabah* (cf. Ezekiel), but they did not dare make of such a postulate an *actual* issue. The prohibition of images had been recognized not only in the Temple but also in private life. For his own time the Chronist does postulate no images whatsoever in the Temple. The only practical postulate which the party he represents possibly had advanced, was that of reintroducing the *Oracle*, the "Urim ve-Thumim." But conditions were such that this postulate, too, had to be withdrawn from actual consideration at the time being and to be postponed, as it were, in the hope it may have a better chance in some future time (Esra II, 62, 63; Neh. VII, 64, 65; cf. Tholdoth I, p. 107). We know that the cherished hope for reinstallment of the Urim ve-Thumin never realised. The Law was reigning supreme.

It was not until the time of penetration of Greek thought and culture into Jewish life that, first in the Temple and then also in private life, a tendency has reached the surface which we may designate as the reawakened desire for plastic arts as a means of expression for religious and other idealistic senti- ments.   But these unlawful tendencies are a later development. The time preceding the Chronist as well as his own time (even the time of the final redactor of the book) was not yet favorable to the reawakened mythical tendencies. The intensified longings for artistic religious expression in wake of those tendencies had to activate themselves as best they could within the narrow confines of the law. The new artistic interest found an outlet in *decorative art*, *literature*, and *music*. How far these higher cultural forms dominated in private life, the scanty information in the literature of the age (Psalms, Proverbs, and, notably, Koheleth) hardly permits any definite judgment.   In the field of religion our period easily signifies the height of development in the sphere of unforbidden art. The wonderful stories about the artistic splendor of the Second Temple (preserved in Graeco-Jewish and talmudic literatures) refer most likely, and exclusively, to the reconstruction of *Herod*.   It is, nevertheless, safe to assume that the spirit of the Priestly Code which favored a certain amount of decorative art in the description of the Tabernacle in the wilderness, pre- vailed to some extent on the occasion of the equip- ment of the Second Temple.

Much more abundant, however, is the information preserved in the literature of our period about the development of *religious poetry* and *religious music*. In that period this question was closely interrelated with the question of the sacrificial ritual:

As to religious *poetry* this interrelation disclosed itself to us in the preceding discussion of the Psalms. But Chronicles permits us a still deeper insight into this interrelation, in that it furnishes us the additional information about the important part religious *music* played in that development. Moreover, it forces the development of music into the fore and concentrates our interest on it as on the key to comprehending the whole complicated situation. The Chronist, expectedly, stands firm on the ground of the law, in all other questions as well as in questions of the sacrificial ritual. He is not engaged in any *messianic = universalistic* thoughts. He belongs to those who implacably resisted intermarriage (in all passages where he accentuates the racial purity of the patriarchs, notably in the passages about the removal of the foreign wives: Esra IX, 10; Neh. IX, 1-3; X, 31; XIII, 23-30). In Chronicles we already perceive the flutterings of that strong particularistic-legalistic spirit, which predominates later, even in Graeco-Jewish propagandistic literature, but most strongly in talmudic literature (eventhough in these literatures, too, profound variations of old prophetic universalism may be found). Of any opposition against the sacrificial cult on the part of the Chronist or even against a certain class of sacrifices, as for instance in Jona and Psalms, there cannot be the slightest suspicion whatsoever. In this he stands wholly and unswervingly on the ground of the law (comp. Esra: VII, 26: the compromise between the institutions of judicial execution and Khareth—שרשי). And if we do find in Chronicles some

deviations in details of ritual, and there are such,
it is always a case of interpretation of some law tending toward more rigid exclusiveness and more special
privileges for the priests. A case in point is the
Passah. Originally the Passah was a house-offering
without distinction of place or land. Then it was
restricted to the houses in the place of the Sanctuary
in Palestine, applying most likely to any large dis-
trict-Bamah. Still later (most likely in Deuteronomic times) Jerusalem was the only place where
the Passah could be offered. Of the injunction,
however, that the Passah should be brought to the
Temple there is nothing in older biblical literature.
The Chronist is the first (and, of course, also the
last) biblical author with whom we find the Passah
as a Temple-offering. Clearly, this is the reflex of
the then incipient and authoritatively favored custom of bringing the Passah to the Temple. But the
Chronist goes here beyond what is justified even by
the custom of those days. In the presentation of
the matter in Chronicles it appears that all functions
connected with the Passah were the exclusive pre-
rogative of the priests. It is, however, a matter of
record that as late as in the time of *Philo* (born about
20 B. C.) the Passah was considered as a *lay-offering*
to be handled by *Israelites* to the exclusion of the
priests. And even if we would not rely upon the
testimony of Philo, there still remains the tradition
accredited in talmudic literature that the slaughter-
ing of the Passah had to be carried out by Israelites,
not by priests (a sacrificial function to which Israelites
were generally admitted). A comparison of this

record of fact with what we find in Chronicles, makes it clear that in Chronicles we have before us a remanant of the literary activity by which a much desired additional priestly privilege was to be established, but which did not meet with success (cf. Geseh, d. jued. Philosophie II, I, p. 209-216; there it was shown that partly at least Philo's contention is borne out also in what we find about the matter in the Talmud). Thus there is certainly not the remotest thought of opposition against any priestly law on the part of the Chronist. Indeed he is considered by all biblical scholars as a staunch promoter of priesthood and Levites. And this unquestionably correct view is based mainly on the fact that in his accounts of political functions in history the Chronist would bring in priests and Levites more frequently than do other biblical historians. On every suitable, and often also unsuitable, occasion he knows to relate of, elsewhere never mentioned, functions and processions at which the priests would offer sacrifices and the Levites would assist them with their music, singing Psalms to the accompaniment of highly developed musical instruments.

However, looking a little beneath the surface we will soon find that the Chronist here, much against his avowed intention, but forced by the inherent force of truth, relates of a movement which really meant the weakening of the whole institution of sacrifices, and which led ultimately to its complete abolition. What we have found in the discussion of the Psalms appears here more intensely illumined. In addition to the movent factors discussed there,

another decisive motive contributes to the shaping
of things. The anti-artistic tendencies of the Jeremian school were given up even by the party of the
Priestly Code within the confines of what was still
admissible under formal obedience to the prohibition
of images. With this limitation, Ezekiel's enthusiasm for artistic expression of religious experience
and sentiment won a great historical victory. There
was a deep yearning for a form of service in which the
artistic receptivity of the higher senses was called
upon to participate. The sacrificial cult in itself did not
satisfy the spiritual demands of the age any more,
as we have seen by the various forms of opposition
to sacrifices as a means of achieving grace (comp.
the book of Jona, end: Prayer, as an expression of
repentance, and not sacrifice, was the means by which
the Ninivites achieved grace). To think of removing
the sacrificial worship was, naturally, entirely out of
the question. It was an institution established by
the Law, and, in addition, it was the outward symbol
of national independence. But there was the possibility to surround the sacrificial worship with an
elaborate artistic program which would spiritualize
it. And this suggestion, growing out of the conditions of the age, was achieved by connecting the
sacrifices with a soul-elevating order of prayers and
recitals in which the national creed and the singing
of Psalms to the accompaniment of instrumental
music was made the center of interest and attraction.

If we stop to consider that sacrifices could be
offered only at the Temple in Jerusalem, while in
the rest of the land God was worshiped exclusively

by prayer, confession of faith, Psalms and music, it is readily seen that a great radical change in the form of worship had taken place: The people at large knew of no form of worship other than prayer and song, and even at the Temple in Jerusalem the sacrificial cult was set into a brilliant liturgical and musical frame, which seemingly glorified it, but which in reality weakened its significance and, consequently, its position as an indispensable element of religious devotion.

And also this development of divine worship may be best understood as a compromise between the different tendencies of the age: Priests and Levites found a welcome opportunity for pompous functions; the adherents of mystical tendencies found, in poetry and music, opportunity for artistic activation of their high-tuned aesthetical sentiment; and the authoritative representatives of rigid monotheism, they, too, found their calculation in the growing importance of liturgy with its consequent spiritualization of the sacrificial cult. If, therefore, the Chronist grants first rank especially to the Levites with their Psalms and their music on the highest historical functions of state, he simply projects the conditions of his time into the past, a procedure which contributed greatly to a more spiritual conception of the past.

Particularly instructive is the way how the Chronist seeks to justify these Levitical functions in the past in sight of the fact that in the national document, the Torah, there is hardly anything about liturgy, practically nothing about song and music with sacrifices, and absolutely nothing about liturgical and musical functions of his beloved Levites (comp. above). Certain intimations in Chronicles suggest that some of the promoters of music in the Temple have played with the thought of revivifying music as an instrument of prophecy (prediction of the future). This may have contributed to bring about the fact noted above that even after the admittance of music into the Temple under exclusion of its mantical sub-feature (comp. above about Urim—ve Thumim), the authoritative representatives of Judaism could not bring themselves to permit the slighest hint at the musical functions of the Levites in the Torah. Thus legally this whole institution had been pending in the air, as it were. It is this inconvenience that the Chronist is trying to meet:

The book of Chronicles, representing, as it is, a conception of Jewish history under the dynastic aspect of the Davidides, ascribes to David legislative authority after Moses. David was the first King of Israel in the period of whose reign the name JHVH was dominating, while in the time of the reign of Saul the name Elohim was dominating, meaning that in his time there was no mercy (comp. I Chr. IV, 10; V, 20.22 with VI, 16.17; also comp. I Chr. X, 13-XI, 1-8). The Chronist relates in a very circumstancial account how *David* introduced the Levitic functions of song and music in the Temple, often emphasizing that this has been created by David through *divine inspiration* as a *legal* institution with binding power. This effort on the part of the Chronist shows clearly that the notion of a Tradition going back to Moses had not yet been conceived, or, at least, not yet generally accepted, in those days. The fact, however, that the Talmudists were strenuously looking for a passage in the Torah on which to base the institution of Levites singing and playing in conjunction with the sacrifices, ignoring the attempt of the Chronist to cover it with the authority of David altogether, shows conclusively that they were hesitating to concede legislative authority to any historic personality other than Moses. At any rate, the attempt of the Chronist bears witness to the actuality of the question in those days as to how to justify later developments in the religious practice.

This imparts to us further insight into the conception of Oral Tradition. Oral Tradition as *interpretation* of the written law evolved from the compromise-combinations of the several law-codes. Oral tradition again as *new institutions* they would ascribe to great historical authorities. In most instances this had some justification in historical reality: In the case of the institution under discussion, we know that the personality of David had been brought into some connection with religious music (cf. above). And even though the attempt of the Chronist to give David legislative authority failed of recognition, the instutition being derived rather, by remote interpretation, from the Torah, it was not altogether unsuccessful: Our Tradition recognizes David as the "Psalmist" and as the *reorganizer* of the institution of Levitical music (Main account of the organization of the Levites for Psalms, songs and music: I Chr. ch. XXV; note verses 1-3: music and

Psalms were introduced by David as a prophetic institution: David's legislative authority for this institution strongly emphasized: 2Chr. XXIII, 18;
XXIX, 25-30; XXXV, 15; Esra III, 10; Neh. XII, 45-
47; other passages: I Chr. VI, 18f; IX, 33; XV, 16.
19-29; XVI, 4-7.42; 2 Chr. V, 12.13; VII, 6; IX, 11;
XXII, 13: a *palace revolution* to the accompaniment
of Psalms and music!   Neh. XII, 27).

The tracing of the institution of Levitical music
is but one case, typical for many others of the same
character.   Most of the new institutions not provided for in the Torah, are the creation of this period,
going under the name of "Sopheric Institutions" or
"Sopheric Commandments". Talmudic tradition knows
of different titles of official legislative and administra-
tive bodies supposed to have existed in our period: "Esra
and his Assistants", the "Men of the Great Synagogue"
then again (for the Greek period) "Synhedrin" or the
"Great Synhedrin", the Great Beth-Din (Court) or
the "Great Beth-Din in the Hewn (Stone) Hall" and
others.   This tradition is rather conflicting with the
information found in Josephus and other Graeco-
Jewish writers.   And there have been many attempts
made to harmonize these traditions or to prove the
correctness of one at the expense of the other.   But
no matter which stand we take in this question, there
can be no reasonable doubt that, except for interruptions in times of radical political or military up-
heavals, there had always been some sort of supreme
religious authority at Jerusalem.   It may be doubt-
ful whether this supreme authority had any compe-
tence in the political and judicial administration, or

whether there were other, secular, bodies alongside the religious authority to take care of the non-religious branches of administration (as, indeed, it was the case, for a certain period at least). But from all we can see in the sources, it was the undisputed function of that (religious) body to sanction all new institutions, evolved either from interpretation or from the conditions of the time, and to surround them with the necessary legal authority by regulating the details and determining the sphere of their validity. By this, however, we do not intend to minimize the evidence of the general tendency in talmudic literature, that the authority of the Soperim in itself did not deem sufficient. This may be due in part to the controversy between Pharisees and Sadducees, when two conflicting traditions were facing each other. But even in cases where there was no opposition, a backing in the Torah is always the much desired source of authority: Usually they would trace a given institution to some great biblical personality, at the same time, however, refer to some passage in the Torah where this or that, new, or enlargement of an old, institution is hinted at by virtue of some hermeneutical rule: They followed the Chronist in the idea of tracing new institutions to biblical personalities, but refused acceptance of his suggestion to recognize any binding legislative authority to any personality other than Moses.

5. Daniel and Koheleth.

These two biblical books, the last to be discussed here, may be very different in content and literary character. Yet, under the aspect decisive here they will be best understood in a joint discussion:

Both of these books deal primarily with the problem of justice. Daniel treats the *national - historical*, Koheleth the *individual*, problem of justice. Daniel arrives at a *positive*, Koheleth at 'a *negative* solution, both, concerning the reality of justice in general, as also concerning the *eschatological* solution. These positive and negative points of contact between these two, also chronologically contiguous, books will impart to us most valuable information about the spiritual, notably about the eschatological currents of their time, currents which produced and determined the eschatological hopes of Judaism for thousands of years to come.

The book of Daniel in its present shape has as its objective the defense of divine justice in history, at the same time, however, paying attention also to the problem of individual justice. And though the treatment of this latter problem here is not nearly as detailed as in Ezekiel, nevertheless Daniel can be best understood out of Ezekiel. The book follows Ezekiel in the doctrine of *angels* and *Mercabah*, and, most particularly, in the solutions suggested and formulated in the defense of justice. In the general solution of the national problem of justice, namely in the prophetic vision of restoration, the final redactor of the book of Daniel follows all previous prophets and writers. But, in addition, he converts the picture of the dry bones in the Valley becoming reanimated by the "Ruah JHVH" and reorganizing to new life, used by Ezekiel as a symbol of political resurrection, into reality. He teaches real bodily *resurrection* of the dead as a part of the working of justice at the time of judgment. National justice will realize in the resurrection of the nation, and individual justice in the resurrection of the individuals, both the just and the unjust. The just will wake up to eternal life, the unjust to eternal torture (XII, 2.3; the national solution in the Visions and in ch. XII in its entirety). This is the only place in the whole Bible where the individual eschatological hope is given such clear and unequivocal expression. This may be explained by the important part this doctrine played in the great martyrdom of the Maccabean period, as evidenced in contemporary Graeco-Jewish literature (Book of Jubilees, Enoch, 2 Maccabean and others).

But in that literature also the other conception of the individual-eschatological solution, namely that of *spiritual immortality* immediately after death, is discussed with fervid insistence. And we have seen that it was this conception of the individual solution which has been suggested in Job and given a more or less definite expression of hope in Psalms. Now if in spite of this indisputable fact, no book, nay no sentence, has been admitted into the canon in which the hope for individual immortality is given such clear expression, as the doctrine of bodily resurrection in the book of Daniel, this had *two* reasons, one *dogmatical* and one *historical*. *Dogmatically* there was

the apprehension lest the doctrine of the individual
continuing life in spiritual immortality right after
death becomes an added incentive to necromantical
practices, which just at that time, under Greek influences, were more in vogue than in the immediately
preceding age.   It is for this reason that the Pharisees preferred to give the people the unphilosophic
conception of immortality: The dead is sunken in a
long deep sleep from which he will wake up on the day
of resurrection. · The *historical* reason resulted from
the controversies between *Pharisees* and *Sadducees.*
The latter rejected bodily resurrection, but not (as
erroneously believed) also spiritual immortality of
the soul.   This accounts for the fact that the doctrine of bodily resurrection had been enacted as a
dogma in Judaism prior to the enactment of the doctrine of spiritual immortality of the soul (cf. for the
whole of the preceding discussion, Toldoth I chs. V-
VII, p. 161-181).

   But that time, the time of the most deep-going
eschatological excitement, and in which, more than
in all the preceding biblical development, justice
was defended with clearly and unequivocally formulated eschatological hopes, was not lacking in
counter-currents of radical despair of the reality of
justice altogether, thwarting all suggested solutions
in its defense, notably the hope of the individual for
eschatological justice.   The great strength of the
individual eschatological hope in those times is accounted for in part by the very efficient succor it
received from Plato, who plays the idea of individual
spiritual immortality as the last trump in his defense

of justice.   And it could not fail to pass that also in Jewish circles a man should arise who felt attracted by the arguments against justice advanced in some of the Platonic dialogues.   And thus one writer undertook it to give expression to these subversive moods, possibly swaying the minds of many in his sphere, in a book.   This is the book of *Koheleth*:

The heretical, or rather semi-heretical, views found in Koheleth are by no means new in biblical literature.   On the contrary, in many biblical books we find views much more radical than those advocated by the author of the book of Koheleth.   This is especially true of the heretical views mentioned in Job and Psalms.   The difference, however, is this: Everywhere else in the Bible those views are mentioned by prophets, Psalmists and writers, only in order to refute them, while the author of Koheleth voices the semi-radical views presented as his own convictions. Of course, in its present shape the book contains some later interpolations, which, wholly or partly, *neutralize* the heretical views uttered.   But if we disregard these few, easily recognized, sentences, the book of Koheleth may be best characterized as the *Jewish Philebos* (Plato's philosophy, being largely the philosophy of justice, swings around the two aspects of the problem: *What* is justice? and *Which* is the *happier life*, that of the just, or that of the unjust?   This is especially evident in The State, the positive result of the dialogue being the answer to the question of justice in its two formulations.   The problem of justice in its second formulation is the problem to the minute discussion of which Plato has devoted his dialogue

Philebos). What is better, *Phronesis* (-Sophia, Wisdom),
or *Hedone* (Pleasure)? This is the problem of
Koheleth: What is better—*Hochma* (Wisdom), or
Holeluth and *Sichluth* (Pleasure; Ignorance — Angoia)?

The general discussion of the problem goes on in
a reflection on all enjoyments life offers, under the
Platonic schedule of the *Three Passions*: *Eating,
Drinking* and *Secsual gratification*, and extending over
the other, subsidiary, ways of spending the energies
of life.   The solusion at which Koheleth arrives, is
different from that of Plato.   The latter arrives at
the positive result that Phronesis, life under wisdom
and justice, is preferable to Hedone and Agnoia, life
under pleasure and ignorance.   Koheleth, on the
contrary, arrives at the negative result: All is Vanity,
both, Hochma and Holeluth, are bitterly disappoint-
ing in the end (cf. Gesch, der jued, Philosophie II,
1. p. 355).

The best philosophy of life. according to Koheleth,
is not to hang after delusions, to enjoy everything
within one's reach, but with temperance and judgment
under the guidance of certain practical rules of life.
Of such rules the author offers a goodly number in the
form of gnomic epigrams, like those in Proverbs:
They are mostly in the nature of practical advise:
Be careful, do not burn the candle at both ends.
Some of them refer to the *political* behavior of the
individual, and betray the influence of the Platonic
idea of the *ideal king*, which we have also perceived
in Psalms and Proverbs (Koh. X, 16-20).

Koheleth starts out with a typical Platonic problem, but his philosophy of life betrays the disposition

of the *Stoic Sage*, with a quite perceptible woof of *Epicureanism* in between. Plato discusses the problem under the definite assumption that one of the two, Phronesis or Hedone, must be the right way of living· Koheleth, on the other hand, while coming to the seemingly definite conclusion that neither of the two can claim the title, refuses to commit himself even to this negative conclusion: It is true, all is vanity of vanities, but do not get excited over that, either. There is nothing that can claim the title of absolute value, but man should bear it resignedly. This is the immutable course of things, in which man may, as best he can, modestly fit in his own little existence, and make up his mind to do it cheerfully at that (Stoic element). To enjoy life? Yes, as much as you just can, but in a way guaranteeing your safety against self-destruction (Epicurean element). God? Of course, there is a supreme divine Being, but Kolheleth has his very own view on the relation of the divine to the human. He differs not only with Judaism and Plato, but also with the Stoics and Epicureans who have influenced him against Plato. Judaism teaches the ethico-cosmological God-conception, the God of justice. So does Plato, who analyzes this doctrine into the three theological postulates which also in the Bible occupy the center of interest: He who professes these three postulates, believing *firstly*, in the existence of God as the cosmological principle, *secondly* in His omniscience and His providence over world and man, and, *finally*, in His impartial justice to be bribed by no human gift, flattery or sacrifice, he believes in the God of justice and retribution. The

Stoics deny divine personality, wherefore the two last postulates are out of congruence with their God-conception. Epicure would admit the first, and perhaps also the first half of the second, postulate, God's omniscience, but denies divine influence on the events in this world, especially in the sphere of man, his activities and relations, wherefore the third postulate is out of congruence with his God-conception. Koheleth, however, admits all three postulates. God exists, He is the creator of the world, He knows everything about it, interferes in the affairs of man, and He cannot be bribed by sacrifices, either. But, maintains Koheleth, the profession of the three postulates by no means permits us to speak of divine *providence in justice.* The very postulate of God not being accessible to any kind of bribe precludes the idea of providence on the basis of man's religious and ethical conduct (note especially IX, 1-3). So the most decisive aspect of providence in justice is self-contradicting. Koheleth follows Plato in centering his thoughts on the problem of justice, but he does so in the opposite sense: Reality imparts to us unequivocally the idea that there is but a very loose relation between the conduct of man and his fate in life, and that, at any rate, this relation does not extend beyond the validity of the practical rules of life. The thought of securing one's prosperity and happiness through a perfect religious and ethical life, appears indeed very remote. Quite likely, God exerts some providence over the world, and possibly there is something to it, to adopt certain commandments and rules of life which are generally considered as divine. In the first place, of course, this refers to the ethical laws,

but there may be some merit even in the ritual pre-
cepts; at times it may even be advisable to bring
sacrifices (comp. IV, 17 and V, 3-4 with the attitude
taken in the book of Jonah and in some Psalms; these
verses, however, may be, or at least contain, later
interpolations).   But the thought that we be in a
position to secure for ourselves divine favor, as it
were, is clearly to be rejected as against the obvious
reality of things.   No doubt, God *has* his plan, thus
far Koheleth yields to the convincing power of the
cosmological proof, as advanced by Deutero-Isaiah.
Job and Plato.   But not only did He fail to really
disclose to us His plan, but, on the contrary, He guards
it jealously as His *mystery*, and all attempts at finding
it out in order to arrange our lives accordingly, are,
from the outset, doomed to failure.   Many tried it, but
reality bears indisputable testimony that all these attempts, as they were unsuccessful in the past, so will
they hopelessly fail in all future (The central problem:
III, 10-17; the last words of verses 14 and 15 decidedly
later additions; V, 1 in the sense of III, 11 and VIII,
17; IX, 5; God's plan not revealed to man; V, 2 and 6:
against *dreams* as a means of communication between
God and man?   Verses 3-4, as also the end of 5
evidently later additions, but not so much on the
score of the angel in 5, as this could well be harmonized with the general attitude of Koheleth to traditional conceptions of things; VII, 15-18: conclusion of
18 later addition; VIII, 14; verses 12 and 13 later
additions; IX, 1-4.11.12).

Expectedly, Koheleth knows all the arguments
advanced in the defense of justice, but he refutes
them as wholly inconclusive:

First of all, the very basis on which the whole idea of providence in justice rests, namely *freedom of man's will*, is quite prolematical (VI, 10; VII, 20; VIII, 4, 11; IX, 1.12).   Of the individual arguments or explanations in the defense of justice, Koheleth would not admit that the *cosmological proof* proves more than divine omniscience, intention and plan, but by no means the reality of what we consider justice.   Of divine mercy manifest in the living nature which the author of the book of Job advances as an argument for the reality of justice, Koheleth takes no cognizance: The evident cruelty in the world of *man* weighs more.   Koheleth denies the doctrine of mercy.   He never uses the name of JHVH, rather using "ha-Elohim" "the God" (comp. Greek "ho-Theos"; cf. Gesch. der jued. Philosophie II, 1, p 179-189).

This disposes of the arguments of *long-suffering*, meant to account for the prosperity of the wicked, and of *family retribution*, meant to account for both, the prosperity of the wicked, and the misfortune of the just (cf. VIII, 12.13, where the argument of long-suffering is evidently a later interpolation).

The argument of family retribution is additionally dealt with in particular, and expressly refuted: Reality speaks against the idea of family account of sin beyond the necessary effects of natural causes.   And also the Epicurean egotistical attitude is brought to bear against the argument of family account: I cannot be rewarded in a future which is not mine own (II, 18-21; VI, 8.13-15; VI, 1.2).

Notably strong are the objections which Koheleth advances against the *eschatological hopes* of the individual as a remedy for the obvious injustice prevailing in *this* world. He refutes the suggestion of retribution in the *Sheol*, bodily *resurrection*, or spiritual *immortality:* He seems to lean toward the view that the "Ruah" (spirit) which animates the body of man, returns to God, at least he leaves this question open. But this would only much the more accentuate the futility of all eschatological hope for justice in the Hereafter: The return of the human Ruah to God extinguishes all individual existence (comp. above to Psalms). Bodily resurrection, again, is altogether out of the question: The body resolves in dust and thus returns to the earth from which it has come (III, 18-21; VIII, 8; IX, 4-10; XI, 5; XII, 1-7; the concluding verse is Koheleth's last trump against the eschatalogical suggestion in the defense of justice: The decay of man's body already sets in with the marasmus of old age, and after death the dust returns to its origin, *Earth*, just as the spirit returns to its origin, *God*. This verse, XII, 7, was taken for a positive statement in favor of spiritual immortality. This then, was found to be in contradiction with III, 19-21. There the return of the dust to earth is positively asserted, while as to the spirit of man there is first a positive statement identifying it with the general animalic principle of breath, and then an unanswered question whether the Ruah of man may not, after all, be different from the animalic breath and "go upward". For this reason some consider XII, 7 a later interpolation. But there is really no contradiction: In III, 21 the higher quality of the human Ruah is reflectively considered, in XII, 7, on the other hand, the return of the Ruah to God is advanced as an argument against individual immortality; cf. Gen. III, 19 and the Psalms treated above, notably Ps. CIII, 14-16 and CIV, 29.30.—Koheleth XII, 10-14 is a later addition in order to conclude the book with a statement neutralizing the philosophy of life genuine to the book.

We know that controversies were going on as late as in the early Tannaitic period about the admittance of the book of Koheleth into the Canon. Now we understand perfectly well the position of the opponents, but the position of those in favor of the book and, most especially, the final favorable decision, is nothing short of a puzzle. There were such controversies also about other books: about *Ezekiel* on account of Mercabeh and some contradicting laws, about *Proverbs* on account of the theory of ideas, about *Song* of *Songs* on account of its erotic character, and about *Esther*, evidently, on account of its advocating the idea that under certain circumstances the marriage between a Jewess and a non-Jewish potentate may be tolerated or even encouraged (and, perhaps, also out of opposition to the celebration of Purim, altogether, quite perceptibly felt in some talmudic sources). The difference, however, is this. We can well understand that the authoritative representatives of Judaism ultimately felt constrained to yield to the popular mystical proclivities and practical demands. But there is nothing on the face of things that may have moved the authorities to adapt, by additions (and, perhaps, also by eliminations), a book as subversive of the essential doctrines of Judaism as the book of Koheleth, to a very much lowered

minimum-standard, in order to force it into the
Canon. Why did they not "take care" of the book
altogether, as in the case of many an other book
which now belongs to the Apocrypha? The most convenient explanation, of course, would be, if we could
say that the authorities desired to preserve for future
generations the literary monuments of all spiritual
currents in the course of the ages. But this would
assume rather too much of a literary conscience in
the modern sense. We, indeed, consider it a most
fortunate contingency that also such a literary product as Koheleth was preserved for us, in which we
learn of the presence in that period of a current of
thought which, whatever its merits, bears testimony
to a highly philosophical capacity of mind. In other
biblical books these currents are presented to us in
formulations conceived by the pious writers for the
purpose of their refutation. In the book of Koheleth,
on the other hand, the views of the opponents of
Judaism are given to us in a certain measure of
systematic coherence not much altered by the later,
easily isolated, pious additions and changes. This,
as has been said, is *our* appreciation of the book.
The authorities of Judaism in the time of the final
closing of the Canon, however, must have had some
more practical end in view in adopting this book into
the Canon. Perhaps we may not go amiss in pre-
suming that in admitting all and any of those books
to which there was strong opposition, the idea was
decisive that to retain the objectionable views within
the Canon and follow them up closely with what
they considered efficient refutations, will be much

more beneficial to the religious development of later generations than it would be if those views were entirely suppressed. This idea, frequently suggested by the Talmudists, sharpens down to the famous imperative of the Mishnah: "And know what to answer to the Epicurean!" The preservation of the book was also made less difficult by the fact that it expounds no God-denying heresy. On the contrary, it is borne by deep religiosity of a very sincere character. The attitude of the book may be styled a systematic elaboration of the very last solution of the problem of justice suggested in the book of Job: We cannot comprehend the divine plan. Thus far Koheleth goes with the author of Job. They differ, though, in the consequences which they draw from this sentence. The author of Job concludes: Justice as we understand it, is a reality, but we do not know how to explain the seemingly contradicting realities. Koheleth, on the contrary, concludes: Man cannot comprehend the ways of God, consequently he has no right to postulate a sort of justice of his own construction, and how much less to assume its reality.

But whatever may have been the reason for retaining Koheleth, and the other biblical books mentioned, in the Canon, to us this decision means an invaluable fortunate occurrence. These books are of so great a value to us not only because they preserved to us some currents of thought deviating even in biblical times from the authoritative attitude, but also for another reason:

These books offer us the possibility to conceive and to comprehend the most relevant currents in the spiritual development of Judaism in the ages to come, out of the different currents in biblical times:

6.   OUTLOOK INTO POST-BIBLICAL DEVELOPMENTS.

Judaism in biblical times, we have seen, was going on developing amid intense struggle with the great world-cultures of antiquity. Babylonia, Assyria, Egypt, the nations of Canaan, Neo-Babylonia, Persia and Greece—these are the great World-Powers of civilization and culture, against which Judaism in biblical times had to fight for a spiritual existence of its own. But these struggles were not merely negative, *defensive*, but rather struggles for the *assimilation of new elements*, throes of birth. From these travails Judaism came out the richer and the deeper. And if we consider that to these great powers of civilization we must add only the *Roman* element to have mentioned *all* historical elements of civilization and culture, it is easily seen why the development of biblical times was preformative and directive for all ages to come. It has been shown in what preceded how liturgy as a confession of faith, as also the conception of written and oral law, have evolved from the conditions of biblical developments. But the preformative impetus of historical junctures and situations in biblical times manifest itself not only in the direct authoritative line of development, but in all currents in post-biblical Judaism, also in times when the demarcation line between authoritative and non-authoritative is almost, even if not altogether, impossible of determination:

Of the *two lines* of development which appear on our horizon as the direct continuation of the biblical development, the *talmudic* is more *authoritative* than the Alexandrian. Nevertheless, the latter may be designated as the more direct continuation of the Bible as literature. Many literary units of the Graeco-Jewish period, known by the name of Apocrypha, appear in biblical garb, and were undoubtedly advanced with the claim to be recognized as such and to be embodied into the Canon. These claims were refused, for many, chiefly, however, for dogmatical, reasons, owing to which even some of our present biblical books barely escaped exclusion. Graeco-Jewish literature, taken in its entirety, is plainly a more intense cultivation of those tributaries and under-currents owing to whose influences the position of the above biblical books in the Canon was very much labile way down into Tannaitic times.

One group of the Apocryphal books cultivates the doctrine of *Mercabah* and *angels* (Jubilees, Enoch, Baruch, Esra Books, and others), while another cultivates the *theory of ideas* in different degrees of intensity and in different formulations, chiefly as the *Logos*-theory, or as the agadistic version of the theory of ideas, according to which only a number of revered things, such as Torah, Israel, Sanctuary and others, were supposed to have had some sort of pre-existence in heavenly patterns (Sirach, Ascension of Moses, the Wisdoms of Solomon, and others). Even more decisively in this entire literature marked as a continuation of biblical literature, by one tendency common to all products of Graeco-Jewish lit-

erature.   It is this the tendency to present matters
in such a light as to make it evident that the *Jewish
Constitution* not only reaches, but even surpasses the
level of Plato's *Ideal Constitution*, and that the philosophy of Judaism contains all that is good in Plato's
philosohpy.   This tendency brought it about that the
problem of justice in this literature forms the nucleus
of all formation of thought, and thus easily links up
with the same phenomenon in biblical literature,
notably in Ezekiel, Job, Psalms, Proverbs, Daniel
and Koheleth.   Considered from this point of view,
the writings of Graeco-Jewish literature may be divided into two groups, one *historical* and one *philosophical*.   To the first belong those literary units
which present the history of the Jews under the
aspect of the ideal constitution, combining the Platonic cardinal virtues with the ideal of the Thirteen.
Their avowed purpose is to show that all historical
development of the world at large had for its aim
the preparation and creation of the Jewish state under the dominion of the Torah as the ideal constitution, and, also, that all historical events, for good
and evil, were, respectively, the effects of obedience
and disobedience to the postulates of that constitution.   These writings cultivate chiefly *philosophy
of history*, in that they treat philosophic problems,
notably those in the sphere of the problem of justice,
in a way subsidiary to their conception of history.
This group of writings which took as their themes
the most prominent events in Jewish history, find
their most comprehensive representative in *Josephus*.
The other, the *philosophic*, group undertakes it to

give a presentation of the philosophy of Judaism or the "fatherlandish philosophy," as some of them say, in such a wise as to accentuate those points in which indeed there is great similarity in Judaism and Platonism. The *historical sketches*, usually at the end of these writings, serve only as illustration. This group finds its most comprehensive representative in *Philo*, whose writings again may be divided into two groups in the same way as Graeco-Jewish literature at large.

These writers take much from Plato, but their philosophy of history is a continuation of the biblical way of thinking. For philosophy of history of this kind there is no model in Plato, or even in general Greek literature. The models for this line of thought they found exclusively in biblical literature. In artistic form of presentation this literature is best characterized as a blend of the biblical *motif of attributes* and the same motif in the dialogues of Plato. In some of these writings this genre of literary composition achieves a very high degree of mutual interpenetration of thought and artistic suppleness of form.

The large majority of these literary products were written not only for *apologetic*, but also for *propaganda*, purposes. They were calculated not only to defend Judaism against the then frequent attacks from Greek writers, but also to win the non-Jewish world for Judaism. By their philosophy of history those writers were led to believe that Judaism is destined to become the *world-religion*. This movement led ultimately to the rise of *Christianity*. At the time, however, when Christianity had become a great power menacing the very existence of Judaism, there were no Graeco-Jewish writers any more to combat the effects of their own creation.   It was then that *talmudic* Judaism, quietly developed alongside Graeco-Jewish literature, stepped in the breach.   Early Christology evolved from, and on the basis of, the doctrines of *Mercabah* and *angels*.   And so the authoritative representatives of Judaism of that age, the *House* of *Hillel*, under the leadership of *Rabbi Johanan ben Saccai*, felt constrained to abandon their reserved attitude, and to cultivate the mysteries of *Mercabah* (מעשה מרכבה) and to formulate these old doctrines in such a way as to combat the aggressive new religion on its own ground.   Later Christology, on the other hand, was based on the theory of ideas, notably on the Logos-theory, in order to further *antinomism*, or anti-legalism, which then had become the most tangible point of difference between Judaism and Christianity: *Jesus* was the Logos, the *Word* of God, the eternal *living Word* of God, which attribute gave him the power to abrogate the Torah, the *temporary word* of God written with perishable ink on the scroll.   In order to combat this new phase of Christology, Rabbi Akiba introduced the mysteries of *Bereshith* (מיעשה בראשית) so as to be able to fight antinomistic Christianity on its own ground.   This is again the repetition of a situation which was preformed in biblical times: Mercabah and Bereshith go back to the schools of Ezekiel and Jeremiah, respectively.

These mystical disciplines were fraught with great danger to authoritative Judism.   Mercabah meant a weakening of the principle of *unity*, and contained in its mysteries the elements of the doctrine of *emanation* of matter from God, thus weakening the principle of *incorporeality*. Bereshith led up to the doctrine of *eternal primary matter* alongside of God, thus to a *duality* of principles, and, within the spiritual principle, to *plurality*, the Ideas having been considered eternal heavenly beings independent of God in their existence, even though dependent on Him as to their activation. Judaism safely resisted these encroachments and victoriously warded off all these dangers. The *Mishnah*, the foremost and authoritative talmudical document of its time (about 200 C. E.), established the principle of creation of all beings outside of God and won for it undisputed authority: Now one could believe in Mercabah, angels, ideas and primary matter, as long as he believed that all these things were creatures of God, not eternal beings as was believed before.

This decisive change from the mystical to the relatively philosophical mode of thinking was greatly aided by the powerful development of the *Halacha* (הלכה), or the legal-logical form in the discussion of the law, not only in its legal branch proper (civil and penal law), but in its ritual branch as well. The logical maturity which resulted from the development of halachistic discussion, bade restraint to all mystical proclivities. In *Palestine*, the original seat of mystical speculations in Tannaitic times, where there was a certain disinclination toward exaggeratedly sharp-minded, hair-splitting, dialectics in halachistic discussion, the mystical disciplines were cultivated more intensely, and for a longer period of time. But soon the center of Judaism was transplanted from Palestine to *Babylonia*. *Rabh*, the founder of this new center of Judaism (about 230) brought with him a fairly well developed mystical system from Palestine. But this system was nearly free from Mercabah elements, being rather a quite acceptable philosophic conception of the theory of ideas, in spite of his insistence on the principle of creation which the philosophical schools in Greece and Rome have found irreconcilable with the theory of ideas. More decisive is the fact that in Babylonia where the dialectical development of the Halacha has reached its zenith, the inclination to mystical speculations was almost entirely absent. Indeed, the field of *Agadah* (homiletical interpretation of Scripture) in general was cultivated but little in the schools and academies of Babylonia. And the little they would cultivate, belonged either to the non-mystical, philosophic, or to the general homiletical, Agadah.

The non-mystical philosophic Agada developed throughout the talmudic period partly out of its own potentialities, partly, however, also by the force of outward circumstances and relations, as the Talmudists often were forced to discuss philosophic problems, such as God's unity, omniscience and omnipresence, notably questions of philosophy of history, with philosophically educated Roman potentates, and with Christian or neo-Persian sectarians of all sorts. In talmudic Agadah, consisting as it does mostly of *aphoristic sayings*, there can be no thought of composition in artistic motifs. But if we investigate into the deeper mutual relations of the aphoristically presented thoughts, we find that talmudic speculation, too, is a system of thought conceived in the combined biblical-Platonic *motif of attributes*. The new departure in talmudic literature, over and above the biblical way of expression, is the development of *logical dialectics*.

This prepared the Jews for the influence of *Aristotle*. After the final redaction of the Babylonian Talmud (ab. 550), in the *Midrashic* literature of the *Geonic* period, we find the mystical disciplines of Mercabah and Bereshith flourishing again. And at the end of the eighth or the beginning of the ninth century a finished product of the theory of ideas appears on the horizon, the "Book of Jecirah (Creation)". The book evidently evolved out of the school of Rabh in Babylonia, and the first philosophic writings of Jewish Middle Ages which made their appearance with the reawakening of the spirit of the Halacha (second half of ninth century), were *commentaries* to the Book of Jecirah. But the Book of Jecirah contains also some (later interpolated) elements of Mercabah, and so it came about that that book had become also, and in a more marked degree, the basis of the medieval mystical discipline of *Cabbalah*. In fact, the Book of Jecirah has been throughout the ages, as it is today, the recognized authoritative *text-book* of Cabbalah.

The development of dialectical philospohy proper toward the end of the ninth century was due specifically to *two factors: One* is the *new contact* of the Jews with *Greek philosophy*, notably with the philosophy of Aristotle. This evolved from the Christian-

Syrian schools of philosophy of the fourth and fifth centuries, in conjunction with the academy in Gondashapur (530-750) and the later developed Arabic seats of learning, science and philosophy. The *second factor* was the *Karaitic movement*. The Karaites attacked the Mercabah doctrines of the Talmudist for their anthromorphic God-conception in order to shake the confidence of the people in talmudic tradition. The Karaites themselves joined the liberal theological school of the Arabs, the *Mutazila*, who professed a doctrine based on the theory of ideas, as against the orthodox school of Arabic theologians whose doctrine was based on Mercabah (both of these parties having built up their theories under Jewish influence).

This led the authoritative wing of Judaism, the *Rabbanites*, to philosophy. And they even surpassed the Karaites in that they rejected not only the theory of Mercabah, rejected by the Karaites, but also the theory of ideas, professed by the latter. They could not remove the incriminated passages from talmudic literature, but they removed their contents by *rational interpretation*. This was chiefly done by the *Eastern School* of Jewish philosophers of which *Saadya* (892-942) was the foremost representative, the *Saadya-group*. This group base their philosophy on Aristotle's *Physics*, which is free from all mysticism. Then, under the influence of the Arabic Neo-Platonic Aristotelians and other mystical schools, there developed the *Western School* of Jewish philosophers, led by *Gabirol* (1021-1070), the Gabiral-group, on the ground of Aristotle's

Metaphysics, which is much nearer to Platonic
mysticism. The members of this group were no
Neo-Platonists, at least as far as the principles go.
But compared with each other we may say that the
Saadya-group and the Gabirol-group are, respectively,
the late representatives of the schools of Jeremiah
and Ezekiel in biblical times. Maimuni (1135-1204)
then tried to unite the authoritatively acceptable
elements of both groups. Then the mystical discipline of *Cabbalah* which during the classical period
of Jewish philosophy (IX-XII centuries) was going
through the preparatory phases in a *latent* development, appeared forcefully on the horizon of Jewish
thought. Now Philosophy and Cabbalah represent,
respectively, the schools of Jeremiah and Ezekiel
of biblical times.

And again both of these schools of thought
develop under the sign of the motif of attributes,
Cabbalah under the combined biblical-Platonic, philosophy under the same, but differentiated by a hue
of Aristotelian, thought. All problems of medieval
Jewish philosophy evolve out of the problem of
attributes and are discussed and solved in intimate
interrelation with it: all after the pattern we know
from biblical times. With some of the representatives of the Gabirol-group the motif of attributes
blooms forth new variations as an artistic literary
motif of composition.

No details could be given in this outlook. But the
foregoing will suffice to confirm our general thesis
that the development of Jewish thought in biblical
times was decisively preformative and forcefully

directive for all future developments. Historical events and relations continuously brought new elements and new motifs in the evolution of thought, but the basic tendencies of the spiritual currents in speculative thoughts and cultural manifestations remained the same. And this can be shown also of the essential formations of modern times.

The full treatment of any one of these periods require s a book for itself.

BIBLE REFERENCES

THORA.

GENESIS.

EXODUS.

LEVITICUS.

Book: xl-xli; I-VII: 89; I-XVI: xxi; I, 1: 188; IV-V: 196; IX, 22-24: 193; X, 3: 187; XI, 44.45: 203; XVII-XXVI: xxi. 210; XVIII, 21: 203; XIX, 1.8.12: 203; XX, 3.7.8.26: 203; 6: 188; XXII, 2-9.10.32: 203; XXV, 17.23: 204; XXVI: xxii; XXVII: xxi.

NUMBERS.

Book: xvii.xxi.xli-xlij; VI, 23-VII, lf.: 193; VI, 24-27: 29; VII, 89: 188; XI, 24-29: 44; XII: 47; 1-8: 44; 6-8: 45; XV, 22-31: 195; 37f.: xxi; XVI, 3.22: 187; 30.33: 50; XX-XXIV: 49; XX, 12.13: 187; XXI, 8.9: 44; 9:65; 14: 81; XXII: 47; 20-35: 44; 22.23: 120; XXV, 11-13: 195; XXVII, 16: 187; XXVIII, 11: 187; XXXV, 16-21: 197.

DEUTERONOMY.

Book: Index.xvii.xxi.xlii.20.22.23.46-48.57-60.72.74.79.83-87. 190.215.217; I-IV: xxi; IV, 8-44: 114; 19: 136; V-VIII: 60; V-XI: xxi.74; V-XXVI: 23; V, 4.5.19-23: 47; 8: 73.77; 9: 58; 26: 49; VI, 4: 41; 5: 84; 9-18: 77; VII, 1-5: 20; 5: 73; VIII, 7-20: 77; 10: 41; 11-18: 49.60; IX-XI: 60; IX, 1: 77; 14: 23; X, 17-20: 59; XI, 26f.: 49.60; XII: 73; XII-XXVI: xxi.60.77; XIII, 2-6: 47.48; 12: 85; XIV, 1-21: 60; 21.29: 59; XV, 12: 114; XVI, 1-17: 73; 11-14: 59; 18f.: 86; XVII, 8-13: 86; 12.13: 85; 16: 59; 17-20: 73; XVIII, 9-13: 58; 9-22: 47; 18: 104; 21.22: 48; XIX, 20: 85; XX, 10-20: 58; XXI, 21: 85; XXIII, 6: 49; 8.9: 59; XXIV, 9: 23; 14.17: 59; 16: 58; 19-22: 59; XXVI, 5: 181; 5-13: 59; XXVII: xxi.169; XXVIII: xxi.23.49.58.72.74; 20: 19; XXIX-XXXIV: xxi; XXIX, 3: 104; 5: 136; XXX, 2: 45; XXXII, 51: 187; XXXIV, 9: 187.

JOSHUA.

Book: xvi.xx.32; V, 13-14: 202; X, 13: 81.120; XXII, 17-20: 195; XXIV: 35; 19: 32; 26: 67.

JUDGES.

Book: xvi.18.32; II, 1-5: 44.45; V, 4.5.23:45; VI, 11-24: 44; 22: 8; 23.24: 195; 24: 194.

1 SAMUEL.

Book: xvi.38; II, 25: 49; III, 1-4: 44; V, 1: 44; VII, 2: 44;IX, 1: 44; X, 5: 78; 12: 239; 16.20.22: 44; XV, 23:46; XVI, 15-23: 78; XVIII, 6.7: 78; XIX, 9: 78; 20-24: 44; XXI, 12: 78; XXII, 15: 44; XXIII, 2-12: 44; XXV, 26.33.34.39: 49; 29: 51; XXVII, 3.6.9.21: 46; XXVIII, 6-22: 44; 6.15: 122; XXX, 7.8: 44.

2 SAMUEL.

Book: xvi.38; I, 17.18: 81; II, 1:44; V, 19-24: 44; VI, 3-12 44; 13-17: 78; VIII, 18-29: 32; XIX, 36: 206; XXIV: 120.263 13: 170; 16.17: 44.202; 17: 120.

1 KINGS.

Book: xvi.38; II, 6.9.: 50; III: 9; 5f.: 46; IV, 11-13: 79; VI, 13f.40f.: 76; VIII, 6-12: 44; XI, 41: 81; XII, 32.33: 66; XIII: 44; 18: 44; XVII-XXII: 44; XVII, 21-22: 51; XVIII, 37: 49; XIX, 7.11.12: 44; 10-14: 195; XX, 31: 57; XXII, 19-22: 44.

2 KINGS.

Book: xvi.38; I-IX: 44; I, 15: 44; II, 1-18: 44; III, 19-25: 58; VI, 21-23: 57; X, 18-28: 91; XI, 25: 122; XII, 17: 84; XIV, 9: 79; 25-27: 93; XVI, 2.4.10-18: 69; 8: 24; XVIII, 3-12: 69; 4: 65; XX, 12I.: 24; XXI: 25; XXII: 71.74; XXIII: 71.74.

ISAIAH.

Book: xvi.36-40.45-46.95; I, 4: 38; 15: 252; II, 2-4: 59.136; 22: 51; III, 2.3: 39; 11.12: 128; 10-26: 77; V, 9: 46; 14: 50.52; VI: 37.65; 1.6-9: 38; VII, 11: 50; 13: 39; 16: 206; VIII, 1-4: 39; 4: 206; 10: 41; 19-20: 53; 19-21: 46; IX, 5: 3ᵴ.194; 16: 38; XI, 2: 40.51; 10: 95; XIII-XXX: 122; XIII, 1-XIV, 23: 138; XIV, 1: 179; 21: 147; XVI, 5: 38; XVII, 7: 141; XVIII, 7: 95; XIX, 1-4: 53; 18-25: 95; XXII, 12-14: 53; 14: 46; XXIII-XXVII: 152; XXIV-XXVII: 138; XXIV, 13-15: 179; 21: 155; XXV, 3f.: 179; 8: 153; XXVI, 14.19: 153; XXVIII, 14-18: 50.52.53; XXIX, 15: 149; 18.19: 38; XXXI, 3: 51; XXXIII, 2-5: 38; XXXVI, 16: 79; XXXIX, 15: 128; XLff.: xx.xxiv; XL-XLVIII: 139.140-142; XL, 1-5.12.14.18.21.26-28: 142; 2: 178; 19.20: 161; 26: 141; XLI, 4.13.20: 142; 5-7: 161; 8.9: 181; XLII, 1-4.19-22: 178; 5.6: 141; 5.9: 142; XLIII, 1-7.10: 142; 1.2.7: 181; 16: 23; XLIV, 1-5.21: 181; 2.6.8.24: 142; 9-20: 161; 21: 178; XLIV, 28-XLV, 8: 179; XLV, 1-7: 140; 3.4: 181; 5-7.9-12.14.18-24: 142; 6.7.12.18: 141; 20: 161; XLVI, 1: 140; 1.6.7: 161; 9f.: 181; XLVII, 10: 149; 9f.: 157; XLVIII, 8: 157.241; 13: 141; 20: 178; XLIX-LIX: 178; XLIX: 179; 1-7: 178; 6: 181; 16: 161; LI, 1.2.9.10: 181; 4-11: 179; LII, 1.4.6.10.11: 179; 4: 181; LII, 13-LIII, 12: 178; LIII, 23: 179; LIV, 7-10: 190; 9· 181; 17: 178; LV, 4.5: 179; 14-15: 55; LVI, 1-8: 179; LVII, 5-8: 161; 16: 104.153; LVIII, 1-14: 179; LIX, 21: 159; LIX, 17-LXVI, 24: 152; LX, 1-7: 180; LXI, 1f.: 159; 5-9: 180; LXII, 2: 180; LXIII, 7f.: 181; 9: 155; LXV, 3.7.11: 161; 11: 180; LXVI, 1-4.12-24: 180; 3.17: 161.

JEREMIAH.

Book: xvi.100-114; I, 5-10: 103; 5-19: 104; II, 3: 101; 4: 114; 27.28: 107; III, 9.16.17: 107; 11.12: 114; 16: 70; 16.17: 113; 24: 110; IV, 1.30: 107; V, 9.31: 111; 19: 110; 20-22: 141; VI, 13: 111; 16.21: 104; 20: 110; VII: 109-112; 3.5-14.17-19.30. 31: 110; 4: 70; 4.8.9.21ff.39: 111; 12-19.29.34: 107; 17.19: 101; 18:25: 24: 104; IX, 12: 114; 22.23: 102; 24.25: 109; X, 1-16: 107.136; 2.23: 104; 10.13.16: 103; 12: 141; XI, 1-13: 70.71; 6: 114; 12: 110; XII: 128; 1f.. 105.125; 15.17: 113; 23: 104;

XIII, 10: 104; 11: 114; XIV, 12: 110; 13-19: 103; 22: 107; XV
15: 105; XVI, 19: 113; 19.20: 107; XVII: 109; 1.26: 114; 2: 107
19-27: 112; 26: 111; XVIII, 12: 104; 18: 111; 23: 105; XIX.
5: 110; 5.13: 107; XX, 7: 104; 12: 105; 14: 106; XXI, 29 30
105; XXII, 9.17.24: 114; 17-19: 106; 28: 107; XXIII, 2.9-40
103; 5.6: 114; 9: 101; 11: 111; 17: 104; 24: 141; 25-32: 48; 33-39
122; XXIV, 4: 114; XXV, 13: 114; 29: 110; XXVI, 4: 114
6: 107; XXVII, 5f.: 108.112; 9: 48.103; XXIX, 1.14.16: 114
5f.: 112; 8:48; 8.9: 103; 26: 239; XXX, 2-4: 114; 29: 78; 34: 111
XXXI, 6.12.14: 111; 15.23: 101; 23: 110; 29.30: 105; 31-33
113; 31-36: 108; XXXII, 15: 112; 31f.34: 110; 34.35: 107;
XXXIII, 18: 111; 20-26: 108; 23: 114; 26: 101; XXXIV: 109;
8-16: 114; 8.18.19: 113; 18: 111; XXXV: 109.113; XXXVI:
114; 4-6.27.28.33: 114; XXXVIII: 108; 16: 104; XLI, 5: 110;
XLII, 10: 112; XLIV, 2.3.5.8.15-29: 110; 8-25: 107; 15-26: 101;
23: 114; XLV, 1: 114; XLVI-XLIX: 113; XLVI, 16f.: 25;
XLVII, 6: 113; XLVIII, 31.36.47: 113; XLIX, 6.39: 113; L:
138; 1.15: 141; 20.23: 114; LI: 138; 5.60: 114; 11.51: 110; 19: 136.

EZEKIEL.

Book: xvi.115-137.132.171.189.226.240.278.288.293; 1: 116.
120.130.201.208; 1: 115; 12.20.21: 123; 24.27.28: 119; 28: 190.
191; II, 2.9.10: 121; 12-14.22-24: 116; III, 5f.: 135; 12.14.22.24:
121; 17-21: 123.127; 18.19: 119; IV, 4-6: 127; V, 11: 130; VI:
130; VII, 3.4.8.9.21.27: 119; 26: 112; VIII-X: 116.120; VIII,
2.3: 203; 3: 121; 12: 125.149; 14-17: 117.130; IX: 202; 3f.:
203; 4.6: 202; 9: 125.149; 16: 118; 21: 119; X: 120; 5: 119; 17:
123; 20-22: 70; X1, 1.5.24: 120; 13-20: 120; 19: 123; 22-24:
116; XII-XIV: 122; XII, 10: 122; 24: 120; XIII: 120; 17-21:
117.120; 19: 118; 22.23: 119; XIV, 2-11: 122; 3-7: 130; 6.14.20:
168; 7: 135.137; 9: 124; 13-23: 127; 14: 117; 14.20: 190; XVI:
136; 3.45.46f.: 117; 17: 130; 27.43.37: 119; 40.41: 133; 59-62:
135; XVIII: 122; 2-20:126; 2.25.29.30: 125; 2f.31: 124; 5-18: 133;
6-12: 130; 21-28: 127; XX, 1.40: 137; 3-31: 122; 5: 136; 5.9-41:
135; 7.28-32.39: 130; 9.22.39.44: 118; 11-31: 133; 12-24: 204;
30.43.44: 119; XXI, 26-29: 121; XXII, 4: 130; 6: 137;
6-12.25-29: 133; 16: 135; 25.29: 121; 26: 70; 30.31: 127; 31: 119;
XXIII: 136; 7-9: 134; 7.14-16.39: 130; 37-47: 133; 48.49: 117;
XXIV, 13: 124; 14: 119; 16-23: 133; 21: 118; 22.23: 120; XXV,
3: 118.137; XXVII, 17: 137; XXVIII, 2-7.12.17: 121; 12.16.25:
117; 14: 116; 22.25: 118; 25.26: 135; XXIX, 13: 135; XXXI: 129;
8.9.16.18: 117; XXXII: 129; XXXIII: 122; 2-30: 123; 8.9.11:
119; 9-20: 127; 15.25.26: 133; 17.20: 125; 24: 117; 32: 131;
XXXIV-XXXIX: 152; XXXIV, 12-24: 137; 20-23: 118; 25.30:
135; XXXVI, 10: 137; 17.19.31.32: 119; 21-27: 135; 25-27:
123; XXXVII: 121.125.129; 1-14: 123; 26.28: 118.135; XXXVIII,
16.23: 118; 16-28: 137; 23: 135; XXXIX, 7.13.21.25.27: 118;
7.21-23.27.28: 135; 12-20: 133; 23-25: 137; 29: 119; XL-XLVIII:
133; XL, 1-XLIV, 5: 131; XL, 18f.: 116; 39: 134; XLI, 18-21:

MALACHAI.

Book: xvi.138; I, 2: 181; 3.4: 168; 6-14: 180; II, 8.10: 181
11f.: 168; 12-15: 180; 17: 128; III, 1: 155; 13-21: 148; 14-18
128; 17-21: 152.

PSALMS.

Book: xvi.xvii.222.229-252.230.259.268.269.271.279.281.282.
285.288.293; *Elohim Psalms*: 32; I, 3-6: 242; II: 236; III: 239;
IV, 2: 252; V, 2-4: 252; VI, 6: 244; VII, 9.10: 232; 12f.: 242;
VIII: 232; IX, 18: 245; X, 4-6.11-13: 232; 16: 250; XI, 4 5:
232; 5.6: 242; XIV, I.2: 232; XV, 230.251; XVI: 230; 8-11:
245; XVII, 14: 242.243; 14.15: 245; XVIII: 236; 16: 245; XIX:
230.251; XX: 236; XXI: 236; 11: 242; XXII, 27.30: 245; XXIII:
232; 1.2: 243; XXIV: 230.251; XXV, 12: 242.245; XXVI,
6.7: 252; 13: 245; XXVII, 6: 252; 23: 232; XXVIII, 1: 245;
2: 252; XXIX: 230; XXX, 4.10: 244; 5: 252; XXXI, 6.18: 245;
XXXIII: 230; XXXIV, 6: 252; 7: 251; 9: 237; 13: 241; 17:
242; XXXV, 5: 237; 17: 245; XXXVI: 7: 252; 8-10: 245;
XXXVII, 9.10.22-28: 242; 9.22.34.38: 251; XXXVIII, 1f.7.16.25:
243; 37.38: 242; XXXIX, 13: 252; XL, 2-12: 252; 5: 232; XLII,
3: 245; 4.11: 232; 5-9: 252; XLIII, 3.4: 252; XLV: 230.236;
21: 234; XLVII: 250; 6.7: 251; XLVIII: 250; XLIX, 5: 251;
6f.: 243; 8: 252; 9.15.16: 245; 21: 247; L: 252; 12: 241; 14: 245;
LI: 230.243; 13: 240; 17-21: 252; LII, 7: 242; LIII, 2: 232; LIV,
5: 232; 8: 252; LV, 16.24: 245; LVI, 13: 252; LVII, 9: 251;
12: 232; LVIII, 4: 241; LIX: 250; LX, 8: 240; LXI: 236; 6-9:
252; LXII, 12: 240; LXIII: 236; 3: 240; 3-6: 252; 26: 251;
LXV, 2-5: 252; 7: 232; LXVI, 8: 250; 13-20: 252; 16-20: 241;
LXVII: 230.250; LXVIII: 242; 2.5: 240; 2.8.10: 245; 29-33:
250; 30-34: 252; LXIX, 14.31.32: 252; 28: 241; LXX, 9: 243;
LXXI, 22: 251; LXXII: 230.236; 5.9-15: 252; LXXIII, 11f.:
232; 16.17.22: 247; 17: 240; LXXIV: 236.240.242; 7-9: 240;
11-18.22: 232; LXXV, 3-8: 232; LXXVI-LXXXI: 242; LXXVI:
250; 12: 252; LXXVII: 236; 14f.. 232; LXXVIII: 236; 8.19f.:
232; 39: 244; LXXX, 2f.: 203; 5: 252; LXXXI: 236; 2.3: 251;
13: 241; LXXXII, 8: 250; LXXXIII: 236.242; 25.26: 245;
LXXXIV, 3: 245; 9-11: 252; LXXXVI, 14: 232; LXXXVII:
242; LXXXVIII: 230; 4: 245; 4-7.11.12: 244; 65: 243; LXXXIX:
232.236.242; 4: 250; 7.8.11: 237; 20: 240; 49: 245; XC, 3.15:
243; 4: 232; XCI, 11: 237; XCII: 232; 4: 251; 10: 247; XCIII:
230; XCIV-XCIX: 250; XCIV, 7-11: 232; 12.18: 243; XCV:
230.242; 2: 252; 2.4: 232; XCVI, 5: 250; XCVII, 5.6: 251;
7: 250; XCVIII, 17.18: 243; XCIX, 1: 237; 6.7: 240; C: 230;
1: 251.252; CI: 236; 1-3: 250; 8: 251; CII, 2: 242; 13.26-29:
232; 17-33: 252; CIII: 242; 1-4.14-17: 245; 14-16: 244.288;
17.18: 242; 19f.: 232; 20-21: 237; CIV: 230.232; 3.4: 237; 15:
243; 24: 239; 29.30: 244; CV: 236.242; 20: 240; CVI, 35: 247;
44: 252; CVII, 21-32: 252; CVIII, 3: 251; CIX, 7: 252; 8-15:
242; 13.15: 251; CXI: 235.239; 6-10: 235; CXII: 235; CXIII:
230.251; CXIV: 230; CXV, 3f.: 232; 5-8: 250; 27: 244; CXVI,

7-9: 245; 12-19: 252; CXVII: 230.251; CXIX: 230 (part);
62.14⁷.148: 252; 126: 70; CXXII: 230.236.250; 1-4: 252; 8:
237; CXXVII: 250; 3: 242; CXXVIII, 12: 242; CXXX, 2-6:
252; CXXXI: 230; CXXXII: 236.250; CXXXIV: 230.252;
CXXXV-CXXXVII: 242; CXXXV, 6f.: 232; 15-17: 250;
CXXXVI: 232; CXXXVII, 2.4: 251; 7: 168; CXXXVIII, 2:
252; 4: 251; CXXXIX: 232; CXLI, 1-2: 252; CXLIII, 7: 245;
CXLIV, 4: 244; 7.8: 250; CXLV: 235; CXLVI, 4: 244; CXLVII:
230.232; 7: 251; 19.20: 250; CXLVIII: 230.232; 1.2: 237;
CXLIX, 3: 251; CL: 230; 3-5: 251; 4: 160.

PROVERBS.

Book: xvi.222.229-252.232.268.282.288.293; II, 7-22: 231;
16f.: 243; 18.19: 246; 22: 251; III: 231; 5-7.19.20: 247; 11.12.31:
243; 12.19.20: 231; 19.20: 239; IV, 10-19: 243; 18.19: 231; V,
3f.: 243; 5.6: 246; 21: 231.233; VI, 15: 243; 27: 246; VIII, 12-14.
22-31: 247; 14-21: 243; 21-31: 239; 21-31.35: 231; IX, 13f.:
243; 18: 246; X: 231; XI, 14: 243; 31: 231; XII, 5.13: 242;
XIII, 22: 242; 25: 243; XIV, 11: 242; 17.21.22.29.31: 237; 27.32:
246; XV, 3.11: 233; 8.29: 252; 11.18: 53; 11.24: 246; 16.17:
242; 18: 237; XVI, 2.3.9.11.33: 233; 5.6.10-16.32: 237; 6.19:
243; 25: 242; XVII, 1: 243; 3: 233; 5: 242; 5.11: 237; XVIII,
10: 237; XIX, 3: 240; 11.17: 237; 21: 233; XX, 1: 243; 7: 242;
8.22.26-28: 237; 11: 240; 12.24.27: 233; 17.21: 247; 25: 252;
27: 246; XXI, 1.2.30.31: 233; 3.27: 252; 13.14.21: 237; 16: 246;
17: 243; XXII, 17.18: 242; 30: 243; XXIV, 12.13: 247; 14:
242; 19: 243; XXV, 2.3: 243.247; 2-4.15: 237; XXVIII, 8: 242;
8.13.20: 237; XXIX, 4: 252; 4.14: 237; XXX, 1-5: 231.239;
2-6: 247; 9: 236; 19: 232; XXXI, 1-9: 237; 4: 243.

JOB.

Book: xvi.132.138.139.142-181.149.151.161-169.171.176-177
182.239.240.242.247.248.279.281.286.290.293; I: 155; 5: 168;
II: 155; III-XXXVII: 143; III, 8: 150; IV, 6-16: 152; 7-12:
144; 12-21: 158; 13: 159; 16-18: 155; 19-21: 153; V, 4-25: 147,
17: 145; 18: 148; VI, 6.10: 150; 7.10: 158; 10: 155; VII, 1.21:
150; 8f.21: 153; VIII, 4.5.13.20.21: 144; 7: 147; IX, 5-13: 155:
13.22: 150; X, 4: 152; 9.12.21.22: 153; 14: 150; XI, 4-14: 144;
12-15: 148; XII, 7f.: 155; 9-13: 143; 10: 153; 27: 168; XIII;
15: 150; XIV, 4.17.21.22: 150; 10-22: 154; 11-22: 153; XV, 14.15:
145; 20-27: 146; 28-34: 144; XVI, 9-17: 150; 22: 153; XVII,
5: 150; 13-16: 153; XVIII, 5-15: 144; 17-21: 147; XIX, 6.11.21.22:
150; 25: 173; XX, 3: 152; 5f.: 144; 8: 159; 10: 147.148; 12f.:
151; 20: 146; XXI, 5f.12: 144.146; 9: 150; 27: 148; XXIII,
12: 150; XXIV: 150; XXV, 2-6: 145; 3.7-12: 155; 6: 153; XXVII-
XXVIII: 144; XXVII: 151; 3: 153; 17: 242; XXIX-XXXI:
169; XXX, 19-23: 153; 31: 160; XXXI, 35: 158; XXXII-
XXXVII: 144; XXXII, 8: 154; XXXIII, 1: 150; 4: 154; 13f.:
159; 23: 155; XXXIV, 5f.: 148; 14-15: 154; XXXVII, 9: 152;
XXXVIII-XLI: 143.157; XXXVIII, 1-XL, 1-6: 158; XXXVIII,
39-XXXIX, 30: 157; XXXVIII, 1: 143.152; 4-38: 157; 7: 155;
17: 156; XL: 157; XLI: 157; XLII, 10-17: 185; 13: 173; 16: 143.

SONG OF SONGS.
Book: xvi.80.166.222.288.

RUTH.
Book: xvi.138.166.169-173.174.175.177.182.226; I, 1-5: 170
8.16.20.21: 171; 16: 113; II, 1-23: 171; III, 1-18: 172; IV, 1-22
173.

ECHAH.
Book: xvi.81.138.288; I, 18-22: 149; II, 1-5: 137; 9.14: 160
III, 1-66: 149; IV, 13: 160; 21.22: 168.

KOHELETH.
Book: xvi.222.262.268.278.281-291.293; I: 281-282; 13.16.17
282; II: 281-282; 1-3.9.10.12-16.19-26: 282; 18-21: 286; III.
10-17: 285; 18-21: 287; 21: 246; IV, 8.13-15: 286; 17: 285; V, 1-6.
285; VI, 1.2.10: 286; VII, 15 18: 285; 20: 286; VIII, 4.11-13.
286; 8: 287; 12-14.17: 285; IX, 1-3: 284; 1.5.11.12: 285; 1.12
286; 4-10: 287; X, 16-20: 282; XI, 5: 287; XII, 1-7: 287; 10-14
288.

ESTHER.
Book: xvi.166.173-176.182.222.261; II, 10.20-23: 175; III
4.5: 175; 8: 176; V, 8: 175; VI, 1-11: 175; VII, 3: 175; VIII, 15:
175; IX, 1.5: 176.

DANIEL.
Book: xvi.6.222.261-264.266.278-281.293; II, 11-23: 263
IV, 5.15.31: 263; V, 11: 263; VI, 11.12: 252; 21: 263; XII: 279;
2.3: 279.

EZRA.
Book: xvi.138.222.261-277; II, 62.63: 267; III, 10: 276
IV, 3: 262; V, 11.12: 263; VI, 9.10: 263; 18: 262; VII, 26: 269
VIII, 21-24: 265; 35: 262; IX: 169; 10: 269; X: 169.

NEHEMIAH.
Book: xvi.138.222.261-277; VII, 5: 81; 64.65: 276; IX, 2
169; X, 31: 169; XII, 27.45-47: 276; XIII, 1.23-30: 169.

1 CHRONICLES.
Book: xvi.79.81.222.261-277; IV, 10: 274; 18f.: 276; V, 17.
81.262; 20.22: 274; VI, 16.17: 274; 18f.: 276; 41: 262; IX, 1
262; 1-3: 269; 33: 276; X, 13f.: 274; 31: 269; X, 13-XI, 1-8.
274; XI, 1: 263; XIII, 23-30: 269; XV, 16.19-29: 276; XVI
4-7.42: 276; XXI: 44.120.263; 16: 120.202; XXII, 27: 81; XXV
1-3: 275; XXVII, 24: 81; XXVIII, 9.18.19: 263; XXIX, 11.12
263; 29: 81.

2 CHRONICLES.
Book: xvi.79.81.222.261-277; I, 10: 263; II, 5: 263; III
10-14: 263; V, 12.13: 276; VI, 8.30: 263; VII, 6: 276; IX, 11
276; 29: 81; X, 15: 265; XII, 15: 81; XVI, 9: 263; XVIII, 19
265; XIX, 5-11: 86; XX, 34: 81; XXI, 12: 170; XXII, 13: 276
XXIII, 18: 276; XXIV, 27: 81; 16: 265; XXVI, 22: 81; XXIX.
XXXI: 69; XXIX, 25-30: 276; XXX, 25: 81; XXXII, 8: 263
19.32: 81; 31: 265; XXXIII: 25; XXXV, 3: 70; 15: 276; 21.22
265; XXXVI, 20-22: 261.

INDEX

A.

Aaron (Ahron): 67.195.240.
Abel: 190.
Abimelech: 5.
Abodah: 257.
Abomination: xxxiii.
Aboth: 256.257.
Abraham: xx.6.23.27.29.30.117.
177.181.190.191.202.203.
Abrahamites: 1.17f.43.66.80.82.
Abrogation: xxv.xxxi.295.
Academy: 297.299.
Account (Retribution): 147.
Acrostic: 235.
Action (-Thought): 241.
Adam: xvii.82.208.261.
Administration: 276.277.
Admonition (Thochahah): xxif.
19.49.56.58.60.72.200.211.
Adonay: 119.120.163.234.
Adult (Retribution): 215.
Adultery: 86.
Agadah: 233.292.297.
Agag: 176.
'Agalim. 65-67.
Agnoia: 282.
Ahabhah Rabbah: 253.
Ahasver: 174.
'Akiba: 166.219.295.
Alexandria: 221.260.292.
Al-hat-Tzadikim (Sopherim) 259.
Amalek: 176.
Ammon: 5.108.171.
Amos: xvi.xx.32.33-34.38.39.49.
52.91-93.279.
Amoz: xxiv.
Andreia (Card. Attr.). 40.
Angels: xxvi.3f.7.14.19-23.27ff.
38.41.44.48f.64.68f.73.75.87.
98.100f.107.115-121.130.133.
136.145.155.160.163.181.187.
191.195.197.201ff.207.209.211.
223f. 237f. 253f. 258. 262-265.
278.285.292.295.296.

Animal:80.86.185.287 (Principle)
Anthropomorph: 38.121.299.
Antinomism: 113.259.295.
Anti-Semitism (A.-Jewish):
xxviii.xxxif.
Anu: 2.
Aphorism: 248:297.298.
Apis: 60.
Apocrypha: 152.289.292.
Arabic: 299.
Arabists: xxiv.
Aram: 36.
Arboth Moab: xviii.
Architecture (Art): 76.
Argument (Proof): 82.83.107f.
230f.285-288.
Aristotle: 298.300.
Arithmetical Unity: 42.
Ark: 67-70.73.75.184.188.192.
212.
Art: 4.76-78.106f.130.161f.163
(Liter.) = 189.198.208. (Arts)
268.272f.297.
Ascension (of Moses): 292.
Asheroth: 63.69.
Ashrei (Happy): 227.
Ashur: 3.69.
Asia: 36.
Assimilation: 175.291.
Assyria (-n): xxiv.2.3.24.36.64.
69.93.95.291.
Astral (Motif): 23.
Astronomical (Motif): 65.
Atheism: 149-151.157.213.290.
Attributes: 3.6f.13.26.28.29.33.
34.39.40f.79.102.108.118f.125.
128.131.140f.147f.154.161.163.
167.170.177.181.185f.189.191.
193.203.222.232f.235.249.256.
263.295.298.300.
Authenticity (of Torah): xxiv.
xxviiiff.
Authority (-ative): xiiif.xixf.
xxvi.xxxt.60.115.185f.216.222f.
249ff.259.264.267.270.273-276.

Definition (of God). 35.39.40.55.
59.102.118.183.187.235.257.
258.263.
Destruction: 138.240.250.256.
261.
Determinism (Free Will): 104.
157.
Deutero Isaiah: xvii.xx.xxi.140-
142.143.148.157.159.285.
Deuteronomy: iv.xvii.xxi.xxii.19.
20.40-42.44.46-48.57-60 63.67.
(School). 71.74.83.85.90.95.97.
105-108.112-117.133.159.161.
163.168.186-191.194.197-199.
205.214-217.222.224.226.238.
249.255.256.263.270.
Dialectics: 296-298.
Dialog (Philos.):   108.164.167.
281.294.
Diaspora: 175.176   (Program).
255.
Dietary Law: xxx.180.
Difference (North-South): 68.
Dinah: 191.
Disposition: 105.
District: 257.270.
Doctrine (Dogma): 223.248.
Dogma: xxvi.164.258.260.279.
280.292.
Dortmund, Germany: xxv.
Drama: 155.164-166.172.
Drawing (Art): 161.
Dream (Proph.):   45-47.103.146.
150.158.159.188.265.285.
Drinking (Three Passions): 282.
Driver, S. R.: xxxv.
Dry Bones: 123.279.
Dualism (Parsism): 140.295.
Dynamic Unity (Monoth.): 42.
Dynasty: 137.169.172.174.262.
274.

E.

Ea: 3.
Eastern School (Philos.): 299.
Eating (Three Passions): 282.
Ebed JHVH (Servant): 112.
Echah: xvi.138.
Eclecticism: 221.226.237.

Edom: 108.168.
Education (Jewish): xxvii.xxix.
xxxiv.
'Egel (Golden Calf): 65-67.
Egypt, ian: xviii.xxiv.28.50.53.
57.59.62.64.66.93.100.110.129.
135.186.207.249.291.
EHJH: 7.13f.28.39.
Eight Verses (Last, Torah):
xvi.xvii.
Eighteen Benedictions (Thephil-
lah): 256.
EJ (JE): 191.
El: 8.-Kanna: 12.35.195. -Shad-
day: 119.191.
Elephantine: 249.
Eli: 241.
Elihu (Job): 144f.165.168.178.
243.
Elijah: 44.51.91.
Elilim: 40.
Elimelech: 170.
Eliphaz (Job):144ff.165.168.178.
243.
Elisha: 44.91.
Eloha: 143.163.
Elohim: 8.13.28.33.34.64.182.
190.191.202.234 (Psalms). 250.
251.274.286.
Elohist (E):   xx.xxii.6.21-22.26.
27-29.32.33.38.41.76.191.202f.
Emanation: 238.296.
End (Justice): 144.164.166.172.
173.197.205.242.
England: xix.
Enoch: 51.207.279.292 (Book).
Ephod: xl.
Ephraim: 94.
Epicure, ean: 231.283-286.290.
Epigram: 39.236.
Equality (Stranger): 135.
Erotic (Sexual): 80.130.288.
Eschatology: 49-59.106.125.129.
150.151-154 (152: Individual).
188.207.244-249.266.278-281.
286-288.
Esra (Ezra).
Essentials (Judaism, Principles):
256.258.260.

CPSIA information can be obtained at www.ICGtesting.com
Printed in the USA
LVOW06s1650260114

371023LV00027B/1458/P

9 781313 779807